THE LAUNDRY GIRL

Spirit of the Boabs

THE LAUNDRY GIRL

Faye Bohling

Copyright © 2015

The moral right of Faye Bohling to be identified as the author has been asserted by her in accordance with the Copyright, Designs and Patents Act 1988. All rights reserved. No part of this book may be used or reproduced, stored in a retrieval system, or transmitted in any form, or by any means electronic, mechanical, recording, photocopying, or in any manner whatsoever without permission in writing from the author, except for the inclusion of brief quotations in a review.

National Library of Australia Cataloguing-in-Publication entry
Creator: Bohling, Faye, author.
Title: The laundry girl / Faye Bohling.
ISBN: 9780992481629 (paperback)
ISBN: 9780992481636 (ebook)

Subjects: Bohling, Faye
                  Mothers and daughters--Biography.
                  Abandoned children--Attitudes.
                  Children--Institutional care--Biography.

Dewey Number: 306.8743092
Book Cover Layout: Marion Duke-O'Callaghan (Pickawoowoo Publishing Group)

All rights reserved.

No part of the book may be transmitted or reproduced by any form or means, either mechanical or electronic, including recording and photocopying, or by any known storage and retrieval system, without the written consent of the author/publisher, except in the case of short quotations being used in a review

The views and opinions expressed in this work are solely those of the author and do not necessarily reflect the views of the publisher, and the publisher hereby disclaims any responsibility for them. No warranties or guarantees are expressed or implied by the publisher's choice to include any of the content in this volume.

Some names have been changed to protect privacy however they reflect real people and events.

Publisher Details

Spirit of the Boabs (ABN 89378673394)
Contact Details: info@spiritoftheboabs.com
Kununurra, Australia
Contact: Sarah Brett
Orders: www.spiritoftheboabs.com

I dedicate this book to my great-grandson,

Reece Patrick Kinnersly,

in celebration of his life.

Introduction

Set in Perth, Western Australia, during the closing stages of World War II, first-time author Faye Bohling has written an autobiography of her life that is full of passion. Called *The Laundry Girl*, it tells of a girl who was abandoned by her mother because she was seemingly considered to have interfered with her often-questionable lifestyle.

Faye tells her story of a ten year-old child, given up by her mother to a Catholic home for wayward women. But there is a marked difference between schoolgirl Faye and the other wards. She should never have been there, as she was a child in an adult environment and where she received no schooling and was put to work in the institutions' laundry.

Through all of this mental and physical hardship, she never lost hope in that some day her Mother would come back to reclaim her.

The Laundry Girl is similar to Albert Facey's *A Fortunate Life* in that it, too, is an honest story told from the heart and despite having spent many years in unfortunate circumstances, Faye still looked positively on life and all that it offered.

The reader gets an insight into life during the war years and a further tragedy in Faye's life when her happiness was once more dashed when her young husband was killed. Having to raise a family of four had its hardships but was also interspersed with heart-warming vignettes of colourful characters, humour and experiences that she met on her life's journey.

The Laundry Girl is a remarkable story of resilience and optimism. It is written in a style that allows the reader to share her trials and tribulations and above all, admire a person who, despite the hand life dealt her, went on to be a loving, caring individual, mother and friend.

Highly readable, it is a heart-warming story.

Dr John Weiland, PhD

Brisbane 2014.

For a short time early in my life, some people had called me Frances. A little later, others chose to call me Lucy. The correct name, however, was Faye, Faye Evelyn, to be precise. I was not Frances and emphatically not Lucy.

Table of Contents

Introduction vi
Prologue xi
Chapter 1 Recollections and Revelations 1
Chapter 2 Through Baby Eyes 15
Chapter 3 Back at Bertram Street 41
Chapter 4 Away from the Wall 53
Chapter 5 Betrayal 1948 63
Chapter 6 Goodbye Lucy 91
Chapter 7 School 1951 101
Chapter 8 Runaway 109
Chapter 9 Pick of the Bunch 117
Chapter 10 Who was Lorna? 135
Chapter 11 Halcyon Days 141
Chapter 12 Heytesbury Road 1957 159
Chapter 13 A Bad House 175
Chapter 14 Ledge Point 1964 181
Chapter 15 We Need a Tomorrow 203
Chapter 16 My Colleen 207
Chapter 17 Essex St Wembley 1964 215
Chapter 18 Earthquake 223
Chapter 19 No Rose Garden 239
Chapter 20 With Dignity 261
Chapter 21 Good Shepherd Revisited 269
    Epilogue 2012 275
    Acknowledgements 279

Prologue

I gazed at the photograph, and memories stirred as I recognised the little figure as myself, but my mother was not there. There I was standing in front of a semi-detached house in Newcastle Street, West Perth. Looking at the tiny, blond, yet untroubled child that had been me, my emotions faltered. Possibly, I was less than two years old at the time; however, I remembered wearing the red cloak with an attached hood on other occasions, later on, when I was bigger. I wondered when the photo had been taken, perhaps after Mass at Christmas time.

My imagination and perhaps vague memories added colour to the old, black-and-white, creased picture. Five or six women stood close by me, all dressed in black, grey or brown overcoats. Possibly the hats that they wore were more brightly coloured. The women stood stiff and unsmiling, firmly clasping handbags to their chests and looking grimly towards the camera. They looked severe and oddly similar to each other and might have been any age between thirty and seventy. At the back of the group stood a tall, thin, upright, old woman, her white hair curling softly around the edges of a small, close-fitting black hat. That was Granny. Next to Granny was a squat, stocky woman wearing a long-sleeved, green-grey, coloured dress. Her short hair was a mixture of black and grey, cut bluntly, with a tortoise shell clip to hold the front of her hair from her face.

That was Aunty Stella. I quickly looked away.

Although it sounded strange, my earliest memories included none of my mother, though plenty of others crowded in. I remembered a pretty lady, who, as she picked me up and put me to bed, smelled of beautiful flowers. However, frighteningly, when I woke up the next morning, the flower smell was all that remained of her. Some other person, not pretty or sweet smelling, had taken her place.

Chapter 1

Recollections and Revelations

I knew, before looking at the small Waterford clock on the dressing table, that the time would be four o'clock, or close to it – the time known to some as the witching hour, when many souls entered the world, or left it, and those of us doing neither were irrationally restless. Sleep and I had never been good companions. Sleep visited me if and when it felt like it, making me feel by its absence as though I had transgressed in some way. The book that I had been reading fell from my lethargic grasp to the wooden floor with a resounding thud. My little black and white cat, which had been sleeping soundly at the foot of my bed jumped and eyed me resentfully for the intrusion. She waited, senses alert, ensuring that I was not going to the kitchen for a midnight snack that might include a morsel for her. She lay there squinting at me for a few seconds before adroitly curling back into herself as sleep overcame her. Lucky little cat, how I envied her quick return to dreamland. Between four and five o'clock in the morning the customary drone of the newspaper delivery vehicle set up the regular howling din of the neighbourhood dogs. That chorus was followed by the hoarse disharmony of squawking crows and the sweet carolling of magpies. Restless now and no longer bothered to try all the self-help strategies for insomniacs advocated by therapists and magazine articles; I accepted that, for me, the night was over. I urged the disgruntled feline out into the early morning chill. She wove around my feet, all soft fur and a cold little nose as I retrieved the paper from where it invariably landed, right in the middle of the thorniest of the rose bushes. Steam moved temptingly from my freshly brewed coffee and, with newspaper in hand, I returned to my bed, which seemed friendlier and cosier now that the dark loneliness of the night had departed.

While leafing through the pages of *The West Australian* newspaper, I noticed a page that I occasionally glanced at but seldom read. The page devoted itself to various organisations and groups advertising reunions, or seeking information about events and people from the past.

A small paragraph inquired: *Were you in an institution as a child? Were you at The Home of the Good Shepherd laundry?*

A shiver of shock and shame washed over me.

Yes I was. Fancy that! I was there through no fault of my own and yet still I burned with shame.

Later in the morning, I copied the number down on a bright pink note and stuck it on the fridge – just in case. No longer shivery, a hot, sweat-inducing resentment burned within me, forcing me to peel my jumper up, over my clammy face, and carelessly toss it aside. I did not like to be reminded of The Home of the Good Shepherd, bringing forth images of women with large, looming, covered figures, and shrouded heads without the softness of hair to frame their faces – only harsh mouths and hard eyes visible to me - the unfortunate target of their wrath. I heard them still, their angry voices, quietly threatening, full of contempt and dislike. Unbidden sadness for the taking of my given name away from me, while in their care, swept over me. Those convent days were long behind me, but the recollections remained vivid.

In the past when watching television footage of men and women participating in ANZAC Day remembrance ceremonies, I had wondered if former prisoners of war who made the pilgrimage back to scene of their incarceration so many years after the event, had felt the need to look again behind the pain and fear. Perhaps they needed to revisit the horror and realise that it had not been so bad after all or maybe to wonder how they had survived.

I speculated who might have placed the advertisement and why. Would it be enlightening to speak with someone who had actually experienced the place? Did other ageing women still bear emotional scars of the treatment handed out by the sisters?

The following day I reached across the burnished, jarrah dining table to pick up the telephone, then dialled the numbers very carefully because if I dialled incorrectly, or if nobody answered, I knew I would never ring again.

Too quickly, a pleasant voice echoed through the phone. 'Hello, Verna speaking.'

My voice quavered and threatened to fail and I was about to replace the receiver without answering, but then I heard my own voice – thin, reedy and childish.

'My name is Faye. I was in The Home of the Good Shepherd.'

This was the first time I ever uttered those words. I waited for some huge reaction from this woman. Perhaps even a Biblical outcome from the elements, but nothing. There was no thunder, nor lightning, no tidal waves, nor the crashing of cymbals. *Nothing.*

With a voice of understanding and encouragement, Verna replied. 'I was about twelve years old, when I, too, was taken to a Good Shepherd institution in another state.' Verna could not recall how long she remained in the institution, but one day a nun told her that she was leaving the home and going to a school. 'However,' Verna added bitterly, 'because I was wilful and confrontational, the *school* turned out to be what they used to call an asylum, a place for the mentally insane.'

Verna seemed to hold much bitterness and, because of the lack of information available to the many victims of the institutions, she was trying to bring those people together, perhaps to seek some sort of recompense, or an apology, or simply to band together with people for mutual understanding of what they had endured. It seemed to me from the way she spoke that it had become a personal battle which resulted in her spending countless, perhaps fruitless, hours pursuing either vengeance or justice. I was invited to a gathering to meet 'other victims'.

As I travelled to the meeting, passing through many suburbs before I stopped in the shade of a parkland tree, I asked myself if I really wanted to be at this gathering. However, after several moments of indecisiveness, I did continue to drive, until a large open gate that led to a sports oval and a long bitumen driveway to a red brick pavilion came into view. The size of the venue led me to think that a large number of people were expected … but only four seats were occupied. A man and a woman sat miserably huddled together and two women sat nervously close to each other at the end of a row of seats in a hall that could easily accommodate a hundred people. I walked past the small assembly towards a woman who sat, chairperson-like, at a table in front of the group. Iron-grey hair framed her face and her gold framed glasses sat beneath bushy brows. She wore a bulky, heavyweight suit, and when she stood and moved from behind the table, it became apparent that she was tall and solidly built.

She came forward to shake my hand. 'I'm Verna. And you are?'

'Hello Verna. We spoke on the phone. I am Faye.'

We sat down; she briefly introduced me to the others. Nobody looked at my face, and their names did not register with me, nor would I have recognised any of them again the next day. The heavy atmosphere and the women's demeanour readily brought back memories of the claustrophobic, disturbed feeling that had existed within the walls at The Home of the Good Shepherd. The women appeared nervous and hesitant to speak without first looking at Verna. One woman attempted to ask me a question, but her words swiftly died when Verna glared meaningfully at her, giving me no opportunity to hear the question or reply. Verna's manner towards me was friendly, but there seemed an undercurrent of anger and repressed aggression which had not been evident during our telephone conversation. Little discussion took place, and it was clear that those unfortunate people had not left the past behind. They were still victims of anyone who exhibited dominance, as indeed was I.

That was no place for me, I thought, no wonder so few people turned up. I left that meeting armed with tapes, compact discs and photographs. There was a recent photo taken of a monument erected at the Karrakatta cemetery to the memory of one hundred and twenty six women. The names on the stone were those of former inmates who had lived, died and were buried from that West Leederville institution, it appeared, without dignity or grace; or without even the fundamental right of an individually marked grave. A representative of Karrakatta cemetery assured me that the practice had been common in the past. The photo reinforced my own, long-held feeling that, without family members who cared and maintained contact, one could have gone into that place and been lost forever.

On the rare occasions that I had ever felt an inclination to speak to anyone about the place, the rigidly instilled practice of *don't tell anyone*, in addition to feeling that I would be disbelieved or thought to be exaggerating, prevented me.

Shame, too, was a most powerful silencer.

However, things had changed. The recently introduced Freedom of Information laws meant that documents previously unobtainable were now available for scrutiny, although many of the old records no longer existed as they had been destroyed. It had all happened such a long time ago, but now I wanted to fit together the jigsaw that I already had and to attempt to unearth the missing pieces.

After many unrewarding phone calls, it seemed that I might get more cooperation by fronting up in person.

I entered a dreary, grey building, and squeezed through one of those revolving doors, that I was always afraid of being stuck in, into a reception area, which was divided at every turn by rails, reminding me of a cattle race. I eventually found my place and stood in a queue that seemingly never got any shorter, despite names or numbers being called stridently at regular intervals. Finally, my turn came to approach a fair-haired service clerk. She smiled at me. 'Hello, my name is Helen. How can I help you today?'

'I need to find out if a person is able to access records between the mid 1940s and the early 1950s,' I replied.

'What sort of records?' she asked.

I answered, 'I think Child Welfare and perhaps Education.'

I was about to add, *and children's homes*, but changed my mind. The Home of the Good Shepherd was *not* a children's home. I explained briefly about being in a home as a child and that I wanted to find out what education, if any, I had received during that time, because I only remembered ironing – no reading or schoolwork.

'Wherever you were,' she replied, 'they would've had to send you to school. That's the law.'

While we spoke, Helen had been writing rapidly on white, unruled paper in a large folder. 'I'll go and see if I can find anything to help you. I may be a while so I will close the counter and call you when I get back. You will probably have time to get a cup of tea from the kiosk: it's down the passage, on the right.'

She was pleasant and thoughtful, but a cup of tea from the kiosk was not what I wanted. I needed information and then I wanted to leave this tightly enclosed, windowless building and go home.

I saw Helen beckoning to me and, as she peered through the opening in the window that separated us, she looked sympathetic. 'You've left your run a bit late. There was a huge clear out of files in the late 80s and records right across the board were destroyed.' She continued in a chatty tone, 'Flora, Fauna, and Fisheries...everything went. Numerous government records, child welfare... all that sort of thing.'

My silence at her seeming dismissal of my existence in no way reflected the shock that surged through me. Surely, my life and that of others from that time and place meant more than to be shredded with the records of the culling of kangaroos, firebreaks in paddocks or the issuing of fishing licences.

I continued making phone calls and writing letters, only to find that a great deal of information had been lost with the passage of time. The building, which was the original site of The Home of the Good Shepherd, had become The Catholic Education Centre. I phoned their office and the person I spoke to was understanding and concilitory, and she readily gave me contact details for their archives in Victoria.

On the floor, I sat cross-legged, beside my intricately carved camphor wood chest, a gift from my sons. I went through the pages and envelopes thoroughly, because I often placed documents or something important, or sentimental between the leaves of a book thinking that it would be safe there. The downside to my habit of secreting memorabilia was that I sometimes lost something important. The book went back on the shelf and I forgot that I had ever put anything in it and at times, the item would not be recovered until much later-sometimes too late.

I was moving house soon, and decided to take the opportunity, while searching, to offload some of my large accumulation of books. I started out diligently, but the enormous decision to part with any of them slowed the process. Those books had seen me through long, lonely nights. They had basked with me in the garden on warm sunny days and they had been on holidays with me. I picked up one book after another, attempting to make the difficult decision of which to part with and which to keep. I eventually simplified the process by first selecting the books that I *did not* want to part with. The writers were like my friends and one did not discard one's friends lightly. As with friends, they were all different – some were funny, others inspiring and others were scary as hell.

Once I had a school report that I was proud of, but a vague memory recalled me throwing it into the fire and burning it. I did not know, then, why I would do such a thing and I hoped that I was mistaken about burning it and that one day it might fall into my lap.

An old Christmas card separated from a bundle and rested in my hands. It was from my mother. She had sent it to me when I was in the home. The date on the card drew and held my attention. In the past, I had often paused to admire the ageing card with its appealing image of stars shining brilliantly above a small, angelic figure. This time though it was not the prettiness of the card, but the year in which I had received it that held my attention. I realised that by writing the date beneath her greeting to me, my mother had unknowingly prompted me to search for a reason for the inexplicable, uneasy feeling, which swept over me each time I held that card.

Strange coincidences! Seeing Verna's notice in the paper and then, despite handling this card many, many times over many years, for the first time the date written on it became truly significant. I looked at my mother's hand writing in disbelief. On my Christmas card, she had written *Happy Christmas darling, love Mummy, Christmas 1948.*

In 1948, I was ten years old, and I received the card while I was in the home. Could it be that my mother left me in that dreadful place when I was only ten years old? The truth was that I had no idea of exactly how old I was at the time nor for how long I had been locked away. Common sense told me that I must have known. However, my common sense did not allow me to probe too deeply. I protected my feelings as one protects an aching tooth – just a gentle touch to see if it still hurts, then a quick, painful jerk away.

I was a child. No one had birthdays in The Home of the Good Shepherd. Therefore, with the unreality of the place and with no one to tell me differently, I had thought I was older when I was put there and that the time I spent there had been about six months. With the understanding of the date on that card, I realised that when I was collected from that home I was twelve.

I came, eventually, to understand how I lost comprehension of the length of my time in there, but what was never comprehendible was why I ever *was* there. The Home of the Good Shepherd had been a closed chapter, never to be spoken of between my mother and me during her lifetime. She would have had no idea of what I thought about my time in that home.

I held a tattered *Missal* and some cards with holy images, which, although they had belonged to my mother, Amy, some of the pictures had the name, Agnes, written on them. The inscription in the prayer book read, *To Agnes from Mother Pierre. 1936*. Was she the Mother Pierre who made my life such a misery? Who was Agnes? And how did Amy get her holy cards?

As I sat puzzling over the contradictions, I pulled out a large wedding photo of my mother from beneath a bundle of photos. She looked so beautiful and I wondered why I was not at her wedding to Con, because I would like to have been there. My mother brought Con to visit me a couple of times when I was in the home, but when they visited, there was no mention that they were married.

That evening, while in an agitated frame of mind, I wrote a letter to the archives of The Good Shepherd convent, explaining that I was seeking any details of myself that they might still have. I told them my present name, my childhood name and I included proof of my identity. With the letter and documents sealed in a registered envelope and, with a sense of inevitability, I watched my letter drop, irretrievably, into the red post box.

After haunting my letterbox daily, and sorting through the junk mail in case I missed their answer, a reply arrived. I took the envelope inside and placed it on the jarrah table. Would the records held unopened in my hand confirm that I had been sentenced to stay in that hellhole at the unbelievably young age of ten? I settled myself on a chair, but then I rose to my feet, and stood up straight, as if awaiting a prison sentence; then I slowly slit the envelope open. I observed the crest at the top of the page, an unusual cross, superimposed upon a heart – and I hastily scanned the contents, picking out the key words:

Name: Faye

Admission: Saturday October 23. 1948.

Date of birth: April 2 1938. Aged 10 years at time of admission.

Place of birth: Perth.

Parents: Mother: Amy Dean.

Father's details not recorded.

Admission: 23 October 1948. Leederville Convent.

Discharged: Left with mother 20 December 1950.

After searching our records for a second time, no other information is available. We have also enclosed the records relating to your mother's time spent in the convent at West Leederville.

I quickly rifled through the documents until I came to another page bearing the same heart and cross crest at the top, left-hand corner. The letter thanked me for my inquiry, and added that the following information was all that they held in their records:

Name: Amy Dean Francis.

Date of birth: 14 years at time of admission in 1933.

Parents: Ernest Francis and Amelia Kandy.

Admission: 20 October 1933.

Discharged: Left for situation on 11 August 1936

Returned: 5 September 1936.

No final discharge date recorded.

My own mother had been in The Home of the Good Shepherd for three years from the age of 14! Was that the answer to who Agnes was? Did the nuns decide that she would be known as Agnes? With no clear date of Amy's release from the home, and as I was born in 1938, it would appear that after Amy left the home not too much time elapsed before she became pregnant. In addition, with that information came the realisation that she left her daughter, Faye, to become Lucy, alone and afraid for seven hundred and thirty days and an equal amount of terrifyingly long nights.

I no longer felt inclined to make excuses for her as I sometimes had when I remembered Stella and Bertram Street – another unfortunate place that my mother had chosen to leave me when I was a child. I had believed that it was not her fault and that she did not really know what Stella was like. However, The Home of the Good Shepherd, she knew well.

Current representatives of the home acknowledged that for a ten-year-old, it was an extraordinary place to be kept.

At that moment of discovery, I fell to my knees and I railed angrily at my long-deceased mother and swore at her in a way I would never have dared to do so during her lifetime. I shouted that she had condemned me to a lifetime of self-condemnation and guilt, never to escape, even in happier times, of forever wondering who I had offended or what I had done wrong. I bellowed at her and asked her to tell me why she made me feel so ghastly that even my mother did not want me.

After some time though, in the bathroom, I splashed warm, soothing water across my face and, when I glanced in the mirror above the basin, I was unpleasantly startled at the image of my barely recognisable, raddled, blotched and aged face staring back at me. I needed coffee and for a moment I envied those who took tablets or drank copious amounts of numbing alcohol in trying times.

Sleep deserted me yet again and, when morning came, my only desire was to remain within the protective, isolated confines of my bed. Crowded shopping centres brought fear and feelings of suffocation and panic; and counting in my head became frantically repetitive.

The knowledge that Amy and Con were already married when Amy decided to let me out of The Good Shepherd made me curious to know when the marriage took place. I phoned the Registrar of Births, Deaths and Marriages and spoke with a helpful, courteous young man who became quite interested in my tale. After lengthy searches and much discussion, he informed me regretfully, that by some quirk of law relating to the Freedom of Information Act, information of my mother's details would not be available to me until sometime in the following year.

'For heaven's sake,' I reacted impatiently, 'this is so ridiculous. My mother died over fourteen years ago, and all I need are details of a marriage. I have her death certificate. I only want a marriage date.'

As I paused for breath, I heard the young man's voice telling me that if I had Amy's death certificate, then the marriage date would be listed there, on that certificate. However, I had once seen Amy's not too successful attempt to alter the date on her birth certificate, so unwittingly the thought crossed my mind. *Not necessarily. I am dealing with Amy.* After I thanked him for his help, I returned to the camphor wood box wondering that if any documents of Amy's would tell the full story. I intended to look, for one final time, at whatever documents and letters the chest held, then to lock it away and put the whole matter to rest for all time.

The soothing scent of camphor surrounded me and I waited a moment before I reached into the box for the certificate. The old-style, large, formal certificate brought home to me how many years had passed by. I saw that the details had been there all along. I had overlooked them. Listed were three marriages. One date leapt out. On Saturday, October 23, 1948, I had been placed in The Home of the Good Shepherd. My mother remarried on Saturday, October 30, 1948. Was it possible that my mother put me in a home *a week* before her wedding day? Was it possible that I had been put away like a puppy in the kennels, to be housed and fed until its owner came back?

Papers and photos flew in all directions until I found the wedding photo again. The elaborate gown made me realise the amount of effort and planning that preceded the wedding. It had not been a hastily arranged affair. The professional, coloured photo showed Amy dressed in an extravagant blue lace, long gown. The *piece de resistance* was a tall, Spanish-style headdress attached to a veil, which cascaded to the floor. An impressive, unusually large bouquet of striking yellow roses with dozens of yellow pansies completed the picture. The photo was reminiscent of the glamorous, alluring, and film star look of the era. The image continued to hold my attention and when I gazed into the brown, kitten like faces at the centre of each yellow pansy, I pictured Amy, strikingly attractive, holding blue lace to her face to see if the colour suited. I imagined an eager-toassist seamstress with her tape measure draped around her neck. I pondered about how long it took her to design and complete the gown and the extraordinary headdress and veil. When all the phone calls to the photographer and the florist, and the finer details of the gown were completed, and with only a short time before her big day, was my mother faced with the almost forgotten detail of what to do with her daughter?

I dreamily pictured myself at the wedding, perhaps dressed in pale, soft, ferny green. But would the image of her lavish beauty perhaps have been marred by the presence of a ten-year-old daughter? Did her new husband know that a ten-year-old daughter even existed?

The thought came to me that if I had not found out that I was only ten years old at the time, I would have maintained my silence. However, my family knew nothing of the real story of their mother. If I kept quiet, I was placing them in the position that I had been in: of, perhaps, finding half-truths, and of saying: 'No, that definitely did not happen. Not to our mother, we would have known.'

After all, though, I thought, did it really matter?

Would my family care, or find my fragile beginnings, interesting?

Yes! I believed they would.

In the words of Ernest Hemmingway ... *My aim is to put down on paper what I see and what I feel in the best and simplest way.*

Chapter 2

Through Baby Eyes

I was born in April 1938. My mother had just turned 19. Because her behaviour seemed so careless and irresponsible towards her baby, and because of her youthful looks, I had always thought that she had been younger when I was born. However, the harsh living and moral standards that prevailed in 1938 built a ready picture of the feelings of hopelessness and fear that the naive and emotionally immature Amy must have experienced when, not long released from The Good Shepherd, she found that she was pregnant and completely alone. The person who fathered me was never mentioned and I am sure that Amy would have liked me to believe in the virgin birth. With no one to turn to and terrified at the prospect of being returned to the dreaded home, or ending up a homeless and shamed outcast with an illegitimate baby, she probably headed to church to confess and beg forgiveness.

Help did come from the Catholic Church in the shape of two of its devout parishioners, whom I came to know as Aunty Stella, and Granny. They were regarded as near saints by the people of the parish, put on earth to help waifs and strays and sinners. Amy must surely have been regarded as all three. My mother gave me into the care of the two women and then disappeared from my life for the next two years. She, no doubt, had no idea of how to nurture or care for a baby and thought that giving her baby to someone else was a good idea. Whilst understanding the difficulties of the era, I would never be able to understand her actions. Amy did not come to see her child and unfortunately, it seemed to me in retrospect, that she was never to lose the notion that any person or situation was expendable when things became difficult.

It was there in Bertram Street that I lived with a woman, whom I called Granny, and with another woman, who was either Granny's foster, or adopted, daughter, whom I called Aunty Stella. There was also an old man, called Mr Cassidy. He did not sleep at their house; he lived in garage of someone's house in nearby Carr Street. However, he came to Stella's house each morning, stayed all day, and returned to Carr Street in the evening. I was never comfortable when Mr Cassidy was around, and I felt safer if he was in one room and I was in another.

Granny seemed to live a good life according to her beliefs. I believed that Stella did not. They both had a strong connection to St Brigid's Church, and the happenings of the parish.

They were, however, no relations of mine.

In the late 1930s, the houses around Newcastle and Bertram Streets in West Perth provided basic rental accommodation for low income earners. Those narrow, semi-detached homes stretched the length of the dwelling from the front through to the back door. One walked along a passageway, passed a bedroom and a lounge room straight into the kitchen, and the bathroom usually adjoined the kitchen. A door from the kitchen led to the back yard where a primitive laundry, at that time called the washhouse, sheltered under a tin roof. Often there were no sides to the washhouse, and the wood-fired copper and rough cement troughs were largely exposed to the elements. Attached to the middle of the troughs was a large hand turned mangle, or wringer. I loved the warm, soapy, clean smell of washday when the steam rose and billowed from the boiling copper. When I was very little, about two years old, I often stood on a rickety wooden box alongside Granny (who I remembered as more kindly and patient than Stella) as she allowed me to put some of the smaller pieces of washing through the wringer. Often I was dressed only in my pants and vest and wrapped in an old cardigan of Granny's because all the clothes I possessed were in the trough for the once-a-week wash. Huffing and puffing I turned the wringer handle with all my might, watching with fascination as the pearly, glistening, sudsy bubbles squished between the rollers and back into the trough. No matter how hot the weather, or how freezing cold and raining, on Monday morning the unsheltered outside washhouse was braved to do the weekly washing.

There was a row of six identical houses in Bertram Street. Each had a small front veranda, generally used for extra sleeping space and enclosed with a canvas blind to afford some kind of protection from the weather. Anyone sleeping in the sleep-out quickly realised privacy or quietness was non-existent. With the bed a mere two metres from the pavement, with only a canvas awning between the two, the sounds of the night were many and varied. Something sounding like the devil, 'coming to get you' was most likely a neighbourhood dog going for a walk and rubbing along the fence as it passed by. Scarier was a drunken person muttering and singing as he wended his shaky way home. He caused me to freeze and hold my breath, so as not to alert him to my presence behind the canvas blind, in case he staggered through the gate again, and up on to the veranda to triumphantly wave mysterious, ugly, dangly parts from his trousers. For many children, the sleep-out was the only bedroom they ever knew.

There I stayed with Stella and Granny until my mother married and took me to live with her when I was around two years old. Unfortunately, circumstances in her life dictated that I would again be separated from her and from my adoptive father when, before too many years had passed, I would be returned to Bertram Street. Amy married in July of 1939 and

Alfredo, her new husband, adopted me legally some months after the marriage took place. It was then that my mother took me with her to live in Kalgoorlie, or rather, at a place called Somerville, about 30 kilometres from that goldmining town. I lived happily there with my mother and adoptive father until I was about four years old.

Alfredo's Italian family were warm, good natured, gregarious market gardeners. Their large property comprised many acres where rich, red tomatoes grew from plants that stood taller than I did, creating for me a tangy, scented canopy as I crept gently through them, hidden from the grownups. The red, loamy soil grew a substantial carpet of small white flowers and lush red fruit, where strawberries nestled among dark green leaves. Beans grew untidily as they straggled up and along strong poles, and grape vines bearing healthy clusters of dark purple fruit stretched so far into the distance that no matter how hard I tried, I could not see where they ended. Further away still, cabbage and lettuce grew in orderly, aligned rows. Down in the paddock, a long way from the house, cows and pigs bellowed and grunted in continuous, ill-timed unison. Once when a mother pig had a new litter, somebody present at the time told me that one of the piglets was my baby brother. In the absence of other children around the place, I found that this was quite acceptable and played and conversed at length with 'my brother' I made up stories for him and, although I did not have his undivided attention as he snuffled around the food trough, I did feel that he was listening. I was allowed to hand feed him apples and I liked the scratchy feel of his whiskery little snout on the palm of my hand. However, the pig grew and soon it was time for him to go to the market. Nobody dreamt up a tale that he was going on a holiday, or to piggy heaven, or some such place. No. He was going, they told me, to market. Although young, I certainly knew what that meant. I missed him. The other little pigs that followed on from him just did not have his sociable nature.

The daytime heat in Somerville baked the ground to a hot, hard, blistering surface. Never would I venture outside without my sandals on.

Sandstorms came and I stood stretched as tall as possible on tiptoe, just inside the screen door of our green and white painted, tiny kitchen, with my nose pressed against the mesh screen. I watched, fascinated as the red sand, thick and heavy, whirled around and around, rising up to streak the sky with fiery orange fingers. Experience had taught me to stay indoors, because on previous occasions, the sharp, stinging sand had mercilessly buffeted me and whipped my legs and face and stung my eyes. At the other extreme, the freezing, frosty weather stung my toes spitefully, turning them numb and blue as I raced across the yard to the outside lavatory and to the wash pump first thing in the morning.

Alfredo had several brothers and sisters who were a happy-go-lucky lot. The women were all attractive and tall with long dark hair. My fair-haired mother, shorter in build and curvier, provided an attractive contrast when they performed and sang with the local theatre group. The sound of them practising their songs and laughing created a wonderfully light-hearted atmosphere. They encouraged me to join in and I adored Alfredo's magic tricks, which I took part in, never knowing if I would end up mysteriously wearing rabbit ears, or finding pennies in my shoes. Alfredo, in addition to working in the market garden, was a popular illusionist and he performed with the theatre group.

I loved to hear my mother's strong, vibrant voice, singing as she pegged the washing on the clothesline, or while we picked strawberries for the market. Ever after, the sweet, summery smell of strawberries and the acidic smell of tomato vines on a still, hot day took me back to that time when life was easy. Remembering my singing mother confirmed for me that, for a short while, for her, and for me, it was indeed a happy time.

War was declared and Alfredo joined the army and departed for Singapore.

Those events heralded the end of Alfredo's and my mother's marriage. Amy and I left Somerville and returned to Perth. I remembered nothing of the packing up or leaving Kalgoorlie, but I did remember the family taking us to catch the train. In those days, trains in the country could be boarded at sidings. The sidings were not stations, just a designated stopping place, seemingly in the middle of nowhere. I scurried on my short, plump legs clutching at my mother's skirt with one hand and my cuddly, big, yellow teddy bear with the other. I recalled the difficulty for us to scramble up on to a huge, shiny, water-carrying pipe that I later learned was the famous Mundaring to Kalgoorlie pipeline.

'Quickly, hurry up,' Amy urged, tugging my arm. 'We have to stand up here if we want the train driver to see us.'

When we managed to get to the top, we balanced rather precariously while my mother waved frantically and continuously to alert the train driver to our presence. Would-be passengers not there in time, or not atop the water pipe, were sometimes left gazing in dismay as the departing train steamed away into the distance. However, my mother's efforts were rewarded. The train chugged rapidly towards us and indeed did stop, though with barely stopping enough time for us to jump on. My mother hauled me into a carriage as the guard leapt to the ground and hurried along, picking up the suitcases. Then the train picked up speed and tore off again. I ran to the window to wave to Alfredo's family as the train rushed off.

When I thought they could not see me anymore I vigorously waved my bear out of the window – surely, they could see him, he was so big. Suddenly, he was not so big. To my astonishment, I saw teddy bear fly off into the scrubby bushes. All that was left in my hand was one of his arms. Through my outraged tears, I saw my mother trying not to laugh. The whole thing probably did look funny to an adult, especially one with her particular sense of humour.

I never did get another bear!

We moved into a large, old house in Aberdeen Street in West Perth, which we shared with other people – a common enough occurrence at that time. One of the other tenants, Mrs Bennett, and my mother became friendly and could be found most days in one or the other's kitchen, chatting, smoking and drinking tea.

Amy and I occupied rooms at the front of that gracious, older-style house, which had formerly been a private hospital. Our bedroom and combined lounge room provided us with plenty of space and I found great comfort sitting in front of the cosy fire, gazing into the crackling flames in the cold weather. The kitchen was just big enough to hold a small table with two chairs and a large cream and green kitchenette that displayed our dinner plates and dishes. Household refrigeration at that time was rare and we had an ice chest to keep our milk from curdling. The iceman came clanging along the road three times a week. Very hot days saw the lady of each house stop whatever she was doing when she heard the jangle of the bell heralding the approaching ice carrier and rush to stand with the front door open.

At Granny's house, instead of an ice chest, there had been a Coolgardie safe, which was a cubic, metal frame with wet hessian bags attached to each side, to keep the food in the safe cool, although in the summer, the butter melted to an oily mess and jellies were rather wobbly. The wet bags usually smelled musty.

Mr and Mrs Bennett, who were 'Ethel' and 'Clarrie' to the adults, towered over Amy as they were both extremely tall and thin. They spoke slowly and their voices reminded me of parrots. I supposed that is what people used to call 'the Aussie drawl'. In spite of her frequent, irritable protests, they persisted in calling my mother 'Ame' or 'Ames'. Most days I played with their two sons, Laurie and Maxie. Laurie was a lanky, tall boy, a couple of years older than I was. His younger brother, Maxie, was a little happy dumpling, a couple of years younger me. He spent most of the day out in the back yard playing games and chortling *Whacko-the-*

diddle-oh when something pleased him. We carted little buckets of water back and forth and sloshed around in the mud, playing near the back yard tap, making mud pies and patting them into neat little shapes. Near the tap, unruly clusters of tawny, red chrysanthemums grew, and when the sun settled on them, they released their tangy, non-sweet perfume. That was where I chose to sit. Chrysanthemums became my favourite flowers and forever after, whenever I smelt them, a fuzzy vision arose of a little me inhaling the green, fresh scent and feeling the warm sun on my back.

Wherever we lived, a visit to the toilet seemed to involve trekking to the furthest point of some heavily overgrown backyard. To avoid that inconvenience at night-time at Aberdeen Street, we had a beautifully decorated china chamber pot – that is, until Amy broke it. One day after she had washed it at the garden tap, she stood for several minutes swinging it around above her head like a windmill to dry it. We both gasped in astonishment as it flew from her hand straight over the fence and into the back lane. We heard it smash and laughed ourselves silly but, unfortunately with coupons, rations and scarcity of almost everything, including chamber pots, we were unable to buy another, so thereafter we used a large jam tin with sharp, rough edges. I hated that jam tin.

In the middle of the house there was an enormous bathroom. I thought the bath must have been the deepest, ugliest bath ever made. I disliked being alone in the bathroom and I found no warmth or comfort from bath time. The enormity and greyness of the rough cement bath made me think of an enclosed submarine beneath the murky sea. I had once overheard Mrs Bennett breathlessly telling my mother a tale of a baby being electrocuted in the bath tub. From that time on whenever I looked high above at a dimly glowing unshaded light bulb, I visioned it dropping into the bath and electrocuting me.

I started going to St Brigid's Catholic School when I was about five years old. The playground resounded with Greek and Italian accents, the sounds of which, even years later, brought me a feeling of warmth and friendliness. No cultural barriers existed there. Willy Wagtails, the little black and white birds that I loved so much, flocked around my feet, cheekily waggling their tails from side to side, as I walked to school. To me, like rainbows and ladybirds and butterflies, they meant happiness. I walked slowly and with care around them as they circled my feet in close little groups.

Sister Laurence gave us a lesson about birds and told us that soon there might not be any Willy Wagtails left, because the councils were spraying some sort of poison on the ground to get rid of Argentine ants, but when the spray killed the ants, the flow on effect was killing the little birds as well. The little birds did disappear for many years until one happy day I thought I recognised the hoppy, cheeky little strut from a distance. I moved closer.

Yes, they were back!

There was an enthusiastic lady, named Mrs Bulbeck, who came to the school two mornings a week to give elocution lessons. With a loud voice, and a determinedly precise manner, she sat in front of us pulling ridiculous, exaggerated faces. With rounded vowels, we repeated, 'How now, brown cow' and 'Coo-ee, coo-ee', and imitated her exaggerated expressions. We enjoyed it though. How strange it seemed. In hard economic times, with no family to speak of, I went to elocution lessons. I had reason to be grateful for those lessons, though, because they gave me the huge advantage of not being forever defined and being judged because of bad grammar and poor pronunciation. Thankfully, for the rather uncoordinated child that I was, I was not sent to ballet lessons.

On February 19, 1942, Australians were horrified and the war brought fear closer to their hearts when two hundred and forty two bombs dropped on Darwin from Japanese aircraft. The town of Darwin had little defence during its obliteration and heavy losses were inflicted on the Allied forces. The raids were the first of almost a hundred against

Australia during 1942 and 1943. As a result, the government declared large parts of Western Australia a blackout area. No street or business light shone. Windows were draped with black cloth, carefully placed, with no chink of light glowing to guide possible enemy planes to any well-populated area. Air wardens patrolled the streets at night, ready to remonstrate with careless householders. The Japanese dropped further bombs on Darwin later in 1943.

From our classroom, we heard air raid sirens and, with the nuns, we all bustled into a trench previously dug in the schoolyard, a huge sandy pit with wooden planks on the side to stop it caving in and with wooden boards above to protect our heads. The structures were optimistically called Air Raid Shelters. Wartime rules prevented us from going home or our parents from coming to get us during an air raid and we stayed in the shelter for several hours after the usual end of the school day until the piercing blast of the safety siren sounded.

On the corner of Aberdeen and Lake Streets stood a general store owned by an Italian family named Bordoni, and on the opposite corner was the Re Store. Similar in style, the two shops stocked all the traditional goods common to continental shopkeepers. My mother became friends with the Bordoni family and we spent a great deal of time in their shop and adjoining home, which was a social meeting place for many people in the district, including detectives from the nearby police headquarters in Beaufort Street. Ironically and tragically, one of those detectives came into my life again many years later. Uncle Bordoni, as I learned to call him used to give me an eggcup full of red wine and a small piece of crusty bread, to 'give the little one the rosy cheeks'. The rosy cheeks were often pinched with enthusiasm.

After school one day, I was with my mother in Uncle Bordoni's shop, when a very showy young man with black hair shiny with brilliantine, whom I found devastatingly handsome, walked up behind my mother and pinched her on the bottom, which was a reasonably acceptable practice by some in those days, to express interest and admiration. She got such a fright she spun around and slapped his face with a resounding whack. He, in turn, got such a shock that Latin-like and volatile, he burst loudly into tears. Then I watched bemused, because she had to hug him for such a long time to console him.

The shop was a magical, jovial place, with much noise, laughter, singing, ten different conversations going on at once and all the customers being greeted like a long-lost cousin. The warm, heady, scent of strong cheeses, ground coffee and Italian sausage hanging from hooks at just above head height and the rich, red wine in huge casks, with its heady, woody, grapey smell, created something extremely evocative and unforgettable. Big tins of loose biscuits sat on the counter waiting to be weighed into brown paper bags to suit the customer's requirements, maybe six ounces or maybe one or more pounds, whatever the customer wanted was all right. My small fingers were never too far away waiting to scoop up the broken pieces. In another section of the store, one found legs of ham.

There were enormous pieces of pickled pork and colourful jars of vegetables and olives. The subtle, sweet tang of sugar mingled with the other aromas as Uncle Bordoni weighed it out from large hessian sacks into smaller bags. Few goods came ready packaged, so it took many hours to weigh and shelve the seemingly endless truck loads that arrived on Mondays, Wednesdays and Fridays – the universal market days. Grocery shopping was sociable and enjoyable, not a noisy, wearisome chore.

The daughters of the Re Store owners, across the road, all went to St Brigid's school. They were a warm, happy family, just like the Bordoni's. The mother and father showed me great kindness and acceptance and, as a family, personified the best aspects of their faith. Their youngest daughter, Aurora, and I were the same age and we usually played together at school and afterwards at her place.

Sometimes I went to their home on Sunday for lunch and, skipping home one day, I was just outside Uncle Bordoni's when I slipped on a banana skin. My head hit the ground with a horrible, sickening thud, which continued to make me feel queasy whenever I thought about it for years later. I lost consciousness and woke up later at home in bed. I apparently had a concussion and the doctor told my mother to keep an eye on me and not let me fall asleep for a while. Not considering the importance of the doctor's advice, Amy went out somewhere and I did go to sleep. When she returned and saw me, she threw herself across me and set up a loud keening and wailing, which woke me.

I sat up quickly. 'Why are you crying Mummy?'

She let out a piercing shriek and cried, 'Oh My God! I thought you were gone!'

From our kitchen window, we overlooked the beautiful, rambling garden of the house of the Greek Orthodox priest who lived next door. His appearance was quite formidable, with his long, narrow, black beard and his large black hat and black clothes. I wondered where this religious man, who seemed not to be a Catholic like us, fitted into the scheme of things.

Other people, mainly men, sometimes came to stay in rooms further down the passage, usually for a short time, before moving on. They fell into the category of people *not to speak to,* only a quick smile and a hello, just enough to be courteous, were permitted because, although living under the same roof, those men were strangers, not friends or family. However, not speaking offered small protection from some of them. One particular person had a nasty habit of sweeping along the passage, naked, with his silky dressing gown unfastened and floating behind him. I hated being in the passage at the same time as him and I hated his sly smile when I tried to duck back into our kitchen if I saw him. I was afraid of him and I was equally afraid of being questioned by my mother, the priest, and the nuns, if I told anyone about him, because young girls were supposed to be pure and good – like the Virgin Mary. Seeing a naked man made me feel less pure and, somehow guilty ... *so I told no one.*

Ambling along towards our house one morning, I looked up to see a smartly dressed telegram boy swing from his bicycle with great aplomb and prop it against our front fence. Wartime telegram boys usually made people nervous and they were greeted with mixed emotions during those uncertain days, because for every time a telegram brought glad tidings, they more frequently brought news of tragedy to the families of soldiers overseas. On that occasion though, he brought the splendid news that Alfredo would be home on leave in a few weeks' time.

Alfredo was coming home on leave! I liked to sing and Alfredo encouraged me to learn a new song to sing for him when he came home. I knew all the favourites of that time: *Oh Johnny! Oh Johnny! Heavens above, White Christmas, Paper Doll* and *Doing the Lambeth Walk.* Nor could I possibly forget the lament of a lonely young soldier: *Kiss me Goodnight Sergeant Major. The Lambeth Walk* involved a dance routine that saw me tramping along the kitchen table, knees and elbows pumping furiously to the beat, and finishing off the performance with a resounding. *Oi!* How must that have sounded? Although, I did once win first prize, singing *White Christmas,* on the Willie Wheaties Saturday morning radio show. Possibly enthusiasm triumphed over talent as I warbled away happily and unselfconsciously.

On the day of Alfredo's homecoming, Amy and I dressed up in our prettiest clothes to welcome him. My mother, dazzling in a beautiful mauve, floral dress, wore white shoes, and painstakingly applied fake leg tan, which rubbed off all over her white shoes and anything else it touched if it was not given time to dry properly. Looking like a Shirley Temple clone, with bouncy ringlets achieved by sleeping all night with my hair wrapped around strips of soft cloth and tied at the end, I waltzed around happily with pretty curls and a sore head.

The train was about to leave from Perth station and we hurried forward, jumping into the first open carriage before the guard blew his shrill whistle and bellowed importantly for everyone to get aboard. The train moved rapidly away from the platform. Soon it gained momentum as it busily clicketty-clacked along, passing through several suburban railway stations on the journey to Fremantle. Beautiful, well-kept gardens, ablaze with the vibrant colours of the blooms of the season, surrounded each station. Pink and red mingled; purple fought with orange; and white, ivory and yellow all blended in riotous glee. With a sky of deepest blue as a backdrop, I was mesmerised as we sped past. The gardens were the pride and joy of the local stationmasters and led to some healthy rivalry between them, particularly as springtime neared. As the train chugged through Mosman Park, we looked towards Rottnest and saw that several ships lay at anchor out in Gage Roads awaiting their turn to enter the harbour. Crossing the railway bridge over the river at the end of Fremantle Harbour, we realised that several large vessels were already berthed. What if Alfredo were already there? We hurried, buffeted by the crowds from the train to the wharf.

The sight of hundreds of jubilant men in uniform, laughing and jostling for position as they came down the gangplank, stirred a huge wave of emotion through the waiting crowd, and cheering broke out. The atmosphere was electric, with families hugging and kissing, laughing and crying such was their relief and joy at being together again, even for a short time. Smiling happily with his kit bag swung over his shoulder Alfredo appeared suddenly from the middle of the crowd, just like one of his magic tricks. Hordes of people milled around, preventing us from connecting with each other. Eventually though, I was swept up high above the crowd into a great, rib-cracking bear hug. After exuberant hugs and kisses with Amy and me, and possibly a couple of strangers as well, we pushed our way through the crowd to catch the train back home. Feeling happy and celebratory, we moved away from the crowds towards the station. An empty carriage slowed and halted right where we stood. We leapt in and hastily closed the door.

My mother handed me a packet of enticing, jewel-coloured jubes. 'Be a good girl and you may have them. I want you to look out of the window at all the interesting things along the way as we go home. I don't feel well and just want to be quiet, so you look out of the window and don't disturb me.'

When I looked at Alfredo questioningly, he looked the other way. It appeared that I was to just eat the jubes and look out of the window. I became invisible to those two people.

I could not help looking around curiously once or twice. My mother was laughing and did not seem sick at all. I wondered why her shoes were off and her floral dress that she was so proud of was all screwed up in a heap.

Confused and lonely, I saw no beautiful station gardens on the way home. I stared out through the window and saw emptiness. Had I been naughty and too talkative? Did I show off and get too pushy and attention seeking? The tears welled and spilled over. I was ill before we got back home.

Oh Amy! Your lollies made me so sick. Sometimes I think that you are not a very nice mother.

His leave quickly over, Alfredo returned to Singapore in December. Two weeks later, the morning sun shone hot and cheery on Christmas morning. No midnight Mass happened for us the previous night because my mother was an occasional and somewhat reluctant churchgoer. Although I preferred being with my mother than not being with her, I did miss the feeling of Christmas that came from going to midnight Mass. Together, my mother and I sat at the small round table, where we usually had our meals. However, that day, the table was covered with brightly wrapped parcels, and cherries and fruit bonbons in a silver dish. When she stood in front of our little tree and said, 'Happy Christmas darling,' and handed me some presents, I felt like a little girl in a movie with a gorgeous film star.

My mother sometimes did try and, in trying, she created some special times and some good memories for me.

Christmas Day moved forward at a leisurely pace. Mr and Mrs Bennett, along with Laurie and Maxie, had come along the passage from their rooms and into our kitchen to share lunch with us. Vera, a friend of my mother's was also there. The table was set with flowered plates and cut glass dishes filled with salad, meat, cheese, and some crusty loaves from Uncle Bordoni's corner shop. I began to feel queasy and disinclined to eat. However, the tempting goodies beckoned me and I feared upsetting Amy by being difficult. But suddenly I feared taking another bite even more.

Vera stood up from her chair, and leaned toward me and put her hand on my forehead. 'Amy,' I heard her say from a seemingly great distance. 'I think Faye is sick. She's burning up and look, she's shaking.'

Mrs Bennett's voice chimed in: 'Oh look, Ame. She is covered in a rash.' She hastily pushed her chair back. 'I'm sorry boys! We have to go!'

That was perfectly normal. Nobody in those days stayed around if there was any suggestion of anything infectious. The rest of Christmas Day passed for me in a haze of sickness and strange half dreams. Adult voices swam around in my head, and I heard words like 'delirious', 'ambulance' and 'hospital'. Through my scratchy, sore eyes, I saw the doctor standing over me and I thought I must be really sick. Fancy the doctor coming on Christmas Day.

My mother cried because the doctor sent for an ambulance to take me to hospital. The devastating childhood disease of Poliomyelitis was in epidemic proportions at that time and it had dire consequences, sometimes including lifelong paralysis. What I did have, though, was Scarlet Fever, so named, because of the bright red, rough rash, which was intensely sore and resembled sandpaper. It appeared on my chest, face and tongue and my raw inflamed throat stopped me from even swallowing water.

I spent eight weeks recovering in the Infectious Diseases Hospital. Evidently, I caught numerous other infections while I was in the hospital and needed time to recover from them.

Visitors were not admitted into the Infectious Diseases Hospital, and babies, in particular, fretted and cried continuously.

One day a boy stood by my bed and, with a big smile, gave me a brooch. I think he said he found it in the garden. Then he ran away. I gazed at it in the palm of my hand and loved what I saw. The brooch was not shiny or glittery: it was smooth and dull like a soft blue eggshell. I did not see the boy for days afterwards and thought that he had left the hospital without saying goodbye to me. I asked the nurse and she assured me, 'No pet. He's just shy since he gave you the brooch.'

To my surprise, I was allowed to keep the brooch. But my ownership was temporary. When the time came for me to leave, I had to leave the brooch behind because nothing from the hospital could be taken for fear of spreading infection. Too weak to walk down the stairs, I had to be carried. My tears flowed, as did my mother's – hers because I was unrecognisably thin and, because an orderly carried me, she thought I was paralysed, and I cried because I wanted my brooch. That happened such a long time ago, but I wondered if a vague memory might have stirred had I ever seen that boy again. I *knew* that I would still have recognised that brooch.

It was a heady time in quiet little Perth when the American sailors descended upon the town. Amy was leading the lifestyle that she clearly desired – that of a single girl with few responsibilities and plenty of good times. I lived with her, but spent time with Granny and Stella too. Alfredo had not been home on leave for a long time. Sailors on shore leave proved to be most desirable companions, being in the main good looking and charming with those cute accents and with money just waiting to be spent.

They took the local girls and women to the movies and to the dances and showered them with gifts of nylon stockings, chocolate and perfume. Those luxuries were unattainable locally, specifically because of wartime unavailability but also because of the requirement for government-issued coupons for most purchases. Necessities such as clothing and food required coupons, as did luxury items. The visiting troops seemed to have no difficulty regarding money or coupons.

The nights when my mother went out were my most dreaded time. Did other people know that I was alone in our bedroom? Nobody came near me and I would never have opened nor gone through the door. I had no way of knowing, when the night fears came, if it would be all right to call Mrs Bennett. I was not to tell anyone that Amy went out at night times; must never mention any particular man friend; and it seemed safer not to talk at all. *So I said nothing.*

An oil-filled night light burned above my bed, not bright enough to be comforting, just bright enough to cast dim flickering shadows. My Catholic imagination, already honed to perfection, ran riot and my thoughts petrified me. I saw the burning and flaming devils of my teaching – the ones that I was destined to meet in Hell if I strayed from the path of goodness. The impish devils darted back and forth in the flickering lamplight, doing a threatening jungle beat dance as they came leering evilly towards my bed. By my turning the flame up in the lamp as far as possible, the room became bright and the shadows went away. However, the scorched wallpaper above the lamp alerted my mother to what I was doing and the lamp disappeared, leaving me in total darkness.

A handsome looking, tall sailor, dressed in a white, stiffly starched uniform, with lots of colours decorating the jacket, was about to leave for an evening out with my mother. They were leaving the room and when my mother kissed me goodnight, he moved forward, bowed from the waist, and gave me some chocolates in a beautiful box. However, wretchedness at being left by myself swept over me, especially as my mother looked so gorgeous in a long, pale, floral evening dress, with a little fur cape around her shoulders. I knew that she would be having a good time and being happy. I was not part of it and I was scared and had no one to talk to, but being scared did not make me feel as bad as not being wanted.

I ate the whole box of chocolates.

Another evening I was alone when I awoke to see a little man creeping by the foot of my bed. For some reason the sight of a little man worried me more than the seeing a normal-sized man. Forgetting the rule to keep silent, I started shrieking. 'Where are you mummy? There's a little man in here.'

Then above my yelling, I heard my mother say through gritted teeth, 'For God's sake, will you shut up? It's me.' Apparently, she had lost her key and had come in through the window. Years later, we laughed about the incident, but I never did find out why she crept across the room on her hands and knees.

It was during World War Two, when a German victory seemed probable and when the Italian Prime Minister and former fascist dictator, Benito Mussolini, joined forces with Hitler, that many Italians living in Australia were placed in internment camps. It was seen that by joining forces with Germany, Italy had become an enemy of Australia. That action caused hardship and heartache to thousands of Italian immigrants, many of whom had lived and toiled industriously in Australia for decades. Luckily, it didn't affect their friendship with most of our locals, although one particularly large, blustering man, who ran the Post Office opposite our house, started walking past making insulting, derogatory remarks at my mother because he knew of her friendship with many of the local Italians. Amy did not take kindly to his insults and she took to hiding behind the blue Plumbago hedge that ran along our fence line. Armed with the hose, she sprayed just enough water to dampen him when he walked by. It took a while for him to wake up to what was happening. When he finally did realise, as he flicked water drops from his head, he came roaring into our garden and there was Amy crouched under the bushes. Never one to back down, she turned the hose on full and completely drenched him. The comments stopped and, from that time on, he no longer walked on our side of the street.

When the war ended in 1945, men, women and children – people of all ages, all religions and political persuasion – crowded *en masse* into the city. The singing, dancing, and jubilation went on for many days. The Town Hall clock chimed continuously and the town's cathedrals' bells rang out joyously. Ticker tape fell from overhead and people watched in amazement as a group of young men bounced cars up and down on the pavement in a display of reckless abandon.

Finally, the war was over.

The excitement of Alfredo arriving back unexpectedly and the joyfulness within hearts and homes and in the streets, because the war was over, made everybody, including me, feel as if the world was on holiday. People laughed and smiled for no apparent reason and their steps, as they travelled to and fro, were light and bouncy. Soon though, an air of melancholy became tangible within the community, particularly when the priest offered prayers at Sunday Mass for those who never returned. Although the hostilities were over, there was inescapable evidence of the damage the war had inflicted upon those soldiers who did return. I averted my eyes and slightly changed direction when I walked along Aberdeen Street and saw a young man with his coat sleeve pinned to his jacket and realised that his arm was missing. I avoided looking into the faces of handsome men in wheel chairs, which previously I had only seen used by old people. The often roughly-constructed, uncomfortable-looking chairs had become a common sight, as men with one leg, or no legs at all, pushed their way awkwardly along the streets. A man that we knew from Uncle Bordoni's, whose name was Oscar, came home, apparently uninjured to much joy and celebrations. Not long after his triumphant return, though, my mother revealed that Oscar was in Heathcote Hospital. I knew that Heathcote was where they took mad people.

I asked my mother, 'Is Oscar mad?'

'No, not mad,' she replied. 'Shell-shocked. It's happened to lots of the soldiers.'

'Will he get better and come home?'

Amy seemed unsure if he would.

My life with my mother had been a mixture of wonderfully good or quite dreadful times. What she considered fun today could swiftly become showy and naughty tomorrow. The inexplicable contrast between the two was often swift and unexpected. Sometimes, she displayed a classic sense of humour and a great sense of fun. However, these delightful occasions were coupled with being slapped if I broke the rule in any way. Mostly I had no idea what had happened to displease her and I dreaded being humiliatingly slapped or yelled at in front of people. There were the outings and having a nice time when she dressed me in pretty, fashionable clothing. I guessed she had decided that if she had to be accompanied by a child, then the child might as well look decent. Patriotically, during the war, I even had a miniature air force uniform with gold buttons and a peaked cap. The little outfit drew praise from adults and made me feel different and grown-up. I also affected a march-like walk whenever I wore it, which too, probably also caused some amused comment.

When I was about seven years old, during one of the times I was staying with my mother at Aberdeen Street, she told me she was taking me with her for a holiday to my grandmother's house, to a place called Diamond Tree, near Manjimup. I had been there to stay one other time, a long time before. My memory of the Diamond Tree farmhouse was of a rough place, a place that, after dark, was lit with kerosene lamps that cast little light and of long shadows that leapt and darted around the room and followed me as I scurried along the passage at bedtime.

During the day, I liked to climb up and across the bumpy bags of potatoes that were stored in a high shed in the paddock. I climbed to the topmost bag, dragging an obligatory water bag awkwardly behind me. Up there I sat, hidden and content, and stared out at the red and green apples in the orchard and at the red, green, and yellow parrots as they pecked ravenously at the fruit. A large kookaburra sat on the same part of the fence whenever I was up there. If he was not there laughing with raucous, delighted lack of restraint, I felt abandoned and wondered why he had not come that day. Lost in thinking about nothing, I breathed in the sweet, scented blossom that ascended from the long, orderly rows of orange trees ... until a distant adult voice hollered for me to come down.

One morning during our stay, my mother and I were alone and she said to me, 'I want to show you something,' and she handed me some important looking papers, which she said were her birth certificate and her mother's death certificate. I read carefully, and saw that my mother had been born in Ireland on March the 18th, in the year 1919, and that her mother died when she was two years old. She seemed proud of having proof of her parentage and of having been born in Ireland.

'My mother, her name was Amelia, died from tuberculosis when I was just two, and my father also died within six months, leaving me an orphan.' Amy paused briefly before continuing. 'My mother had four other children. There were George and three girls. Their names were Lorna, Blanche and Rose. From what I was told, which was precious little, they all went to different places in England, but your Nana Maude, who was Amelia's sister, and her husband, Alf, had been planning to come out to Australia with their own boy, Harry, and they decided to adopt me and bring me with them.'

I pondered over the fact that Maude was not my real grandmother. No feeling registered when I heard that. Maude was a stern and forbidding presence to me, not sweet, as I imagined grandmothers to be. My unknown grandmother was dead and the man I knew as Granddad was not my grandfather and Uncle Harry was not my true uncle.

'Who does Chris belong to then?' I asked her. Chris lived with Maude and her husband, Alf. He seemed around their age and I liked him the best of the three. He was patient with me, rarely speaking unnecessarily and never harshly.

She replied, 'Chris? Oh, Chris is a sort of cousin of Maude's.'

There seemed to be a few *sorts* of cousins in our family.

Captivated by my mother's story, I followed Amy when she wandered through the house and out on to the front veranda. Perched attentively beside her on a cane chair, I basked happily among the mixed fragrances of the cottage garden flowers surrounding the veranda. I found that being with her in that relaxed atmosphere was heavenly.

Amy frowned when the sun moved across her face and she stood up to go inside. We were sitting in the kitchen when the fly screen door squeaked behind us as it opened and Maude came in from the garden. She took some cold milk from the ice chest and put it on the table. She cut some slices from a fruitcake, put the pieces on to a flower-patterned plate and placed it beside the milk.

'Help yourselves, you two. I'll be in shortly,' she said, as she left the room. Amy wrinkled her nose, as she often did when Maude was around. The pair of them often bickered, and appeared intolerant towards each other.

Through the window, I was able to see Maude's tall frame that tapered from narrow shoulders to a considerably broader lower half as she bent and pulled carrots from the dark, brown soil.

Maude barged noisily through the screen door and into the kitchen again, holding up the front of her long, floral apron from the bottom to form a carrier for the vegetables, which she dumped heavily on to the table.

The next morning, Amy came and stood beside me, as I stood idly in Maude's vegetable patch, eating a fully ripened tomato that I had just picked. She lit a cigarette and the smoke drifted over my head, mingling quite pleasantly with the smell of tomatoes and farm animals.

'I want to talk to you.' Alarm bells rang in my head. I did not like my mother wanting to talk to me. It usually meant trouble. She smiled briefly. 'There's no need to look like that, and you've done nothing wrong. I told you that Maude adopted me.' I nodded agreement as she continued, 'I suppose you think that I should be grateful, but I'm not grateful at all and I often wish that she had left me behind. I was never able to satisfy her. I was no better than a servant, nothing like a daughter, or even a niece.'

We walked on a little, and then we both stopped and rested our arms on the rickety wooden fence between the vegetable garden and the chicken coop. In places, the fence leaned drunkenly towards the ground and showed the scrappy, peeling remnants of long before applied white paint.

Amy's voice continued, 'Maude resented me and her own son, Harry, being friends and she tried to drive a wedge between us whenever she could. She believed herself to be an important person; someone of note and influence in the district, especially within the Catholic community.'

Suddenly, her face contorted with anger, Maude's furious voice erupted from behind the chicken coop, her words indistinguishable, because the chickens had taken fright and twenty flapping, squawking birds drowned out her voice.

When the noise subsided, Maude turned to me, 'I'll see you inside, young lady.'

I wondered nervously why she wanted me. I followed her and Amy closely followed me. Maude imperiously waved me towards a chair and told me to sit down.

Although uninvited, Amy sat down too. Maude positioned herself in front of the warmly glowing wood stove and folded her arms. Fixing her eyes upon Amy, not me, she spoke coldly.

'I have listened to your mother talking all sorts of nonsense out there, but let me tell you, young lady, I have been good to your mother. She was the wrong one; wilful and selfish and would listen to no one. I could do nothing with her, nor could the sisters, or the priest.'

The two women glowered at each other angrily, but no one spoke.

Moments passed, and I asked tearfully, 'May I go now?' No one answered, and I slid from the room, thinking Maude an unkind person, who was not nice to my mother at all.

Chapter 3

Back at Bertram Street

Without warning, I found myself back at Bertram Street with Granny and Stella.

I could not remember my mother telling me that I was going back to them, I just seemed to find myself there one day, going to bed at night on the front veranda and hurrying across the road to school each morning. Again I sat through the seemingly never ending Mass in St Brigid's Church on Sunday morning and, on Sunday evening, I sat with my head banging on the back of the pew as I tried to keep awake during the Benediction. One morning though, my heart leapt and the sound of the priest's loud ramblings became a distant murmur, because about three rows in front of where I sat, I saw Alfredo kneeling in prayer. I fixed my gaze on the back of his glossy, black hair and prayed hard for him to look around and see me. I imagined his face lighting up with pleasure. The time came to go to the alter rail to receive communion. The people in the rows ahead stood and so did the handsome, dark-haired man. And when I saw that it was not Alfredo at all, I lowered my head quickly before anyone noticed the threatening tears.

One day Granny took me outside and into the back yard. There were no garden chairs or anywhere to sit, so we stood awkwardly facing each other amid the unruly plants. Granny told me in a hushed voice that Alfredo and my mother were going to be divorced. I was upset and I cried, because I had been taught that getting divorced was a terrible, sinful thing.

Stella's way of dealing with me when I returned to the kitchen was to say, 'Don't waste your tears. He is not your real father anyway.' That made me cry more, but I experienced no curiosity about my unknown, real father.

It was Christmas time. Midnight Mass was peaceful and I prayed during the mass for my mother to come and see me and to take me away with her for Christmas. My mood was expectant, surrounded as I was by the glorious church decorations, the flowers and the music. Earlier that night, dressed in my best clothes, I stepped out into the inky darkness to walk across the road to the church with Granny and Stella. I gazed at the misty, mysterious glow shimmering around the streetlights and at the glittering star set high upon the church steeple. The beautiful sound of Christmas carols streamed towards us across the chill air as we came around the corner.

We entered the church through the front door and I glanced to my left at the immense statue of Jesus, torn and bleeding, in the arms of Mary Magdalene after he had been lowered from the crucifixion cross. I did not look for long. Not at Christmas time. The priest's white vestments and the covering chasuble, lavishly embroidered with gold, looked rich and celebratory, and the perfume of white Christmas lilies, banked upon the main altar and placed in front of the many statues around the church, rose and blended headily with incense. The priest was mellow and peaceful that night and spoke gently, instead of roaring about hell.

A chore of mine was to dust and polish the large, ornate dresser in the lounge room. It was difficult to clean, with grooves and curly bits all over the place. One day just before Christmas, while dusting away for dear life, I spotted a wrapped Christmas parcel with my name on it. Stella was outside so, very quickly, in case she came back, I took the long box and gave it a little shake. It rattled a bit, and I gleefully realised it was a tea set. The time finally came to open gifts after Mass. I missed my mother and I was suddenly worn out. I just wanted to get my tea set and go to bed. Fortunately, nobody appeared to be looking at my shocked face when my tea set turned out to be an ordinary, not-at-all-exciting game of *Snakes and Ladders*.

My mother did not come that Christmas. I went to bed and cried quietly into my pillow because, although Granny had none of Stella's brutal behaviour, she was strict, so crying for a missing mother or a non-existent tea set would hardly have found sympathy.

I told myself that I did not care if Amy never came again, that she was mean and cruel and hurt me. Then, out of the blue, there she would be, breezing in through the front door looking so pretty and glamorous that I would have forgiven her anything. We would spend some time together, but we rarely went out. That is what my mother was doing – visiting. I longed for the chance to beg her to take me away, but as I planned how to word my plea, suddenly amid another flurry of hugs and kisses she would be gone again. I would immediately begin to rehearse what I would say to her next time. I just knew that it only needed me to tell her how lonely I was and she would come and take me away. She just did not realise, I thought. I got into the habit of sitting at the front gate in the evening after dinner. I shivered with cold, but I could not go inside in case she came around the corner and I missed seeing her. In the half dark, I often thought that she was walking towards me, and hope would rush through me, but when I blinked hard and looked again, she was not there at all. The weather got colder and I was forced stay inside. By the time I saw Amy again I would have forgotten my carefully-rehearsed entreaty.

At school we were taught during Catechism instruction that when a child is born into a Catholic family the child must be baptised immediately to absolve it from the stain of original sin, the sin committed by Adam and Eve, which, according to the teaching of the church all children were born with upon their soul. To me, that was most unfair and not a reasonable belief at all, that a newborn life could be blamed for being sinful before they had lived long enough to do anything wicked. By the age of seven, Catholic children were deemed old enough to receive their first communion. This formal acceptance into the church was based on the premise that at seven years a child knew right from wrong. Little Catholics were supposed to be mature enough to understand and accept the teachings of the Church, to know what was sinful and to confess their sins on a regular basis. In the dark, claustrophobic confessional box, with a tiny space in which to kneel, a small wire grille covered with a filmy black curtain separated us sinful children from the priest. The curtain was no doubt placed there so that penitents remained anonymous as they confessed their wrong doings, although probably the priest recognised each voice in the parish. While I squinted through the misty barrier trying in vain to see what lurked behind in the dimness, the voice of the priest often burst forth with, 'Hurry up child, get on with it.'

If my list of misdemeanours seemed too short, the priest usually instructed me to spend a few moments examining my conscience. Despite dredging up every wrongdoing imaginable, it was a difficult task to be bad enough to satisfy him. Sometimes I would add, 'I was disobedient three times,' or 'I was envious twice,' in order to hasten my exit from the stifling, cavern-like atmosphere.

First communion was a momentous event. I, along with the other girls, wore a white dress and veil. We assembled self-consciously at the church in dresses that were as lavish and as expensive as the families could afford, like a miniature wedding. The incense, strong and pungent, swirled above my head making me feel heady, light, and saintly. I knelt before Father Scully as he murmured unintelligibly. I opened my mouth and he laid the wondrous wafer upon my tongue. I panicked in case I bit it. We had been told many times during religious instruction that the wafer was the body of Christ and we were forbidden to bite into it. I could not swallow mine, so it remained stuck to the roof of my mouth until I escaped into the school grounds and found a tap. I washed the wafer down with water. I was not sure if that was allowed and I guiltily wondered if God knew what I was doing.

The busy, bustling ladies of The Sacred Heart Sodality excelled themselves. Competition was strong. All were eager to impress the visiting cardinal and his entourage, as well as hoping to find favour with the resident priest and the nuns. The women bustled around importantly, dispensing red cordial or homemade ginger beer in paper cups and offering little triangle shaped sandwiches made of Peck's paste, or tomato and ham. Delicate china plates sat piled high with wonderful, rich, buttery cakes, iced and creamy. Each time I took a cake, I knew Sister Lawrence's beady eye was fixed upon me. It did not lessen my enjoyment though. I was deliciously shocked to see the priest drinking beer. The day drew to a close and with all the excitement and fun over, I went to bed blinking hard and biting back tears.

My mother had not been there to see me.

Soon after the first communion day, Granny became ill. For a long time she stayed in her bed, eating little and becoming frail and gaunt. People from the parish visited Granny almost daily, and while they were there, I welcomed the break from Stella's temper. I appreciated, too, that Mr Cassidy stopped touching me all over and trying to tickle me, as was his way.

I was asleep on the veranda early one morning, when Stella vigorously shook me awake, 'Get up! Granny is dead! Go to the telephone on the corner and ring Dr Wheeler, and Father Scully, and tell them what has happened.' I did not even think, *poor Granny*, because now she was dead, I was scared of her.

Stella called to me to get moving and I jumped from my warm bed, my feet trembling with cold and fright as they hit the freezing cold linoleum. I feared the lurking presence of death inside the house and I stayed on the veranda to put on my clothes. Stella came and handed me four pennies, two for each phone call. With the money, and a corner piece of an old envelope with the phone numbers written on it clasped in my hand, I stepped out into the early morning gloom. My shadow loomed eerily before me as I hurried along. I had never been outside alone before the sun had risen.

I phoned the doctor. I must have woken him too early, because he answered with a gruff, 'Hello.' Then silence. I stuttered out my message. 'Aunty Stella wants me to tell you that Granny is dead.' The doctor always made me nervous, and I found it hard to get the words out. What more should I say to him? Suddenly he put the phone down. I did not have spare pennies, and I worried that if he misunderstood my message he might not turn up at the house. I dropped the remaining two pennies into the slot above the telephone to speak to Father Scully, he responded with, 'Oh the poor dear lady. I must say a little prayer for the repose of her soul'. Much nicer than the doctor, I thought. To my relief the doctor did arrive later in the morning chattering away to the priest as they came through the front door together.

Donned in his surplice and waving the incense burner the priest administered the last rites to Granny. I understood that the last rites were a blessing given to Catholics before they died. The blessing absolved the person from sin and, ensured them trouble-free entry into heaven. I wondered why the doctor came, after all, Granny was already dead, what was he there to do? Father Scully told me that the doctor came to issue a death certificate. He explained that it had nothing to do with the church. It was the law.

Groups of people from the church came and sat for hours praying and saying the Rosary. The priest told me that this was called a vigil, because sitting and praying with a departing soul comforted the soul and helped speed the journey into glorious eternity. However, when darkness fell, I wanted my mother. I did not want to sleep anywhere near a dead person. Someone must have thought that it was not right for me to sleep on the veranda, with dead Granny in the front room, and I went to spend the night at the Newcastle Street home of Granny's sister.

The next morning, I walked back across the short road. Stella stood at the front door with her hands placed on her hips. 'What took you so long? I have been waiting for you. Come and say your prayers and kiss Granny goodbye.'

Stella always made me afraid and I was more frightened than usual when I saw that, apart from Stella and Granny (who wasn't alive), the house was empty. The women from the church who came to prepare Granny for burial had gone. Stella's hand firmly grasped the back of my neck and guided me towards the lounge room. I stiffened against her touch as I felt myself abruptly thrust forward into the middle of the room. *Don't look Faye, just don't look. Help me someone. I'll be good, God.*

Granny was lying stiff, and looking uncomfortable, across several wooden grocery boxes of varying heights, that were covered with sheets and pushed together to form a long, narrow bier. Bewilderment momentarily overcame my discomfort. A sight more macabre than anything I could possibly imagine was that of Granny, as she lay there swathed in white sheets with a bar of green soap under her chin secured with a bandage tied into a large fancy bow around the top of her head. I wondered what possible reason there could be for tying a bar of soap to her face. Father Scully told me that the weight of the soap tied firmly under her chin supported her jaw from dropping open. Her face looked sad as I leaned over to kiss her. But as I moved close, and when her greyish, waxen image was only inches from my own, she didn't look sad any more. She looked awful. An uncontrollable shudder rocked me as a cold chill rose from Granny's body and I inhaled the tangy scent of eucalyptus soap.

Stella observed me from the doorway without a word.

I thought, *I don't think children should see a dead body.*

At the funeral, the long Requiem Mass dragged on, with oppressive, dirge-like droning from the choir. Stella propelled me by my neck towards the edge of the grave and I stiffened, afraid that she might push me in. I stood beside the large mound of earth at the graveside and watched the coffin bearing Granny gradually disappear from sight. A horrible dream of Granny rising up and down from her grave was to haunt me for many years.

Life for me was going to get awful. I knew it. Stella's cruelty, once held in check by Granny, could now run rampant. She swung me around by my long plaits, viciously using them as weapons against me, banging my head on the wall as I was flung across the room. My legs and backside were usually covered in welts and ached painfully from thrashings with the yardstick. I felt very sad as I walked slowly and sobbed inwardly on my way to school each day. I had thought that the dreaded stick was called the yardstick because it came from the backyard. Another of my chores was to light the kitchen fire as soon as I got up in the morning, I never minded doing that as it seemed to be a grown up thing to do and it was not difficult. I threw copious amounts of kerosene on to the kindling until the wood was blazing. On more than one occasion I singed the front of my hair and eyebrows, until I learned to toss the kerosene, throw the match from a distance and bolt for the back door.

The toilet stood at the furthest possible corner of the back yard, which backed on to a laneway. A visit out there at night challenged the bravest of souls. Stella had a trick that apparently afforded her great amusement. As I perched nervously in the dark, Stella – who had followed me quietly, would hold the door handle firmly from the outside so that I unable to get out. As I begged to be let out, a deep, harsh voice answered, 'I am a drunken man and I won't ever let you out. You can stay there in the dark all night.' The silly thing was that I knew it was Stella, but the knowledge made me no less afraid. After a while, she would tire of her game and wander back inside leaving me to tear breathlessly through the back door behind her. I never forgave her, *ever.*

Next door, a wood yard filled the remainder of the small street. Wood from there was chopped and carted to houses all over the district. The place was unoccupied on weekends and the yard was zealously guarded by a nasty-tempered, wire-haired Airedale dog. He terrified me by baring his yellow fangs and clawing my legs, making them bleed, when Stella used to hoist me over the fence to pick up bits of wood to throw back to her. Stella, from her safe position would call to me as I tried to clamber back over the fence, while trying to kick the dog away from my legs. 'Don't be such a baby, he's only playing.' I wondered did she steal wood every Saturday morning and confess every Saturday afternoon?

One day the owners of the wood yard nailed a sign to their front fence, notifying nearby residents that they intended to fell a large tree. The notice warned that there might be considerable noise and vibration as the tree hit the ground. The day arrived and neighbours stood around waiting for the momentous occurrence. The men chopped and sawed, stopping to size up the situation every few minutes. After some time they began running and waving and tugging on ropes to guide the tree away from the fence. Their shouting became a roar. Then silence. With some disappointment, I realised that the tree, with an unremarkable little plop, had hit the ground. I had been expecting something akin to the disastrous earthquake scene that I had seen in a movie. I asked Mrs Hill, the lady who lived next door, 'Is that it? It wasn't very noisy at all, and the ground didn't shake like they told everyone it would.'

'Yes dear,' she murmured, laughing as she walked away. 'That was it. A lot like life really.'

I hurried home from school each day and when I walked through the house to the kitchen, I was surprised to see Stella holding a plump, fair-haired, baby boy in her arms. She told me that his name was Tony and that he would be staying with us. His mother probably thought that the church-going woman that she was handing him over to would take good care of him. Or maybe she never minded one way or the other. He was not a tiny baby, though he did still sleep in a cot. Stella said that he was partially blind, as well as being deaf, and I noticed that his legs did not work too well either. I loved him completely and I would have taken a beating every day if I could have spared him from Stella's temper. I longed to stop his tears and make him laugh. His downy, soft hair brushed against me when I picked him up and his tiny hands were so soft and chubby when he gently patted my face.

Sometime after I left Stella's, a quirk of fate led me to overhear a conversation between two adults and I learned that Tony had died. I could not show my sorrow because I was not meant to have heard the comments, but the pain was unbearable.

A lifetime later, the memory of Tony remained with me, still unbearably poignant and tears fell whenever I thought of that beautiful little soul. He warmed my life as he returned to me the love that I gave to him. I loved him and, by returning my love, he made me feel worthwhile. That was his everlasting gift to me.

With little enthusiasm one Sunday morning after church, I swept the path at the front of Stella's house. Convinced that I would go crazy if my mother did not come to see me that day, I shoved the broom listlessly back and forth along the pavement and I remembered hearing that she had moved to a house in Cleaver Street, which was not far away. I had passed it often when I had travelled on the tram along Newcastle Street. Without stopping to think about the consequences of my actions, I tossed the broom over the fence and took off along Bertram Street and around into Newcastle Street. I ran along Newcastle Street until I came to the corner of Cleaver Street, telling myself breathlessly as I ran, that I would find her and we would stay together and be happy. Fortunately, Cleaver

Street was not very long and I had only knocked on five doors, saying to whoever opened it: 'I'm looking for my mother. Her name is Amy. Do you know her?' when an old lady at the door of a large red brick house, with a low brick fence and a lot of lawn that had not been cut for a long time, said, 'Hang on pet I'll get her for you.'

To me, what I had done was not out of the ordinary and it never occurred to me that I would not find Amy, or that she would not be thrilled to see me. She came around the side of the house and up the steps to where I stood. She was smiling.

'How on earth did you find your way here?'

I answered, quite proud of my ingenuity. 'I heard Aunty Stella say that you lived in Cleaver Street, so I came to find you.' It was a strange visit. Once I was actually there in front of my mother, I found myself tongue-tied and unable to say all the things that constantly simmered in my mind. My mother treated me kindly and courteously, as she would any visitor, albeit an unexpected one. We had biscuits and cool drink and then we walked back to Stella's house. I never got into trouble over the escapade, nor was I invited to visit again.

My eighth birthday came and my mother did not come to see me. I had not seen her for a long time. Tears of despair frequently fell, especially as day ended and night shadows darkened the house. I still went to St Brigid's, but apart from seeing the girls from the Re Store at school, I saw none of the people from Aberdeen Street. As well as missing my mother, I missed them as well. I was never to return to live in the house in Aberdeen Street and it was many years before I saw it again.

Chapter 4

Away from the Wall

One morning – it was a Saturday – Stella and I waited at the Newcastle and Fitzgerald Street corner for a tram to take us into the city centre. Ten minutes later, we left the tram at the corner of William Street and Stella marched me along the street to Boans department store. I writhed in embarrassment and hoped that I would not see anyone from school as she placed her hand on the back of my neck and propelled me forward. I absolutely loathed being pushed along by my neck in public.

Gloomily I trotted along and recalled the last time that I had accompanied Stella to Boans. It was to buy shoes. I really liked the black shiny pair with little straps across the front. Stella handed me a pair that laced up and looked like gardening boots. I tried them on and my heart sank when they appeared to fit me. 'They are a bit tight,' I said hopefully, looking pained, and with all my strength willing the sales assistant to go and look for something else. Stella said they would do, and those nasty shoes became mine. When we arrived home, Stella asked me if I liked the new shoes.

'Yes thank you, Aunty Stella, I do.'

She replied, 'If you don't like them as much as the others, you should say so because God can hear you. If you are telling a lie, you will be punished.'

I was a gullible little dope. I opened my mouth and out came, 'Well I did like the other shiny shoes with the straps.' Before the sentence was completed, she flailed me about the head with the shoes, screeching about selfishness and about poor children who had no shoes at all. She bruised my face and hurt me and I was very wary after that whenever we went shopping.

The first I knew that I was going to a boarding school in Lesmurdie was when Stella said to the sales assistant, 'I want to see the uniform for St Brigid's College in Lesmurdie.' I had never heard of Lesmurdie and wondered how far away it might be.

I did enjoy the fuss and attention of the friendly sales lady whose name badge announced her as Mrs Docherty. However, I knew better than to be too pleased, or showy, or I would be in trouble.

The crest on both the hat and the blazer for the school displayed the motto: *Virtus Sola Nobilitat.* Virtue Alone Ennobles. They and the rest of the uniform were expensive items for someone who would need them for such a short time.

Wherever I was going, I felt it must be better than living with Stella. I had grown to hate her sly way of luring me into a seemingly ordinary conversation with the express purpose of leading me into saying the wrong thing and causing trouble for myself.

I never knew then, or, indeed, ever, the circumstances that took me to Lesmurdie. My mother did not appear to be involved. I had ceased to think of her as a rescuer, or expect her to come for me.

The nuns at Lesmurdie were strict. Heaven help you if one of them took a dislike to you, but they were angels compared to some that I would unfortunately encounter later in another place.

On that first bewildering night, I woke up cold and uncomfortable and realised, to my intense shame, that I had wet the bed. What would happen to me when the sister in charge found out? I had the unbearable thought that all the girls would hear and make fun of me. With no idea of what to do, I stayed in the soggy bed, which prompted one of the senior girls to ask me, 'Why aren't you getting up? If Sister catches you still in bed after the bell, she will give you hell even though you are new.'

Mortified, I burst into tears and told her of my shameful lapse. She showed me to the bathroom and told me clean up and get dressed and to remain there quietly until she came for me, because if I was found there, *we would be in a lot of trouble*. I waited scared that I would be discovered sitting in the bathroom when I should have been in church.

Later, one of the girls, her name was Margaret Dillon, told me that she and some other girls had taken the sheets, and rinsed them in the bathroom and draped them over some bushes behind the kitchen to dry. When I returned to the dormitory that evening, my bed was clean and fresh and I heard no more about the incident. I remembered those girls in my prayers every day for a long time.

My life seemed to be following a pattern of inexplicably grim times and, sometimes, unexpected, uplifting kindness.

They called me Frances during my time there. I never knew why, but I thought it was probably because Faye was not a saint's name.

I made friends, but I never became close to any of the girls as I was afraid that I would accidently blurt out that my parents were divorced. I knew I must not say anything like that while attending a Catholic school. When conversations about mothers, fathers, brothers and sisters took place, I never joined in or spoke of my parents in the way that the other girls did. Nor did I talk about the continuing absence of my mother and certainly not about my life with Stella. It became so much easier to remain silent than to be fearful whenever I opened my mouth. Being rather quiet meant that I did not attract attention, so consequently I rarely got into trouble. Religious studies, English, reading, or arithmetic filled our days. We learned by rote, chanting prayers and lessons repeatedly in a repetitive singsong manner until the information became embedded in our minds forever. A book, any sort of book, always proved to be my best company. Unfortunately, music notes with quavers, semiquavers, clefs, breves and all the rest baffled me. I struggled to understand the music teacher, but we both often ended up teary and upset before the lesson was over. I never understood, and she could not understand why I did not.

Sewing proved to be an area where I definitely did not shine. On one occasion, from a pattern, we were to cut material into the shape of an apron, hem it by hand and embroider it. On completion, The Mother Prioress would inspect our efforts. As the girls tried to outdo each other with beautifully worked flower gardens, ladies in crinoline dresses and picturesque cottages, I settled on the outline of a black cat. I laboured over my apron, refusing to show it to anyone until I completed it. My secrecy unintentionally led the girls and the sisters to expect something special. My black cat took far longer to finish than the elaborate, intricate stitching produced by most of the other girls. We stood in high anticipation, eagerly hoping for a favourable comment as Mother Prioress strolled along imperiously, stopping to inspect and remark on each girl's effort. 'Oh Mary, how exquisite, you are a clever girl.' or, 'Regina, we simply must show that to Father on Sunday after Mass.' Then it was my turn. I waited expectantly. It took a while, but eventually, with a big smile, she exclaimed, 'Oh Frances dear, I see you chose a plain-Jane, no nonsense approach.'

Daily gargling with *Condi's* crystals, a purple, foul-tasting antiseptic that Sister Josephine told us would protect us from infection, was compulsory. Because we hated this ritual, we all huddled under bushes behind the laundry and, making loud gargling sounds accompanied by much coughing and spitting, we then threw the awful stuff into the bushes. Of course, one morning we were caught. A nun, one whom we rarely saw around, suddenly leapt from behind the laundry door. The many layers of her all black habit swirled around her, and her white wimple slipped sideways as she frantically waved a ruler and screamed that we were *as bold and as brazen as brass*. Lined up, hands outstretched, we each received a hard, painful whack from the ruler.

The most powerful memory that I have always carried of my time there is visiting Sunday. Visiting day on the first Sunday of the month saw families arriving between one o'clock and two thirty, depending upon whether they came by car or bus. Most came by bus, as fuel was still in short supply after the war, and many women did not drive cars anyway. On visiting Sunday, it was customary for all girls to go to the refectory for afternoon tea. With our ears eagerly attuned, listened until, as if by a pre-set signal, the gradual distant drone of vehicles became audible, one after another crunching on to the gravel forecourt. A busy, almost carnival-like atmosphere greeted them. Gracious, ever-smiling nuns milled around.

The families approached with a flurry of anticipation, smelling sweetly of perfume and bearing gifts of special cakes and biscuits. We girls all remained in the refectory, gulping our drinks down as we rapidly crammed the last bites of biscuits into our mouths. Then, lined up against the wall, we waited as, one by one; the names of girls with a visitor were called by the sister in charge. Time after time I stood there, hopeful, yet hopeless, as I prayed for someone to visit me. Although deep in my heart, I did not expect that my name would be called. I, and the other girls without visitors, bit back our tears.

We knew that everyone else knew that we had nobody. *That we were nobody!*

One glorious day though, my mother did arrive, accompanied by Alfredo. I heard my name called and joyfully I stepped away from my familiar spot by the wall and walked forward giving little thought to the other girls still left standing. That day, I was not left anxious and waiting. I became just like everyone else. I had somebody.

My visiting somebody was blonde and pretty, wearing lovely perfume and looking glamorous; and she was accompanied by a dark haired, good-looking man – Alfredo! Proudly I set off with them for a long walk outside the school grounds through a gate normally forbidden to me. Bright orange and lemon trees, laden and heavy with fruit and smelling sweetly of citrus blossom, bent towards the ground. Delicate bush orchids clustered around the mushy base of old, gnarled trees and brilliant, deep Blue Leschenaultia trailed over ochre brown, gravel patches. Hand in hand, we ambled along slowly until we stopped at a roadside stall to buy me some tangy, sweet oranges. I enjoyed one of the best days of my life, seeing them both together. We continued walking, but all too soon the shadows began to lengthen and I watched as the sun gradually descended below the hills and the sky took on the dull, purple, melancholy hue that signalled the end of day. I knew that very soon I would be returned to school. Dusk, followed by darkness, would arrive and my perfect golden day would be over.

Soon after that memorable day, I became unwell, with a painfully discharging ear accompanied by burning shakes or freezing shivers. The Sisters seemed not to realise the pain I felt. They probably thought that any sign of malaise among the girls was due to homesickness, rather than illness. Eventually, though, they arranged to send me to Perth. *Back to Stella's.*

I reluctantly returned to the dismal, cheerless existence of living with Stella. I missed Lesmurdie and the companionship of the girls, and I disliked Stella more than ever.

Dr Wheeler, whom I had been visiting for many weeks, patted me on the head one morning, and told me that I needed to go to a specialist about my ear.

Sometimes Stella accompanied me, however, from the Fitzgerald Street corner, I mostly caught the tram and went alone to Dr Gray's rooms in St George's Terrace. He was kind in the detached way of many adults of that time towards children. The doctor's treatment was to give me sulpha tablets, one of few antibiotics available in the mid 1940s, before the use of penicillin. The huge tablets usually caught halfway down my throat causing me to cough and make my ear pound. Every second day I went to have my ear swabbed with cotton wool, wrapped around a long needle-like probe. That resulted in pain and some tears. With eyes tightly shut, I prayed and counted in my head until it was over. I then left the surgery, walked along St George's Terrace to William Street, and caught the tram back to Stella's.

One morning, I heard the doctor tell the nurse he needed to take some X-rays. I was not scared until I looked up and saw the machine. A terrifying, circular monster hovered above my head. I struggled to escape as the fearsome object bore down towards me. I started to count in my head. Rapid and repetitive counting stopped me from thinking about the machine and being frightened of it. I stopped struggling and waited for the machine to crush and kill me.

The nurse was unsympathetic, 'If you don't sit still, we will have to do it all over again and doctor will be awfully cross with you.'

How different the frightening experience might have been if the nurse had simply explained that the X-ray machine was a doctor's camera and that it would not even touch me.

It appeared that I had a damaged mastoid bone, caused by an untreated infection, possibly from an old injury. The doctor decided that I needed an operation and asked me if I remembered ever hitting my head really hard. *Could it have been Stella?* She bashed my head against the wall.

Alfredo came to visit me at Stella's, a rare and special treat for me. He came to take me to the pictures, but my excitement quickly turned to dismay. Because of my messy ear and the fact that I was to go into hospital the next morning, I was unable to go with him. I had not seen Alfredo since the splendid day when he came with my mother to Lesmurdie. Because he and Amy were divorced, I did not fully realise at the time that I was not going to see him again, except for a few brief moments a few years later. The reason for his visit and the outing to the pictures was a farewell, as he was about to remarry and I would not be part of his life anymore.

The next morning found me waiting at the front gate for a taxi to take me to St John of God hospital in Subiaco. I peered in through the window, because I hoped that my mother might be sitting in the car, but it was empty except for the driver.

Stella offered no comfort and I sat, rigid, on the cold leather seat as far away from her as possible as we travelled towards the hospital.

Cold and starchy sharp sheets strained against my legs and held me so tightly bound that movement was impossible when I woke up from the operation some time the next day. Pain tore through my head, making me yell as I tried to sit up. I spent a lot of effort at various times, trying not to cry. That time though, as I thought to myself that no girl should go to hospital without her mother, or someone who cared for her, I could not stop and I let the hot tears splash down my face as I remembered the previous day when my long hair fell to the ground. I fell asleep and when I woke up, stiff and still cold, I spent the rest of the day watching the door whenever I heard footsteps approaching. Deep in my heart, I did not really expect to see her. I could not help hoping though. I lay flat on my back with my feet freezing and my cold nose breathing in the cloying smells of ether and medicine.

At last, I was able to sit up. My head wobbled under the unaccustomed weight of the bandages and multi-layers of dressings. I was hungry, and waited eagerly to hear the squeak and laboured rumble of the food trolley bringing the meals. I knew that dinner would be fish, because it was Friday and at that time Catholics, adults and children, were forbidden to eat meat on Friday. I was not prepared though, for what met my gaze when I stared at the food on my dinner plate. A horrible, grey fish, with one dull eye, sitting on pale green, chunky cabbage, looked back at me. The only type of cooked fish that I knew was the scrumptious, golden, battered fish from the fish shop. A shudder of distaste rippled through me as I turned away. I knew that I would be given no other choice. As a Catholic, it was the one eyed fish, or nothing.

'What's this then, not eating your dinner?' The woman, who took the trays away, muttered to me, 'the starving children in Africa would like a nice dinner like this.'

I thought, perhaps they would, but I still did not want it.

The young girl taking trays from the other side of the ward looked over at me and smiled. I smiled back reluctantly and slid down between the cold, stiff sheets that prevented me from feeling warm, night or day, and continued to read my book. A few minutes later, the young girl returned carrying a plate with two sausages and some bread and butter and another dish with jelly and custard. I burst into tears and told her that I could not eat the sausage because it was Friday. She told me they were special sausages made especially for sick little girls, and that the Pope agreed that it was okay. Unexpected kindness!

My mother never came see me in the hospital.

When I left the hospital, a nun walked me to the bus stop – no taxi that time – and I caught the trolley bus back to Stella's house.

Weeks later, I thought I heard my mother's and Stella's voices echoing along the passage. I listened carefully and I was right. She had come. However, my joy quickly faded when I heard her angrily demanding, 'Who gave you the right to put her in a hospital? Why didn't you tell me?' Stella replied in a flat tone, 'Nobody could find you, and she was very sick. What were we supposed to do? What gives you the right to appear and disappear whenever you feel like it, anyway?'

As I walked towards them they stopped talking, and Amy embraced me gently, as if I might break. 'Oh my poor little darling, what have they done to you? I have been so worried since I found out. Don't worry about your hair; the lopsided plaits will soon even out.' However, her tone when she spoke to Stella remained angry, and I felt rather relieved when it was time for her to leave.

I stayed in Perth for the doctor's visits until he said that I could return to Lesmurdie, where I remained for, I think, two or three months before returning to Stella's.

Stella told me one day that Alfredo paid money for my clothing, upkeep and schooling. Possibly the reason that he and Amy were together that wondrous day when they visited me at Lesmurdie, was to discuss the payment of fees with the Sisters. Perhaps it also explains the reason for my untimely departure from the school. Without any laws in place to force him provide for me indefinitely, Alfredo probably stopped contributing to my upkeep when he remarried. A thoroughly good man, it was no doubt vital to his new marriage and for a peaceful life to cut all ties with Amy and, consequently, with me. Did he visit that evening, before the operation, to see me and take me out, or to sign a permission form for the operation as my legally adoptive father, in the absence of my mother? I was never to know.

In spite of this separation, nothing could diminish the joy of having Alfredo and Amy visit me at school that day, enabling me to step away from the wall.

Chapter 5

Betrayal 1948

The days turned into months and I dreamed of returning to my mother, or at least to Lesmurdie and away from Stella, but no reprieve came. I continued to live at Bertram Street and go around the corner and over the road each morning to St Brigid's school.

On a particular cold, sunny Friday afternoon in October, dressed in my best going-to-church clothes, I waited for my mother outside the front gate of Stella's house. My red tartan dress with the pleated skirt brushed softly against my legs as I jumped up and down with my skipping rope to keep warm. Jumping vigorously also stopped me from thinking about how awful it would be if she forgot to come. My hair, freed from its customary plaits, was tied with large ribbons. I hoped that my mother would think that I looked nice.

My mother did arrive and she looked gorgeous and happy. Because we saw each other so rarely, her prettiness registered anew with me. She told me that we were going to the pictures and then out for tea. From the Newcastle Street corner, we clattered and rattled our way into Perth on the tram. We strolled along Hay Street to His Majesty's Theatre, which showed films at that time, and we bought ice cream and chocolates before entering the magical world of make believe. I remember the movie, *Mother Wore Tights*, vividly. It starred Betty Grable in a story about a glamorous showgirl. She was blonde and beautiful and reminded me of my mother. I sat lost in the bright musical show happily munching chocolate almonds. Tucked warmly beside my mother my life could not have been better. Forever, though, whenever I remembered the movie, or saw the name Betty Grable, the joy of the memorable day was tarnished by my feeling of betrayal.

The early spring air was soft and balmy when we left the theatre and, as I held my mother's hand, I prayed for the evening never to end. We walked from the theatre and through the small crowd across the road to the Star cafe for tea. I was fast learning to store moments, like a small bank deposit, when something companionable or nice took place so that I could recall them later when loneliness came. I ate slowly, trying to stretch the time for as long as possible before I had to return to Stella's house. Then a wonderful thing happened. Instead of getting on the tram at the corner of William Street, my mother walked me right past the corner and continued along Barrack Street, and down to the river's edge. With no word to me she gave a man dressed in a uniform some money and, in return, he gave her two tickets and we clambered on to a waiting ferry. I did not know that people could go on the ferry at night-time. The city lights created a fairyland that twinkled brightly in the background as the ferry gently made its short journey across the Swan River. When we left the ferry though, I heard a lion's roar and a caged dingo barking from the nearby zoo and I shivered apprehensively.

We wandered around in semi-darkness looking for an address that my mother had printed on a small piece of pale, blue paper. 'Oh by the way, you will be leaving Aunty Stella soon. You will be going somewhere different,' my mother informed me casually. I did not ask her where I was going. Not even when I hoped something good might be going to happen did I ask.

Before I had time to feel any reaction to her news, she found the address she was seeking and knocked briskly on the painted, wooden door. A pink faced, cheery looking woman, wearing a white apron over a blue and yellow floral dress and holding a huge ginger cat tightly in her arms, opened the door. I wandered off while they talked thinking that this looked like somewhere that I would like to live. The house was big and old with a wide veranda going all the way across the front and down the sides. A tumbledown garden looked mysterious and interesting. I thought it would be a perfect place to hide with a book. From the parts of the murmured conversation that I heard, I gathered that Amy was inspecting the house with a view to renting it. My spirits soared. Okay, a different school, but I would be with my mother in this exciting place called South Perth, where one travelled back and forth on a ferry.

The next day I was anxious as I waited to hear from my mother.

I had no premonition of what a dreadful, life-changing day it was going to be for me. As I walked into the kitchen, Stella said. 'Your mother is coming for you later. Gather your clothes and put them in there.' She pointed to a worn, brown suitcase. I was cocooned in a happy little daydream about ferries and the zoo and of being with my mother.

The hands on the ornate mantle clock moved so slowly that morning. It sounded its single sonorous chime every fifteen minutes and on the half hour, as if purposely reminding me that the morning was passing. At last, from my splintery seat on an old wooden fruit box by the front gate, I saw my mother come around the corner and she was carrying a suitcase.

With no warning, I was about to go to another place. I wondered where. If I were returning to Lesmurdie, surely one of them would have told me. An uncomfortable frisson inched icily over my scalp and body. Amy and Stella's demeanour towards each other was hostile as Amy tossed my clothes from Stella's suitcase into the equally tattered brown one that she had brought with her. They barely spoke to each other, or to me. Stella gave me a fleeting, distant embrace and pressed a prayer book into my hands.

'Goodbye. I will remember to pray for you.'

I did not look at her face, as I scurried out the front door behind my mother.

A lengthy walk took us to a bus stop in Cambridge Street. My mother was not too chatty, but I felt happy enough as we waited for the green trolley bus to come into sight. It stopped alongside us with a cushioned *whoosh, whoosh* sound as the brakes were applied. The bus driver pushed his green cap jauntily to back of his head, and leapt from his seat to take the suitcase. Amy glared at him when he asked in a jovial manner, 'Going on holidays are you love? Want to take me with you?' When we left the bus only a matter of minutes later, he again helped us with the case, giving an unfriendly Amy a cheeky grin and a wave as he drove off.

As I walked along in silence with my mother, being with her again, South Perth, and the zoo, did not seem to be in the plan. My mind skipped around between small hope and huge dread. I didn't think we were going to be together at all. Maybe the special time the previous evening was her way of doing something nice for me before she sent me away again. We came to a large, walled, church-like edifice. The walls were made of rough stone, thick and grey, not neat, red brick, like most schools and churches that I knew. The sign on the outside wall read: Convent of the Good Shepherd. I had never heard of it. I walked beside my mother and we passed through the tall, wide gateway and along the shrub lined path, past beautiful rose bushes and, seemingly, miles of green lawn. I had no inkling, as I walked that long pathway towards the unknown, that I would not see those roses or that green lawn again for an unimaginably long time.

The significance of the suitcase began to register uneasily with me as I plodded towards the imposing building. Amy tugged a cord, and I heard a bell echo hollowly from behind the immense, imposing timber and stained glass door. After a long wait, during which time my mother never spoke and looked around, anywhere, except at me, loudly jangling keys broke the silence and the large door swung open. We crossed the threshold and, although bewildered, I noticed that the floors and all the furniture were rich and dark looking, shining glossily and smelling of furniture polish. A tall, severe looking nun greeted us unsmilingly and gestured for us to enter the grand room. She was quite different in appearance from the nuns at St Brigid's, for they wore a neat, black compact habit. This one was dressed in a cream, voluminous habit and wore a white veil. She loomed over me and she seemed to be covered with such a lot of clothing, I had the impression that the person belonging to the face was lost somewhere inside, far below the surface.

My mother appeared nervous. 'Mother Pierre, this is my daughter, Faye.'

How did my mother know what to call her?

The nun looked at me disdainfully, 'Well, young lady, I hope you know how to behave yourself.'

I hoped she was not going to be my teacher!

Whatever further conversation took place went unheard by me. I went away into my mind, counting faster and faster. *Four, eight, twelve, sixteen.*

My mother stood to one side, almost as if waiting for permission to leave. She moved towards me and her soft perfume enveloped me as she clasped me in her arms. Her hair brushed my face as she hugged and kissed me and I clung to her in panic. Surely, this was not where she was going to leave me, with this stern-faced old woman? I watched, paralysed, as she started to walk away.

My tinny, hollow voice echoed around the room.

'Please Mummy. Oh please. Don't leave me here. Take me with you. Where are you going? I'll be good.'

She kept walking and did not look back.

The one called Mother Pierre seemed to have gone. Another nun, much younger, smiled as she took my hand and led me towards an existence that should never have happened. I began to cry but it did not sound like me, it sounded deep and moaning. Mother Pierre appeared silently beside me. She put her mouth close to my face, 'Behave, and stop all the silly nonsense this instant.'

Four, eight, twelve, sixteen ....

From a seemingly great distance, I heard the floating voice of the young nun saying, 'To be sure, to be sure, you'll be wakening the dead if you do not hush up.'

Where did they keep the dead that I might wake up?

'Take her away until she stops that noise and, for goodness sake, give her a handkerchief,' Mother Pierre muttered.

The young one rushed off and, with my heart beating a ragged tattoo loudly in my ears, I followed further into the unknown world behind all those closed doors. Holy statues, recessed in alcoves along the walls, stood watchful, rigid and shadowy. The nun's pace quickened as we passed brightly coloured, stained glass windows as she urged me to hurry. Up a steep, slippery, spiral staircase we went. It required concentration to stay on the widest part of the steps and I held the banister rail firmly in case my feet slipped. I went behind her into an attic-like, deserted room. Slivers of sunlight shone weakly through small, square windows set high in the wall. Little particles of dust spun in the sun's rays and danced crazily around the room in dizzying, never-ending circles. Along one wall, garments hung untidily on clothes racks. The nun told me to stay where I was and she left the room. I was momentarily distracted by my knees, which I could see shaking and banging together beneath my skirt. The room troubled me. I didn't want to think what might happen to me next. I might die in there and no one would ever find me.

Time dragged by. I counted my numbers and stared in fascination at my shaking knees over which I had no control. A heavily built, square shaped, strange looking woman, with peculiar eyes that did not quite look at me but, rather eerily, passed my shoulder as if something or someone lurked behind, clumped into the attic. The nun also came back into the room and told me not to be afraid of Winifred. 'She's not quite right in the head, but she won't hurt you.'

The woman called Winifred, pushed some clothes at me.

'Here put these on, and then give me your things,' she muttered in an odd, rusty, unused-sounding voice.

My clothes were warm from my body and smelled of Cashmere Bouquet soap. I clung to them trying to find comfort by hugging the warmth to my chest. I held on fiercely as Winifred determinedly loosened my fingers and took my things from me and locked them in my suitcase. I wanted to take my case with me, but when I went to pick it up, she shouted, 'Leave that. It stays there.' A different nun – tall and thin – accompanied by three other women, came into the attic room. Winifred stood, silent and sullen, leaning against the wall.

They gave me a pink cotton dress that looked like a nightgown and told me to put it on. They gave me some big, ugly, thick stockings and some elastic to hold them up. The nightgown Winifred handed to me was huge and heavy with a high neck and long baggy sleeves. I knew real terror as I took the gown from Winifred's hand. A nightgown meant bedtime. The thought of bleak, black darkness and the notion of getting into a bed hammered at my brain. Then the comforting numbers took over.

Another nun walked me towards a group of women and then left me and walked away. The women stood staring at me curiously until one of them spoke, 'Hello. When did you get here?'

Mute with fright, I stared at her and she said, 'We're going to church; you'd better come with us.'

Who were these people? Where were the other children? Where were the classrooms? Why was I wearing their old woman, strange clothes?

We moved in a tight-knit group towards the church, along a colonnade with arched openings along the sides. As we walked, I was able to see a small part of the front of the convent and briefly to glimpse some parts of the garden that I had walked along earlier and for a moment, hope surfaced. It could not be that bad if I was able to see the garden. I soon found, though, that the only place where the outside world was visible, but not accessible, was on that short, accompanied journey to church.

A bell rang in the distance and a woman told me that it was teatime. I remembered nothing of what I ate, or if I ate at all. I had thought that all the adults and old people that I had seen around were in charge of the place, but when we sat down at the meal table and I looked around properly, I saw that they were all adults and old people. There was no one there of my age at all and bleak despair washed over me, because I didn't know where I was, or what was going to happen to me.

What I did know though was that I was locked in with no way out.

Afterwards, we all trudged up an outside wooden staircase to an enclosed balcony. I recognised Mother Pierre smiling at me from her large, throne-like chair, which was situated at the top of three polished wooden steps. Even when she smiled, she still managed to look chilling. Everyone was looking at me. I was the new girl. Ten or twelve women took their places on chairs that were placed around the balcony. The radio, playing softly in the background, made things seem a little more normal as I sat in the cool of the evening with a couple of girls talking to me. Mother Pierre clapped her hands three times and beckoned me to her. She spoke little, but she beckoned and clapped a lot. She pointed to the nearby dormitory, and told me that was where I was to sleep. She then added, 'While you are here, you will be called Lucy. Don't forget that.'

I did not want to be called Lucy. I worried that no one would ever find me in there if I were known by a different name. I counted sixteen beds, eight on each side of the room.

Fifteen strange strangers and I still had not seen any children.

I probably have to stay with the old people until I learn the rules. I had better say my prayers.

Throughout the night, the women moaned and fretted as they wrestled with their demons. Many of them loudly repeated the Rosary with droning monotony. I wondered if I was crazy and if that was the reason for me being there.

When exhaustion finally claimed me I slept, albeit fitfully.

Clap. Clap. Clap. I woke up, and with a sinking, trapped feeling, I immediately remembered where I was. Six more bad-tempered claps. It must be Mother Pierre. No, it was not. This one was a little, gnome of a person, crabby-looking and irritable.

Aidan, the woman in the next bed, was what I came to know as a Consecrated, advised me to, 'Get up now. Mother Pascal will keep clapping until everyone has their feet on the floor.'

When I stood up to follow the other women, my feet tangled around inside my nightgown, almost tipping me over, but no one seemed to notice as I staggered along after the herd. The women brushed their teeth and washed their faces in cold water in a big basin. We each had our own basin so I copied what they did.

On my bed I saw a dark green beret with the number six stitched in red coloured cotton on the inside band. The beret was to wear to church and the number six was the number for my clothes.

How terrible. I was number six and my name was Lucy!

As the days passed, I found that nobody in there retained her outside name. No wonder I never spoke about the place in later life if it was such a disgrace to be there that one had to hide behind a secret name. To my ear, there were some strange sounding names. There were women called Thecla, Ignatius, Dolus, Celestine, Dagmar, Aloysius and Fidelas.

Mother Pascal told me that we had a bath once a week, on Saturday afternoon, and that I had to be careful not to catch nits, but neglected to tell me how not to catch them. She also warned against keeping what she called bad company. I was to keep away from *not-right-in the-head* people. However, in that strange place, I initially found it difficult to tell the difference.

The most I remembered about any reaction to me was some curiosity because I was new and, possibly, because I was so young. Some of the women thought that I sounded English, and deduced that I was an English war orphan, but could not fathom why I was in that institution and not in some sort of children's home.

When I had been there for two, or maybe three days, someone, called Ignatius, told me I was to follow her to the ironing room. I expected that I was to be shown where the women worked and perhaps to see the class room, but another girl, Rita, told me that she was going to show me how to iron clothes. Rita seemed nice and *all right in the head* as well. The room was hot and noisy, and the large, strange looking irons clanged backwards and forwards on to metal stands, as the women flicked the garments over to iron the reverse side. The irons stood in a long row, attached by rubber tubing to metal gas pipes above. Rita told me that the irons were large and different, because they were powered by gas, not electricity and that they were for industrial, not household, use. The acrid smell of gas and of the waxy tapers, which were used to ignite the irons, lingered on the hot, still air. Rita shared her basket of ironing with me for a while. Then I got my own!

Nobody saw me as a child and I received the same harsh treatment as the rest.

From the ironing room, we went to the refectory for lunch. I remembered little of any food that I ate while I was there, or if I liked or disliked it. At breakfast time, twice a week, we were given Epsom salts, a potent laxative that had a disgusting, lingering taste – its vileness indescribable and unforgettable. Same dose for all.

The woman seated next to me at mealtime was large in build, and very tall. Her name was Dolus and I did not like her. Her size was intimidating, but more worrying to me was her air of menace.

She wore a black modified version of the habit that the nuns wore, but was not a nun, and there were several other women dressed like her. They were called Consecrateds. They ate, worked, and slept with the rest of us but were a little higher in the pecking order. I did not think that they were novices, or that they advanced to become nuns. Perhaps they were women who without anyone on the outside chose to remain in the home voluntarily. At mealtime Dolus frequently muttered about, 'greasy dings,' 'garlic munchers' and 'wops.' She spoke close to my ear in muted tones because only I was supposed to hear. I remembered my Aberdeen Street friends and thought longingly of Alfredo, and I always ended up crying. I wondered why she took delight in slyly taunting me.

Spending the days in the ironing room was something I slid into without a great awareness. It no longer seemed strange. I seemed to find within my discomfort, a level of uneasy acceptance that made each day bearable. Not the life I wanted. Just the life I had.

Unceasingly multiple heavy irons thumped over the clothes, then clanged loudly back on to the metal stands. The place was never quiet. The excessive, continuous din was agonising. Gas frequently escaped from the tubing that fed the gas from the overhead line to the iron. Then the gas caught the flame in the iron and ignited the surrounding area. Although the flames scared me, I did daydream about being burnt – not hurt too much – just badly enough to be dramatically rushed to hospital, then my mother would have to come and see me and take me away.

In the ironing room were two Consecrateds, Marguerite and Irene. Although they ironed sometimes, they also spent a lot of time in the folding and sewing room. They appeared to have free time, and some degree of autonomy. Those two women were quite kind to me. There was also Angela, who was only about as tall as I was and seemed incredibly old. She was supposed to be our nurse, but did not seem like a nurse to me, although she may have been one in another life. She now wore the habit of a Consecrated.

Monday to Friday, I ironed. Sometimes I was sent to the laundry to sort the clothing and linen as it arrived in huge baskets. The baskets were so heavy that it took two men to hurl, without actually lifting them, from the truck to the laundry floor. The worst days, for me were when the dental clinics sent their white coats and towels. The smell of blood, antiseptic and ether stung the back of my throat and made my eyes water. All the clothes and linen had their own embroidered insignia somewhere on them to prevent confusion and mix-ups. Baskets arrived from Catholic colleges, some whose names I knew, and recognized. Aquinas Boys College, I had heard of, and Castledare and Clontarf Boys Homes. The Adelphi and Esplanade, and O'Brian's Court Hotel, and the Savoy were some of big hotels whose names I saw regularly.

The laundry was a terrible place in which to work, the gigantic machines roared constantly, discharging intense heat, steam and fumes into the air. There was never any relief from the unbearably hot and steamy atmosphere, even during the coldest days of winter.

Those machines claimed their victims. I felt ill and moved away quickly the first time I saw the pink, withered skin, from the hand to the elbow on the arm of one of the women.

The laundry workers had a more defeated, exhausted air than the rest of us. Viewed along the length of the laundry, their faded cotton dresses and dull hair gave the appearance of a parched, arid garden, deprived of water and nutrients in a heat wave. Their overall appearance was not improved when they rolled the thick stockings, which we all wore, down over knotted, veined legs and bulked them around their ankles in an endeavour to feel cooler. The tight elastic garters, worn just above our knees, left deep, unsightly, painful grooves in our legs.

The arrival of the large noisy trucks at the laundry gates, bringing the overflowing baskets of washing and mending, caused the nuns to become alert and watchful in case any of the girls attempted to talk to the male truck drivers or send out messages or – even worse – try to escape. Inmates did get away sometimes.

At recreation one evening, two or three of the women were talking about one of the others. I sat and quietly listened to the gossip. They laughed about a woman and said that she slept in her cardigan, as if it were an unusual and unhygienic thing to do. A few days later as we waited to go in to tea, the same person that they had been talking about remarked that she was freezing cold and that she could never get warm.

Before I had time to think, out of my mouth came the words, 'Yes. You even have to sleep in your cardigan.'

Her eyes glittered. I was scared and I knew that I was in trouble. She flew at me and grabbed my hair so hard that my feet came up off the ground. My head hurt and I felt mortified as everyone looked on at us with interest. I had not been in trouble with any of the girls before and now that I was, all I could do was pray for the tea bell to ring.

I never was, and never would be, familiar enough with those girls to joke or exchange banter about anything. Why did I step outside my comfort zone and say what I did?

Later that night I stood at the dormitory window, uncomfortable in my large nightgown, and I longed for the cool, silky pyjamas that I had when I lived with my mother. I liked looking out of that window, when I thought the others were asleep, but I would have preferred it not to have bars on it. I stood in the corner, close to the wall and hoped that no one would see me there. I had been lucky so far. Distant lights twinkled prettily around a mass of water forming a circle, like a sparkling necklace. I didn't know how far away the water and the lights were from where I lived when I was small and went to St Brigid's, in Aberdeen Street, but I remembered seeing it before. I liked to remember nice things, but the remembering hurt badly.

I hoped that the next day would bring no repercussions from Mother Pierre. The next morning my head was sore, and the Epsom salts was affecting me drastically.

Then, just before lunch time the next day, when grey clouds hung low, as if the weather was in a bad mood and not quite sure what to do about it, a Consecrated materialised beside of me. With an air of great importance, she announced, 'Mother Pierre wants you, immediately'.

I knocked on the door and stood close listening attentively to hear her voice. Not knowing what to expect, I stood outside her door for so long that my legs started to ache, and I did not dare think about wanting to go to the *doogee*. What a place – even the toilet did not have its proper name! Mother Pierre finally opened the door and I entered a small, sparsely-furnished room. Two chairs stood on either side of a large desk that took up most of the space. The only items on the desk were some prayer books, and some writing paper, a bottle of ink and a pen. On the wall was a picture of The Sacred Heart and in front of the picture, there was an ornate *prie-dieu.*

With her brow and mouth turned down in a perfectly symmetrical frown, Mother Pierre suddenly turned her face, suffused with anger towards me. She grasped my collar and shook me backwards and forwards as if I were weightless. Her angry voice whispered hoarsely, 'Get on your knees.'

Was I going to have to say prayers for penance?

'Down, down to the floor you go. You will kiss the floor until I say you can get up.'

Three times, I went to get up and three times, she roughly pushed my head down to kiss the floor again. I saw the knobbly grain in the wooden floorboards and the little diamond shapes carved into the chair frame. The corners of the floor were dirty and bits of fluff and dust hung like dusty little curtains around the skirting boards. Her polished black shoes, laced tightly across her pudgy feet, were shiny. I also noticed that the hem of her cream habit was grubby and ragged. At last, I was allowed to stand up and I wobbled uncertainly to my feet.

Although afraid, I turned to her, and asked, 'Mother, why did you call me a wicked girl? Is the girl who hit me and pulled my hair going to get into trouble? I never touched her at all.'

Her hard eyes glared back at me from behind her enormous, black-framed spectacles.

'I don't explain myself to you. Now leave this minute. You remind me of your mother. She also had too much to say for herself.' *What did she know about my mother?*

I seethed and hated that cruel, unfair woman who bowed so piously and who was so holy around the priest and visitors, but was capable of such viciousness.

I returned to the ironing room. Rita looked across at me as I miserably bit back tears and relit my iron and she said consolingly, 'Uh oh! It looks as if you not only had to face the music, she expected you to do the dance as well.' Then she added, 'Think carefully about repeating what you see or hear, about *anything*.'

The convent had quite a few cats. An enormous, bushy tabby named *Zacharias* was a great favourite with all the girls and with Mother Pierre in particular. He used to sit adoringly at her feet, and when she left the room, he stretched his large body along the length of her footstool and there he remained until she returned and shoved him off. We all laughed dutifully at these antics so that she would remain in a good mood. I got into trouble over *Zacharias*. It appeared that someone had cut off most of his whiskers, and because I used to play with him whenever I could, I became the prime suspect. Although I denied it repeatedly, I still came under suspicion. I knew that cats had whiskers for direction and that it was important not to touch them. Besides, I loved him. Because of my affection for the cat, I was more upset about his missing whiskers and that someone had hurt my warm, non-judgmental little friend than I was about being in trouble. Any house that I had ever lived in, or stayed at, had always had a cat. Their soft fur and smoochy ways had comforted me on many occasions, earning my enduring love for their species. Now one was going to get me into trouble. I was upset too because nobody knew me well enough, or cared enough, to say, 'Lucy wouldn't do something like that.'

However, I was not Lucy, I was Faye and they did not know me.

Saturday was the day that I, with some of the others, scrubbed the long, splintery floorboards of the ironing room. Our skirts were caught up behind, and secured with an enormous safety pin and our hideous stockings were rolled to our ankles. I would have done anything to avoid plunging my already blistered hands into the hot water, which contained volatile, burning caustic soda. I did penance and paid far greater retribution than my sins warranted.

After finishing the ironing room floor, I went with Mother John to the main convent building where I polished the long, glossy wooden boards in the main corridor. Being taken to polish the floorboards and to be in this most restricted part of the convent was a privilege. Polishing the floor was something I did not care much for but I did like being with Mother John. She was gentle and I did not find her upsetting. No matter how much polish I put on though, I could not make the floor shine. I kept dragging the heavy cloth up and down and I hoped that before Mother John returned the waxy polish would disappear and that the floor would become shiny. I rested back on my heels and wondered if I was getting close to finishing. With relief, I saw that there was only a short piece of the passage still ahead of me. I reached the end and still on my hands and knees, I looked up and found myself face to face with a massive door. Jesus looked down on me from his high cross. I recognized that door and I knew the shocked, pained feeling that I got whenever I accidently touched the hot iron. I knew that I was in front of the same door that I came through on the day my mother left me. Seeing the door made me remember many things about my mother. Where was she? Why hadn't she been back to see me? I hoped that she had not gone to another country. I wondered if the big door was ever left open by mistake. I could not look away from it. Mother John came back to see how I was getting on with the polishing.

She stopped, as though in shock, and she seemed upset. 'You may go now, Lucy.'

That was it. I could go. Did she think that I remembered the door and that I might be planning to try to run away? The real cause of her dismay, however, was the fact that I believed more polish meant a shinier floor. I battled unsuccessfully to remove the layers of polish that I had slathered on so thickly, but I suspected that Mother John might have been the one who had to finish the polishing. The next time Mother John stood and watched me. Being hopeless that first day did not mean that I did not have to learn how to do it properly the second time.

I looked at the door every time I went to polish the boards after that, I recalled the day my mother walked away from me and I tried to have good thoughts about the day that I would walk back through the door to leave that place.

In the convent, I never knew what month of year it was. Time became suspended and it was difficult to place the timing of any event, such as how long ago Christmas had been, or how long ago it had been since that first terrifying night that I spent in the dormitory. In the sameness of our existence, something may have happened a few weeks, or many months ago. The passage of time was marked, not by months, but by feast days.

Although I knew the exact date of the feast day of St Lucy, I did not know my own birthday. I forgot how old I was.

Sundays were miserable and terribly lonely. Lonelier, it seemed, without the crushing routine of the week days. It was the time of Lent and soon it would be Easter. Lent is a sombre time in the Catholic Church, preceding Good Friday and the crucifixion of Christ. Sacrifices are expected and the altar in the church has no flowers, and the altar vestments are the ancient colour of mourning: deep purple. It was a time of repenting. I did not like the time of Lent and I did not care for the purple in church, or no flowers. Going to church all the time was bearable only because of the beauty of the decorated altar, and the huge vases of glorious flowers. Kneeling in church one morning, my back ached until I could tolerate it no longer and I slid back on to the seat, hoping that no one would prod me and tell me to kneel again. I looked around and forgot to pray. The church was divided into sections and across from the front altar, we, from the home, faced parishioners from the outside neighbourhood as they sat on the opposite side of the altar. I longed to sit with them but separated as we were by the altar, we might have been on opposite sides of the ocean. I wondered what they thought as they prayed with downcast, reverent eyes. Did they feel sorry for us and pray for the 'bad' girls? My mind wandered aimlessly, and I was seized with a terrible longing to be free. My imagination made it seem that it would not be so difficult to slip unseen across in front of the altar, over to the other side, while everyone had their eyes closed praying, and then mingle with the normal churchgoers and escape.

If I did that, though, where would I go?

During Lent, different priests came to the convent to celebrate Mass and give sermons. Marguerite, one of the Consecrateds, told me that they were there to retreat from the world for a time and to pray and find peace. But because of *their* retreat, *we* spent a lot more time in church.

One of the visiting priests was a dark-haired man with a red, coarse face and an extremely loud voice. He told us all about being pure and holy and in the confessional told us we must confess if we had impure thoughts. He told the story of a woman who used to sleep with no clothes on, and of how offensive that was to God. One night the woman had a terrible dream. In her dream the devil, fiery and dragging burning chains came clanging up the steps and burst into her room. The fearsome devil stood over her for a time and then disappeared. The woman awoke with a sigh of relief, glad it had only been a dream, until she saw a fiery handprint burned right through the wood of her dressing table. The priest's face went from red to purple, and his voice rose to a thunderous roar startling us all into straightening up rapidly, 'That sinner offended God, and the devil came into her life, as he will surely come into each and every one of your lives if you don't obey the almighty Lord.'

He was the priest who caused the women and girls to laugh and make jokes about him. They said that in the confessional, they made up sinful, shameful things to tell him until his breathing got so heavy it could be heard all over the church.

At the front of the building in a large room that was normally set up with looms for the renowned lace-making that was carried out at the convent, we sometimes saw a movie on a Saturday night. It was not often, but we knew when it was going to happen because we were called to the move the looms and sewing machines to the back of the room, and to line chairs up in straight rows. Visitors were also received in that room. One day I was summoned, and I walked hesitantly into the room, not sure if I was there to move chairs, or if I had a visitor. I moved no chairs that day.

My mother had come to see me. I cried like a little baby when I saw her waiting for me. She looked so pretty, and her perfume was beautiful and full of memories. Nevertheless, I felt a funny feeling, a feeling that I sometimes felt when I looked at Mother Pierre. I did not think I loved my mother that day. It had been unfair to bring me there, leave me and never explain the reason. I did not think she was fair or kind not to visit me. I was not excited to see her in the way I would have been when I was at St Brigid's convent. Too much had happened. I sat awkwardly not knowing what to say to her, ever mindful of the sisters strolling around, never far away. Hurt stopped me from caring as deeply as I normally would have done and now that she was there at last, I had no words.

The silence dragged on and I became lost in thought, wanting to ask. Why am I here? Do you know that I work in the ironing room with the women all day? With not even a book to read. Why do you never come to see me? How can you not know that I am not doing any lessons? My mother stood up. It was time for her to go.

Do not go yet! I am sorry for my bad thoughts. I know you do not mean to leave me all the time.

No words came from me, and she kissed me and left.

Betrayal 1948

It was not long before my mother visited me again and on that occasion, she was accompanied by a tall, good-looking and friendly man whose name was Con. My mother looked very fashionable. I was a bit embarrassed though, because her dress was sleeveless and cut quite low, a style frowned upon by the nuns as being immodest and showy. I worried that the nuns might be annoyed with me because of my mother's style of dress. Con joked with me and made me laugh, although I never had a lot to say, because I was never sure when I might say the wrong thing. Unlike St Brigid's, there was no dispensation that allowed us to walk in the garden. Nevertheless, I enjoyed the day and, when they left, I hoped that I would see Con again.

Back in the ironing room, I dreamed of another place. I was not sure where it was. It was a pleasant place with pretty gardens and I was not lonely. I dreamt to remove my mind from the worrying thought that that day might be the day when someone, who was mad about something, might thump me again. Or when one of the epileptic people might suddenly start foaming from the mouth and thrash violently around on the floor. When those things happened without warning, my garden vanished and it was hard to find it again.

The morning was already hot and everyone appeared weary and fed up before the day had even begun. I needed to keep quiet and keep out of the way, because tempers were likely to flare on a day like this. I hoped that today they would put the metal drums of cold, red drink with the unusual flavour outside the ironing room and laundry. Rita told me that the tangy taste was something called quinine. I did not mind the taste. Tasting cold and sweet was all that mattered to me. Oppressive heat from the previous day still lingered in the ironing room. The nights were made unbearable by the inescapable and pervasive fumes of *something awful* burning in a large drum at the end of each dormitory. I inhaled the disgusting smell that caused my throat to clench and my stomach to churn and I thought that it came from outside somewhere. I did not believe Irene, when I asked her where the smell came from; until she showed me the drum and told me tersely that, they used burning *cow shit* to get rid of mosquitoes.

'Surely they wouldn't do that in the room where we sleep.'

'Yes, they do,' Irene replied. And her face revealed that it was not only me who found it disgusting.

Miserably, I attempted to relieve the pressure on my toes, standing first on one leg, then on the other and wriggling my feet around inside my uncomfortable, ill-fitting shoes as I pushed the iron around listlessly. Day dreaming of my flower garden was not helping that day and relief swept over me like a cool shower when I heard Irene call to me to go to the sewing room with her. Although I hated the ironing room, I felt a quiver of concern at the thought that they might be going to put me in the sewing room, where I felt that my ineptitude with a needle could keep me in trouble forever. I followed Irene past the women whose task was to fold the huge mounds of ironed and pressed laundry. Unrestrained laughter abruptly burst forth, and Irene and I both smiled as we looked about to see the cause. Two of the women had become tangled around each other and ended up screeching with laughter on the floor as they tried to fold an enormous bedspread. It probably was not so funny to anyone else, but hysterics of one type or another were never far away, so for the moment, with no one to *shush*, clap, or frantically beckon, they were enjoying themselves.

We went past the folding area towards the centre of the room where the sewing and repairs took place. Large cardboard boxes filled with buttons stood along the wall, and bigger boxes filled with reels of cotton, mostly white, stood alongside. The sewing machines hummed busily and the women did not glance up from their work as we walked by. Others, not at machines, sat replacing buttons and repairing seams.

Irene bustled past all this activity with me scurrying along a couple of feet behind her. We continued towards the back rooms where we entered a small-screened area. Marguerite beckoned me in with her sweet smile.

'Hello, Lucy. I need to take some measurements. You may need new clothes. What you are wearing is getting a bit small for you.'

I had never heard of anyone being measured for clothes. Anything unusual made me apprehensive. As I twisted and turned, my inches were scribbled in pencil on the back of a brown paper bag. Marguerite looked into my face, 'Lucy, don't look so worried. Keep being a good girl and one day you may get a nice surprise.'

A few days later, the same breathless Consecrated who led me to Mother Pierre the last time I was in trouble, told me to follow her. Her quivering eagerness reminded me of the German Shepherd puppy that I sometimes saw running along the outside of the high wire fence at the back of the laundry. I left the ironing room and walked along the shaded section of the veranda to the wooden outside steps that led to the dormitory. The aura seemed friendlier and less threatening in the daytime.

Mother Pierre stood perfectly straight outside Mother Pascal's little cell with her hands clasped in front of her. An assortment of clothing sat on a chair in the passageway. Mother beckoned me forward, smiled and indicated towards the clothes, meaning for me to try them on. I was pushed and poked in and out of different tops and skirts while the two nuns nodded like fashion gurus and gave their opinion on what looked best on me. I did not know what to think and I feared to be too hopeful about what it all might mean. So I thought nothing.

When I returned to the ironing table, Rita leaned over and murmured quietly. 'It looks as if you're going home.'

I felt no excitement and I had no presentiment that anything was about to change. I had learned my lesson too well to become overly hopeful about anything. After not receiving a visitor for a long time, I had recently seen my mother twice within a few weeks, and on those occasions, she was accompanied by Con. When I remembered those visits I did begin to feel a bit more hopeful, surmising that Con may have had been brought to meet me and perhaps pass judgment before a decision was made about me leaving the convent. He probably thought from the imposing exterior and impressive rooms where visitors were greeted that he was visiting some sort of school.

The following morning, after breakfast, as I was leaving the dining room, a girl that I did not know told me to remain in the dining room until someone came for me.

Only a second later, Sister Cecelia, the nun whom I had first seen on the day of my arrival, suddenly appeared at my side.

'Now come along little one, we are going to get your things.'

She walked briskly and I tried to keep pace with her as we hurried along the long corridors that I had learned to polish so capably. She unlocked the door at the end and we went through. Once again, we passed the stained glass windows and the statues of woebegone, long-suffering, pious-looking saints. As we entered the attic room, it appeared to have been frozen in time. It seemed that the clothes draped over the rails were the same ones that I had seen before and the suitcases seemed not to have moved away from their place along the wall except for the old, brown, scuffed case, held together with a long leather strap: that was my case. Emotion struck me with a stunning force. Memories of my mother and her sweet perfume swirled around me. *Oh Mummy, please come and get me.*

I longed for her to hug me hold me and make me warm on the inside. I wanted to feel her soft blonde hair against my face again and to breathe in her perfume. The pent-up loneliness and fear broke through the barrier that I had lived behind for so long and I howled when it hurt so terribly.

Sister Cecelia told me to calm down and, as she had done on the day of my arrival, handed me a handkerchief. I sobbed and hiccupped while she helped me gather my clothes and put them into the case. I opened the lid and, when I saw inside the case, a feeling of joy swept through me as I recognised my books and pictures. I had not realised how I missed those books until I saw them again. There was no time to see more. Sister urged me to hurry up and decide what I wanted to wear.

The rest went into the case. I sat alone in a large room until Sister Cecelia came in and said to me, 'Well, Lucy, there seems to be a problem. We hope we can sort it out today. Mother Pierre is doing all she can for you.'

Was I going from there, or not? I did not even know with whom I was going. Was I going back to Stella's house? Would the next morning see me back in the ironing room?

Nobody came into the room. I had been summoned after breakfast at about eight thirty. I heard the lunch bell ring a long time after that, so I reasoned that it had to be now being around one o'clock. Another long time passed in the semi-dark room, chills, and hunger pangs gnawed at my stomach. It was just as well that I did not dwell on thoughts about lunch, because nobody brought me any. Besides, I knew that I would not be allowed into the dining room while I was dressed in outside clothes. The room grew cooler and a little darker as the sun changed direction. My heart thumped rhythmically, pounding, loud and insistent in my ears. In the stillness, I heard the sound of jangling of keys, and then I heard the swish of the voluminous garments, as the door flew open, and Sister Cecelia rushed in.

'Hurry, Hurry! They are here. You are going now. God Bless you, little one.'

With that, I felt a small shove in the back, into a room where my mother stood gazing with little interest at a vivid painting of cherubic infants.

My mother! There she was, dressed in a white linen two piece suit and her blonde hair beautifully waved. She turned towards me, and I became aware of another person in the room. It was Alfredo! Overjoyed, I knew that they had come together to get me.

It was not quite like that though. I learned that when Amy arrived earlier in the day to collect me a last minute hitch occurred when the nuns realized that because Alfredo had legally adopted me, Amy needed his sanction to take me away. No mobile phones existed in those days so it had taken all day to find him and bring him to sign the necessary documents. I wondered if she needed, or had, his agreement to put me in there. I did not think that either of them was happy with the situation. Because the problems involving my release took up most of the day, our reunion was a bit ordinary. I was happy beyond words to be with my mother and to be getting out of the convent, but I was cautious about getting too comfortable until I knew what she really planned.

Although she tried not to show it, Amy was furious about having to seek Alfredo's permission for my release. It had been a long, frustrating day, the kind of day that might have had her thinking. Why am I bothering? With a curt nod to the other people in the room and a brief smile at me, Alfredo abruptly stood and left the room without speaking. I worried that he might not be able to find his way through the maze of passageways.

Amy hugged me. 'Come on, darling. It's been a hell of a day. Let's get going.'

Mother Pierre rattled keys as she swished along ahead of us, along my polished boards towards the forbidden door. I wondered who would help Mother John with the polishing now that I was going. Keys jangled futilely until, with a small grunt of satisfaction, Mother Pierre withdrew a key measuring about six inches long from the depths of her large pocket. The door swung open and we hastened from the ornate room that I remembered from the day of my arrival. I did not look around. I just wanted to leave before anything stopped me. Mother Pierre promised to pray for me. More key searching, another door reluctantly swung open. *I breathed in freedom!*

The high walls behind me cast late afternoon shadows as I walked away, too stunned to even feel happiness. I moved one foot after the other in step with my mother. We did not speak. Angel statues, chipped and cracked, gazed sightlessly down from their eternal place atop colossal, cement plinths. Brilliant, emerald green grass smelled sharp and fresh as a worker pushing a lawnmower disappeared behind a small bank of trees. The perfumed rose bushes, committed to my memory, bloomed vigorously and vibrantly. Sounds fractured and split, becoming individual and distinct. With startling clarity, I heard bees buzzing lazily around the colourful flowerbeds. A black car, its motor humming gently, drove at slow speed past us towards the front of the building. Dreamily, I hoped that no one was being taken there to be left behind. Further away, the powerful sound of a motorbike revved and thudded, its deep growling rumble gradually fading to a soft drone as it moved rapidly into the distance. I lugged my case and I once again passed through the imposing, double gated barrier that separated the institution from the outside world. We were heading towards Amy's world. She appeared to be about to embrace life with her new husband and include her daughter.

I never forgot the day I left The Home of the Good Shepherd. The sudden exposure to life outside walls was almost unbearable. I experienced a dazzling, over-heightened sense of reality, broadening, magnifying and vividly colouring everything that surrounded me, reminding me of a medically-induced, euphoric release from severe pain.

Chapter 6

Goodbye Lucy

'Never tell anyone about where you have been.' That was what my mother said to me after we boarded the trolley bus to take us to where she now lived. *Don't tell anyone?* No words were ever to pass between my mother and me about where I had been. I was never permitted to speak to her, or ask her for an explanation about why I had been left.

Once again, I found myself travelling on a green trolley bus, but this time I was going in the opposite direction along Cambridge Street towards the city, quite unaware that it had been *two years* since my last journey on a bus.

The trolley bus moved along smoothly and I sat in an agreeable trance-like state, gazing at the brightly coloured, storybook world through the pane of the dust-streaked bus window. My eyes and ears feasted on the sights and sounds of freedom and my eyes lingered on the fantastic shapes of the trees that lined the street in orderly rows. Some were smooth branched and others gnarled and knobbly. They stood in contrived symmetry, one tree aligned precisely to each red-roofed house. Neat gardens were protected from passers-by and meandering dogs by small, white, picket fences. We paused briefly outside a small, corner shop, which had a brightly-coloured, orange, yellow and green, striped awning pulled to the halfway mark. One person got on the bus and two people got off. A few minutes later Amy stood, wavering unsteadily and tugged the bell cord sharply. The trolley bus stopped at the corner of Cambridge and Sutherland Streets and we both stepped cautiously down the narrow, metal steps. My mother and I crossed Sutherland Street and walked to a large house on the corner of Havelock Street.

We stepped through the gate to my new home and crossed a short strip of lawn before climbing up some crumbling limestone steps. I followed Amy along a wooden veranda, which led to a large, impressive, old, timber door. Captured forever in glass on either side of the door, images of two vibrantly pink flamingos gave the entrance an air of faded, old-world grandeur. The house was immense and Amy and Con, along with other tenants, rented rooms there. It had formerly been a private hospital, as our previous place in Aberdeen Street had been. This house was desperately in need of repair though, with its glory days long departed.

My mother acted as if we had just returned from a daily outing and she appeared to feel no awkwardness. Amy led me into the front room of the house and said, 'Con and I are married, you know, and we have been for a while,' I felt nothing, except to momentarily wonder why I had not been allowed to be at the wedding. I would be living with them, it seemed, and I was shown the lavishly decorated room where she and Con slept. The largest bed I had ever seen was covered with a burnished-gold, ruffled, satin bedspread, adorned with piles of matching, bouffant pillows and cushions – also gold in colour and trimmed with rich turquoise embroidery. In an alcove at the opposite end of the spacious room, russet-coloured easy chairs, placed in front of a small fireplace, looked comfortable and inviting. Centred in pride of place on the mantel was a large, dark brown radio. A Singer sewing machine stood by the door and the whole effect was warm and inviting.

My inexperienced eye found it quite splendid.

There was a jaunty rap on the bedroom door and my mother opened it to a woman whom she introduced to me as Mrs Campbell, the owner of the house.

'Mrs Campbell, this is my daughter, Faye.'

'What a pretty name,' the older woman exclaimed.

Faye! It sounded joyous and somehow young. I wanted to hear my name over and over. What a pity there was no song with that name in it. I would have sung it all day.

Mrs Campbell was a talkative widow of indeterminate age, and wore clothes that were colourful, floating and feminine, and her tightly curled hair was especially dark. She reminded me a little of her house: a faded remnant of earlier, perhaps-more-affluent days. That first night home, and for some time afterwards, I slept on a spare bed in Mrs Campbell's cluttered bedroom, which smelled muskily of the various perfumes and make-up that sat piled in some open, and some unopened, bottles and jars on her dressing table. In another part of the house, Mrs Campbell's sister, with her husband and their two teenage daughters and a son, shared rooms.

Before I awoke completely the next morning, I knew that I was somewhere different. No angry clapping assailed my ears and no pungent odour of manure stung my eyes. Instead, I heard, 'Good morning love, did you sleep all right? I hope my snoring didn't disturb you. Do young girls like you drink tea? Would you like a cup? Do you have a dressing gown? Here, borrow mine.' I shrugged myself into Mrs Campbell's wonderfully soft, ancient, pink dressing gown, and wrapped it around myself. Barefoot, I trailed after her to the kitchen.

Mrs Campbell placed two pennies in the coin slot attached to the side of the gas stove, then lit the gas jet and placed a battered, enamel kettle on the flame. I never forgot that morning. There I sat, rugged up in a kind old lady's gown, drinking tea and eating deliciously hot crumpets dripping with butter. Better than all the cake and ice cream in the world, I thought.

'Hello darling,' my mother chirped, as she came into the kitchen. 'Good God! What have you got on?'

'Mrs Campbell loaned me her dressing gown,' I told her, drawing it comfortingly around myself.

'That's nice of her,' she said, smiling a little uncertainly. 'Tomorrow, I will take you shopping.'

I had thought earlier that I had seen a cat wander by and, as I sat with Amy while she drank her tea and smoked the first of her many cigarettes of the day, a cat did stroll into the kitchen.

Freckles, this dark brown and orange, tortoiseshell, female cat caused Amy a great deal of anxiety because of her refusal to come in at a respectable hour, curl up like a good cat, and go to sleep. Freckles appeared to feel no shame about being the neighbourhood Jezebel.

At the end of my second day out, I waited at the front of the house for Con to arrive home from work. The trolley bus rounded the corner and as Con swung from the bus to the pavement, his overall appearance really registered with me for the first time. With masculine, Greek good looks and dark hair, which he wore fairly long, he was extremely tall and powerfully built. He had about him a slightly lack-a-daisical, easy-going approach to most situations and people who he encountered. He was a gentle person; there was no apprehension in his manner and he was very funny. He never became my father but, better still, he became my friend and supporter. He teased me mercilessly as we played backyard cricket, using a kerosene tin for the wicket, and I quickly learned to hit the ball over the fence to get six runs without exerting myself.

I learned that Mrs Campbell liked to gossip about her sister to Amy and about Amy to her sister, though her manner towards me was warm and kindly. Friday and Saturday nights saw Mrs Campbell elaborately dressed, sweeping through the front door on the arm of an elderly man dressed in a shiny, navy-blue suit. Mrs Campbell's relatives shared a large dining room with Amy, Con and me, and they took it in turns to cook in the separate kitchen. A frequent cause of disagreement between the residents was the coin-operated gas stove. A penny placed in the slot provided enough gas to cook a quick meal and perhaps boil the kettle. However, arguments often arose if someone felt that they hadn't had their penny's worth before another person came and used the stove.

I hadn't yet been taken out at night, and one evening, shortly after I came home, Amy, Con and I went into the city on another green trolley bus. We left it at the corner of Wellington and William Street, and as we crossed the road to the opposite corner, I was intrigued by the strange name in front of a quaint, old-fashioned building, and wondered what they sold there. Con, observing my questioning look at the words written in elaborate gold lettering on the window, W.A. Apothecaries told me that an apothecary was a dispensing pharmacist. That evening was probably the beginning of my life-long curiosity of interesting and unusual words and their meaning.

The sight of the bright advertising signs that continuously flashed red, blue, and green, illuminating the windows of department stores and cafes and casting vivid patterns across the pavement, for me, after so long in the darkness, was glorious. We wandered along and I gazed through the windows of the milliners and the dress shops. I feasted my eyes on gorgeous full-skirted dresses with narrow shoulder straps and wide waist cinching belts: clothes that I would love to wear, and probably would, if I could only stay with my mother for long enough. I had not realised that it was so close to Christmas until, in every shop window, I saw the decorated and illuminated trees. We passed by Boans' department store and it brought to my mind the wonder of the Christmas decorations and of going to see Santa Claus in my other life, a long time ago. We wandered around to Hay Street just in time to be tangled up with the crowd pouring out on to the pavement from the Ambassadors Theatre. I had been to the Ambassadors with Laurie and Maxie to the afternoon matinee when I was little. It was there that a pianist played on the stage during intermission. Suddenly, my mother clutched my hand and pulled me along to London Court. The clock was about to chime and the small Crusader figures on horses that circled the base of the clock on the hour were about to appear. As a little girl, I had stood there many times holding her hand, waiting for the little Crusader men on their horses to appear. *Did she remember?*

Con rubbed his hands together vigorously and, declaring himself starving, suggested that we go to a cafe on Wellington Street. Several girls, all with their long hair drawn back into ponytails, sat high on chrome and green laminex stools, with layers and layers of starched skirts spread around them. Alongside each chatty, laughing girl sat a boy, looking offhand and confident. They each drank with a straw from a metal, milkshake container or from small glass bottles of Coca Cola and, although seated, they bopped and clicked their fingers to the popular music of the early 1950s. I could not imagine what it would be like to feel that sort of confidence and I hoped they didn't look our way and see me looking at them. That would have made me feel vastly out of place and self-conscious. We sat comfortably on painted, white, wooden chairs as we waited for attention. To distract my gaze from the teenagers and, to overcome my feeling of awkwardness, I studiously inspected the red checked cloth and glass, salt-and-pepper shakers.

My mother leaned across the table and lightly tapped my hand.

'Don't twiddle your fingers like that; it makes you look a bit simple.'

I was relieved that no one could hear the rapid counting going on in my head!

Many people were frankly astonished to meet Amy's *big* daughter. Con's relations knew that Amy had a daughter, but they clearly expected a child considerably younger than me. However, whilst Con's family warmly accepted me as one of their own, I did have a little wish now and then that I was not such a large, eye-opening surprise whenever I met new people. Con's Greek family had the same appeal for me that I remembered from Uncle Bordoni's Italian family. Con's father was not exactly jovial, but I sensed that he liked me and did have his own Greek sense of humour. He often spoke rapidly in broken English and gesticulated wildly when in conversation with me, and then he would look enquiringly, awaiting my response. Embarrassed and baffled, because I had no idea what to say, I would look hopefully to Con for help, until one day, Con said, laughing fondly at his dad, 'Poppa, you behave. She is only a kid. Don't tease her.' Despite his heavily accented voice, I quickly grew to understand Con's Poppa, and when he joked, or teased, I came to recognise the sneaky look in his eye. Sometimes he and I would beg off eating more food, or playing cricket, and sit on the front veranda together where he pointed out plants and flowers and told me their names.

Mother Mae, as I came to call her, was large and gentle, and soft in nature and features, with a truly beautiful complexion and, to me, was a bit like a fairy godmother. I sensed, though, that Con's family thought there was more to the story behind my sudden appearance. Of course she was curious. I was nowhere to be seen when her son married my mother and her conversations with me occasionally took on a questioning tone. My attitude became wary and withdrawn whenever even a seemingly innocuous enquiry arose because, with my mother's words echoing *Don't tell anyone,* I was afraid of saying too much, leading people to perhaps think that I was aloof, or extraordinarily shy, or maybe *even a bit dopey,* when I answered in monosyllables.

Just along from their family-owned cake shop in Walcott Street, there was the news agency and it became my favourite place. Christmas was near and the shop glittered with tinsel and shone with sparkly cards. Santa Claus and delicate, angel ornaments dangled from the ceiling and sat piled upon the shelves. It was my own Christmas fairyland; I especially admired one Christmas card, which pictured a jolly, red-robed Santa leaning on a sleigh full of presents against a snow-covered background. The card, brightly covered with sparkle, was the loveliest thing I had ever seen and I wanted to buy it for my mother. I wanted to show her that I loved her and, of course, I hoped that she would realise that she loved me.

When I had left the convent barely a week before, I had not known how close to Christmas it was. How amazingly a life could change in a week.

Christmas day was truly a family experience celebrated with Con's four sisters, one brother and their families. Exotic Greek dishes shared the table with traditional English fare. We continued to nibble the delicacies as our Christmas day passed into evening and we all remained together. Nobody left to be anywhere else. Being together with their family on Christmas day was the only place they wanted to be. The beauty of that Christmas and the close feeling of belonging in Con's family, added to the recent sudden and dramatic change in my life, overwhelmed me. I had only been out of that other place for a week. The release was so sudden and, although happy, I found myself weeping quietly in one of the bedrooms.

Years later, as Amy's relationships foundered, I lost many splendid influences from my life including, eventually, Con and his family. But what would my life have been and what sort of person might I have become had they not been in my life at all? I cherished being part of those family gatherings.

Peace around Amy was fragile, ready to shatter, inexplicably, at any time. But I gave thanks daily that I was not still in the ironing room.

One Sunday morning my mother brought up the subject of me going to Mass. 'After all, you are a Catholic.' She seemed to forget that we both were and did not offer to accompany me. I went to St Joseph's Church, in Subiaco, twice, but I was uncomfortably aware that it was perilously close to the place that I recently had left, perhaps less than a mile away. I never returned to St Joseph's, or went into any church for a long time. I gave thanks and sometimes still implored God, but from a place of indoctrination and habit, rather than faith, and I was not at ease in the cloistered atmosphere which reminded me too vividly of the place that I hated.

I had just celebrated a glorious Christmas in honour of the birth of Jesus and yet, there I was, just a few short weeks later, uncomfortable in the Catholic Church. If those two attendances at the church of St Joseph achieved nothing else, they helped me resolve *for myself* the issue of my seemingly double standard. I had two points of view. To me, at that time, the Catholic Church represented nuns and other cruel people who were devout Catholics. There were the priests who roared from the pulpit condemning their parishioners, including children, with terrifying threats of burning in hellfire for all eternity. Understanding the link between a benevolent, forgiving god and the angry god who was prepared to cast me into hell with the devil, was difficult. At Christmas time, though, the church put aside the threats and intimidation, for a short time, being gentler and more caring to the innocents around them. If only that spirit of kindness had prevailed after the festive season. Therefore, I had the two faces of the church. Childishly, at that time, I accepted one and rejected the other. I had a long talk to Con about it and he said, 'Sounds reasonable to me.'

Con was a keen fisherman and on hot, summery evenings, he frequently went to fish from the wall outside the Swan Brewery, the local beer brewing company on the bank of the Swan River – the belief amongst anglers being that the brewer's yeast used in beer making attracted fish to the area. I often went with Con. The actual fishing never thrilled me, but I liked the camaraderie amongst the other fishers, and watching Con battle to land a huge glistening Mulloway one evening, was exciting. We later carted the dripping, slippery monster, wrapped in a hessian bag, home on the bus. Some travellers avoided coming close while others inspected the fish admiringly and inquired where we scored the splendid catch. One wit once asked if we had paid its fare. The bus conductor ignored our transporting a fish.

Amy accepted me into her life and we went about our days as if our existence had always been so. I enjoyed the ritual of Saturday afternoon when Amy and I went to the garden, and washed our hair in a bowl of warm water. Then with an alarming array of metal and plastic curlers attached to our heads, we kept to the furthest corner of the backyard in case an unexpected visitor dropped in. We filed our nails and hand washed our underwear, and then cleaned our shoes and sandals ready for the week ahead. I liked to think that for both of us, for my mother, as well as for me, it was an enjoyable time. However, just as nature decreed that summer must inevitably pass through autumn and turn to winter, so it was with my mother. Changes were inevitable, regardless of how well and pleasant things seemed.

I had no wish to part with my newly-found freedom and I pushed away the anxious thoughts about my imminent enrolment and subsequent attendance at a school. I could not begin to imagine what might lie ahead. Eventually, the decision was made that I would go to a non-Catholic school nearby. Amy must have approached the headmaster and told him something about where I had been. I could not have gone back into the system without any reports or explanation, could I?

However, my mother knew exactly how long it had been and cast me back into the system to cope the best way I could. After two year's absence, I started at a new school, aged twelve – nearly thirteen – as if I been away on holiday for just a few weeks.

Chapter 7

School 1951

The school case banged awkwardly against my side, my clenched knuckles stark white against the brown handle as I gripped it tightly. Nervousness walked beside me with unwelcome familiarity when I crossed the basketball court towards the main building of Thomas Street School on that first day.

My steps slowed. The thought of being in a classroom, of fitting in and trying to make friends terrified me. What if they thought me odd and completely ignored me. Why do I have to face all these rotten changes by myself all the time? I stood, seemingly invisible, near some steps, while dozens of boys (*boys!*) and girls milled around me.

A severe looking woman, dressed in a plain grey skirt and a pristine, white blouse with a large cameo brooch on the collar, came towards me. 'Faye, I'm Miss Larney. Come with me. Because you weren't with us last year, I am going to give you some aptitude tests before we decide where to put you.'

I went into Standard Six, which was the equivalent of Grade Seven in the twenty-first century. At the time, I did not think it was such a great achievement, but back then, I did not know that I had missed two years of schooling.

Miss Larney walked with me across a wide hall, stopping only when we reached a group of three classrooms clustered together at the end the hall. A tall, male teacher stood with some boys outside one of the rooms and to my astonishment Miss Larney ushered me forward. 'Mr Ryder, this is Faye, your new girl.' My face must have spoken volumes when I saw a male teacher and boy students. I had seen some boys when I arrived, but never dreamt that we would be in the same classroom. I remembered little of what happened next, or indeed, had any clear recollection at all of the next few weeks as I returned to the classroom. Mostly I struggled, not with the lessons, but with fitting in. I did not feel like the other students. I felt like a much older person with nothing in common with any of them and was embarrassed that they all knew more than I did, not just about school work, but about everything.

I discovered that by the end of the first week in the classroom that when I looked at the blackboard or a book for any length of time, my vision became so blurred that the only way I was able to see was to continually look away and blink rapidly for several seconds. Mr Ryder noticed my difficulty and sent a note home to my mother. I had worn glasses from the age of about seven, but I so heartily disliked them, that when I went into the convent without them, it didn't bother me. Without schooling, the only reading I did was the prayer book, most of which I knew from memory, so I had been able to get by without them. A visit to Dr Arndt, the same specialist that I saw when I was little, soon had me back in the dreaded glasses.

Mr Ryder was a sophisticated looking man. However, he did not have a suave attitude at times. The teacher had a furious, quick temper, which often saw him hurling the blackboard duster or a book at some unfortunate boy's head. The girls escaped having anything thrown at them, but they were subjected to his sarcastic, albeit, witty comments, about everything

School 1951

from their lack of brains to their lack of beauty. He did not often single me out other than to instruct me about something, and he never reprimanded me. He cast a long shadow as he towered over my desk as he took time to explain and make sure that I, and the others, understood the lesson. If I were slow to grasp the point, he would say consolingly, 'Well, you went to a Catholic school and we all know that they teach nothing but prayers.'

I was sure that the other kids saw me as an oddity. I was self-conscious and overly aware of people and of their reaction to me. The short, unfashionable, and possibly unflattering, red-plaid coat that I wore to school every day, summer and winter, would never have established me as a trendsetter. Everywhere I went I took that coat. Without it, I felt vulnerable and exposed. My plaid coat was my security blanket. Even Amy gave up trying to separate me from it.

One day at school, as we sat in the lunch shed, one of the girls must have said something unkind to me – maybe a comment about the check coat – but the strangeness of being at school and my sense of being different engulfed me and I put my hands over my face.

To my surprise, my face was wet and tears were streaming from my eyes. One of the girls came over and sat with me, the others joined her and endeavoured to console me. Those girls were all right. It was not their fault that I was withdrawn and afraid to open my mouth. From that time I was part of the group and did get along in a friendly, casual way with all of them. Reading was my life though. Any sort of book meant that I did not have to be careful with what I said because, when you read, there was no need to talk, or even look at anybody.

A hollow, shaky feeling, as though I had missed a step went through me when I came home from school one day to see my bedding and pyjamas piled on the kitchen table. Life was okay and I was not ready for any changes. It transpired that I was not going far, only to the side veranda. Mrs Campbell and Amy had had some sort of disagreement, which resulted in Mrs Campbell saying heatedly, 'And you can take your daughter out of my room too.'

Overgrown shrubs rioted around the side veranda making it barely visible from the street. It resembled a large cubby house. I was not nervous at all as I lay wrapped up warm and safe, gazing out from behind the tattered canvas blind. I believed I was safer there than I ever was when with living with Stella. I watched the moon shining brilliantly on some nights, or beaming dull and golden on others. The glittering stars were comforting, as was the sound of the rain, sometimes violently pelting and shaking the veranda posts and, at other times beating like a soothing, hypnotic drum. Freckles slept on my bed, her dear little heart beating in unison with my own.

One morning, the postman's whistle blew cheerily as he dropped some letters into our rickety, leaning-over letterbox. Amongst the mail was a letter from Amy's mother, Maude. Amy recognised the writing, 'What the hell is she writing to me for? We haven't spoken for years, not even a Christmas card.'

I found out then that a stony silence had existed between the two women for several years. In spite of her seeming indifference, Amy slid her long fingernail under the envelope flap and withdrew a one-page letter from which she read aloud:

'You hear of the poor devils wanting to escape from the terrible destruction brought about by the long war. Their homes are in ruins and they do not have the money or the will to begin again. The government is offering cheap passage by ship for eligible families to migrate here. For some time now, I have been corresponding with your brother, George. He lives in London with his wife, Clare, and their son, Ronald. George and Clare have written me several letters begging me to act as a referee and sponsor for them and Ronald to come to Australia. I am not sure about this, as I barely remember them. I don't know what sort of people they are and they will have to live with me until they are settled. George has expressed a desire to meet and get to know you after all this time. I take it that you are not against the idea of seeing your brother, George, and his family settled in Australia after all that they have been through.'

Amy continued to read snippets from the letter but my mind had closed to her voice, as I idly wondered what George, Clare, and Ronald might be like. I hoped that they would come and I pictured a joyful, moving reunion between my mother and her brother.

I had not seen Maude since I had last visited Diamond Tree with my mother when I was about eight. Since that time Maude, Grandad, and Maude's cousin, Chris, who lived with them had moved to Bunbury.

No further letters arrived until one day, months later; I took a beige-coloured envelope from our mailbox and recognized Maude's large, rounded handwriting. Amy took the letter and slit the envelope with a carving knife that rested handily on the nearby breadboard. Maude wrote that George and his family had arrived in Australia and were living temporarily with her in Bunbury. She invited Amy, Con, and me to stay for Christmas and to meet the newcomers. The thought of having family arrive from so far away was enticing and I waited eagerly for the opportunity to go to Bunbury to meet them. I also felt that my mother was looking forward to meeting with a link to her past.

The Christmas holidays arrived and we caught the train to Bunbury to meet the English relatives. Chris met us at the station and, quiet as ever, he loaded our cases into the boot, and then drove home at a very modest speed.

Maude stood in the doorway; her hands clasped graciously, and welcomed us all with a big smile and a hug. 'Come in, come in, and have a cup of tea and a sandwich. Alf, take Amy's case.'

Maude had not met Con, nor had she seen my mother or me for a long time, so it appeared that all was forgiven. It was time to play happy families.

A well-built, tall man walked into the kitchen, he and Amy looked at each other uncertainly before clasping and clinging to each other emotionally. After several moments the tall man walked towards me. I met his eyes and thought what an impressive-looking person he was with his military bearing and large moustache.

'Well, you must be Faye. Aren't you a sweet girl?' he boomed loudly, in a British sounding voice that reminded me of a radio newsreader. 'Clare, Ronald, come and say hello to Faye.' Ronald, I thought, was about ten years old and he remained where he was, shyly leaning against the wall with his hands tucked firmly in his pockets.

A tiny woman sashayed happily towards me. 'Hello dear. I'm your Aunt Clare.' She spoke in a husky, almost hoarse voice, while in her hand, she held a cigarette. Her thick, grey hair frizzed cloud-like around her head and, although she seemed almost diminished alongside George, of the two she appeared to be considerably older. I found her amiable and friendly though, and she eagerly held on to my hand while we sipped tea.

The kitchen soon filled with visitors and my heart leapt when I realised that the young boy standing looking expectantly at me, was Paul. I had not seen him for a long time. Paul was Uncle Harry's and his wife, Dorothy's son. When Paul was three or four years old, we used to play together and I adored him. I found that when I was with him I enjoyed the rare, unworried sensation of being just a little kid. He had an old wind-up gramophone, and we vigorously cranked it up and played a song called. 'Once in love with Amy.' There was another old scratched record that we also played endlessly: 'Eleven more months and twelve more days and I'll be out of the calaboose.' When we weren't frantically winding up the machine, I read stories to Paul, as he sat behind me and brushed my long hair. (It was a simple time, but I suspect that our pleasures were more simple than most) I remembered my previous discussion with my mother about her family and I wondered if Paul was my cousin or not. I was rather short of relatives and quite enjoyed having someone to call cousin. I asked Con what he thought.

'To tell you the truth, I find that the whole issue regarding who is who with them all is a bit confusing. But yes, I believe that Paul is your cousin.' He paused, thought, and then said, 'Second cousin.' I was happy with that.

With still another week of holidays to look forward to, I spent as much of that time as possible with Paul. Once again, I read to him and, once again, he brushed my hair.

The afternoon was hot and humid. I sat in Maude's lounge room reading and not really listening to Amy, Con, and the others as their voices drifted through from the kitchen where they sat discussing Ireland, England and complicated family relationships. Suddenly though my ears pricked up, as George's voice, loud enough to break my concentration with my book and engage my full attention, said to Amy, 'Amy you do realise, don't you, that I am not your brother? Lorna, Blanche and Rose are my sisters, but you are actually my niece. Lorna is your mother.'

He paused, but no one else uttered word. Then he continued.

'When the family realised that our unmarried Lorna was pregnant, with no prospect of her being saved from what they saw as the ruinous disgrace of being an unwed mother, your grandmother, Amelia, took the baby to bring up as her own child. That baby was you.'

'However,' George went on, 'my mother died of tuberculosis when she was forty two and her sister, Maude – your great-aunt – decided to adopt you and bring you out to Australia. So, although I love you, you are not my sister, but my niece.'

By then, I had put my book completely aside and was listening to a far more interesting tale.

Interesting as I found it all, the raised voices disturbed me and I started to feel uncomfortable. I walked outside to sit in the sun and gaze though the neighbour's fence at the enormous, plate sized, prize-winning dahlias that grew in their garden. The haughty looking tabby cat from two houses down strolled by, then came back and sat beside me, purring contentedly as he waited to be patted. Granddad wandered past, whistling tunelessly. He seldom seemed to sit inside with the others.

In convent idiom, I thought, *Holy Mary, Mother of God. What a mess.*

When those inside seemed to have quietened down, I went back into the house. I saw that Maude and Amy, who were both known for their quick tempers, were clearly furious. Con looked bemused and Chris looked fed up. George and Clare took hold of Ronald and went off in another direction. The carping between Amy and Maude, resumed. Whatever took place that day caused a major rift between them all and the honeymoon period of grace seemed over for the new arrivals. It was clear that some of them did not like each other. Upon occasion, I wondered if they liked me.

We returned to Perth. Maude and Amy did not speak to each again for another long time. George and Amy remained friends, though, and continued to refer to each other as brother and sister. Which appeared to indicate that no one really knew what was what, or who was who.

Our family tree was a tangled, thorny, bramble bush.

Chapter 8

Runaway

Twelve months passed by quickly and I left Thomas Street School at the end of the year without any qualms. I felt no sense of loss at moving on. I had not formed close attachments and the others from my class were leaving Thomas Street to go to different high schools anyway. For once, I was not the only person moving out of the sphere. I came nearly top of the class in all subjects, probably due, in part, to Mr Ryder and his easy-going, tolerant demeanour towards me. For many years, I cherished a school report with my results, but shame swept over me one day and I burnt it when I realised that I was a year older than the other students in the class were. I regret that act. I had no inkling that the day would come when I might want to flaunt that report with pride. My mother was quite pleased with me, but never breathed a word about my missed schooling.

After the summer holidays, my mother enrolled me at Girdlestone Girls High School. My results showed that I was a good, average student. I enjoyed learning, but school was never going to be a comfortable place for me.

It became usual for me to wait at the corner bus stop for Con to come home from work, when I raced towards him and we hugged exuberantly, theatrically and jovially, before walking the short distance around the corner to the house.

That was until one day as I walked towards the front gate, Amy said to me, 'You need to stop hugging Con when you meet him after work. It doesn't look right.'

I stopped hugging him and I stopped going to the bus stop.

Tension arose between Amy and Con. Her face was often angry and her disdainful looks towards him were nasty. Although Con mostly feigned good-natured tolerance, when he did occasionally let the mask slip it was clear that he was puzzled and disliked the change in her manner towards him.

Amy came to me as I sat eating my breakfast one morning, 'I think I am going to need you to go Bunbury to stay with Maude. Just for a little while.'

I may have called Maude Nana, but I knew she was not my mother's mother and she did not seem grandmotherly at all to me. I did not relish the thought of staying with her. I had no words of reply and remained silent.

Eight thirty on a cold August morning found me shivering at the Perth railway station. Overhead signs showed information. The one above my head told me that I was on Platform Two, and that the train would depart for Bunbury at nine o'clock. Amy had gone for a cup of tea and I heard her high-heeled shoes tap-tapping on the terrazzo floor as she crossed the vast, almost deserted platform. She came towards me bearing thick, china cups of tea and, of all things, a meat pie each. She flopped down on the wooden bench, 'I know a pie is not exactly breakfast, but it's all they had.'

I liked pies.

As in previous times, we didn't have a lot to say to each other and I had given up praying for divine or magic intervention. Amy gave the impression of being uneasy and of wishing to escape as quickly as possible. I wondered was there any feeling of regret at sending me away once again?

The idling train began to huff and puff importantly and steam hissed and spat spasmodically from the engine. Passengers scurried forward. Amy hauled my case up and urged me towards an empty carriage. The only other person to get in with me was a middle-aged woman who, like me, was quite happy to make short remarks occasionally and then return to her reading. The journey took about four hours as the train travelled south and passed the lush green, rolling paddocks dotted with dairy cattle and sheep. The peaceful scenery and the rhythmic clicketty-clack of the train wheels as they sped along lulled me into a sleepy state. The movement of the train slowed and as we passed the sign for Bunbury the pretty station gardens came into view and a moment later the platform appeared. I continued watching, and amongst the sprinkling of people standing expectantly waiting, I saw Chris, Maude's middle-aged, bachelor cousin, peering anxiously into each carriage. My travel companion and I smiled at each other as she hauled her luggage from the overhead rack.

Chris and I greeted each other reservedly, but he smiled proudly when he ushered me into his new car, a light-olive-green, coloured Austin A40. We spoke little on the short drive home.

Maude was a harsh, sometimes-difficult woman, not one to display warmth or affection. When I arrived at the house, she showed me my bedroom – just as my mother had acted when I returned from the home – as if I had only been gone for a few weeks, Maude now, apart from directing me to the bedroom, acted as if I had always lived there. Also living in the house were Granddad and Chris. They seemed a mismatched group, but they existed together quite agreeably and accepted me into the house without questions or discussion – at least none that I knew of – and we all existed in cautious harmony. Even so, it was a strange existence. There was Maude's surprise religious change. After a life time as a devoted Catholic and as a matriarchal figure within the Church, Maude abruptly turned her back on Catholicism for reasons known only to her and had become a passionate believer and follower of the Jehovah's Witnesses.

Maude spent many evenings and Saturday afternoons sitting around her large kitchen table with other church members, earnestly reading from their church's magazine, or dissecting and rehashing tracts from the Bible until the Bible conformed to *their* beliefs. Granddad, Chris, and I did not participate in these activities, nor did we go to church.

I loathed the country high school to which I was sent. I disliked the male form teacher intensely. I found his bright, carroty-red hair repellent and his strange, uncomfortable manner when he spoke to me and looked at the floor, rather than my face, left me foundering. Plainly, he did not know what to make of me and his noticeable attitude carried over to the students. I failed to understand how it was possible that anyone who felt as awkward and as obvious as I did could apparently be invisible to teachers and students alike. I walked alone along the walkways and when I sat in the school grounds praying for lunchtime to finish, no one saw me. If any of them had been aware of me, they probably would have seen a painfully shy, awkward girl who rarely spoke, who came from Perth, who was definitely not one of them and who lived with an old grandmother.

It was early December and school was soon to break up for the year. I panicked, because when I found it too unbearable, I sometimes missed classes after the lunch break. I walked away from the school grounds and spent the afternoon alone, walking or reading in the welcome solitude of the nearby bush. Would those missed classes reflect my overall performance? I knew that they would. I was coping well, but not so well that I could afford to miss vital learning time. I was fearful of the consequences when it was discovered that I had not regularly attended school and the certainty that, because of my absences, I had not achieved good results. So I took what I felt was my only option. I did not go back to Maude's after school on the last day of the term; I went to the station and caught a train to Perth. I never planned to run away. It just happened. That was possibly the single most foolish thing that I had ever done. That decision, and what followed because of it, could easily have landed me back behind the convent walls, almost validating, to some, a reason for me being there in the first place. Running away was a most serious transgression. Many of the girls in The Home of the Good Shepherd were there because of running away from home or from a less secure institution.

Although, in my mind, I was not running away, I was *returning* home to Havelock Street, the only home I had known for a long time. I did miss living at Havelock Street. I missed its random assortment of characters, I missed Freckles, the cat, and I grieved for Con's mateship and cheeriness. I had become used to, and enjoyed, the easy-going acceptance of the other people living in Mrs Campbell's house. I also liked sleeping on the side veranda, lying on my back and looking up the stars as I drifted into peaceful, untroubled sleep.

When my mother found out, in a rare long distance phone call from Maude that I had not returned home after school, she travelled to Bunbury. Con remained in Perth and the next day, thinking that I might be on a train, went to wait at the Perth railway station. He finally saw me, and he thought I had just emerged from a railway carriage.

The truth was: I had spent the previous night in a toilet on the railway station, after having been sexually assaulted. I had not planned to run away and when I got to Perth I had no idea know of what I was going to do. Too scared to go Havelock Street, the realisation that I was a runaway hit me. It was about 6 o'clock in the evening and when I walked through the station entrance, I saw taxis lined up along Wellington Street. A driver called out and asked me if I needed a taxi. I hesitated, because I had little money left over after paying the train fare. Then the driver was standing beside me, with one hand, he opened the front passenger door of the car and with the other, he removed my small bag of belongings from me. I slid into the car seat. He possibly would have seen a clueless young girl, with a small bag and no idea of where she was going and with apparently no one around to offer her protection.

He jumped into the car and asked, 'Where to?'

I replied, 'Havelock Street.'

As he eased the car into the traffic, he said. 'That's not far but the traffic is heavy. How about I go up St Georges Terrace and cut along that way?'

I was not familiar enough with Perth, or where I lived, to know that our end of Havelock Street was along Wellington Street and under the West Perth subway, and not along St Georges Terrace toward Kings Park.

The taxi driver chatted amiably, and asked if I was new to Perth and where had I come from. I told him I had been staying with grandmother in Bunbury for a while.

'Now you have arrived back and there's no one to meet you. That's a shame; didn't you have anyone to pick you up from the station?'

I mumbled some reply and as I did the car swung around the monument at the entrance to Kings Park. 'Have a quick look at the city from up here,' the taxi driver said. 'Travellers from all over come up here to see this view.' But he drove past the view to a secluded area within a canopy of trees. When he stopped the car, I was puzzled, but not afraid. However, when he slithered across the bench seat until his leg was pressed hard against mine, and then I knew I was in terrible trouble. The car became noisy with the sound of his raspy breathing and his hand roughly tore my blouse away from the waist band of my skirt. Then he was pinching my breast and inner thighs painfully. My terror came, not from what he might do to hurt me, but that what he might do to me would make me a bad girl. I did not want to be called a bad girl, a girl who belonged in a home.

Oh, please God! Someone help me. I didn't mean to run away. I do not want him to make me a bad girl.

However, I was not saying all that in my head. I was screaming loudly. Although the canopy of trees sheltered the taxi, it was still daylight and

I must have made a terrible din. He probably did not expect me to start screaming to God and Mary to help me, because he suddenly righted his trousers, the buttons of which were undone, and turned on the car ignition.

He drove quickly back to the station, clearly anxious to get rid of me. He stopped the car and leaned across to open the door from the inside. I leapt from the car towards the protection of the bustling crowd. The taxi driver appeared at my side and placed my bag at my feet. Then, without a word, he drove away. He asked no money for the taxi ride.

I walked back past the ticket collector, who was still seated behind a metal grille. He did not ask for a ticket and, because I had no idea if I needed one or not, I kept walking, trembling badly as I went passed him. The station seemed safe and, more scared than ever to go home, I went into the toilet and decided to hide there. The night passed slowly as I huddled in the small cubicle breathing in musk scented bowl cleanser and the strong odour of urine emanating from the cement floor. As I fought against terror at being enclosed in such a small area, and of the shock of what had happened with the taxi driver, I counted non-stop *four eight twelve sixteen* and, while I gasped for breath, I reminded myself that although locked into the small space, I could slip the latch and walk out any time. Footsteps passed by the door throughout the night. I prayed that their owners would not stop and rattle the door and demand to know who was in there.

The sun had risen, after the longest, coldest night of my life, when I eventually emerged from my hiding place. Walking along the platform, not knowing what to do next, I was cold, hungry and very afraid at what I had done. I looked up, and there was Con. I did not know how long he had waited at the station with the expectation that I might turn up there.

He walked towards me, and asked, casually, 'Good trip? Your mother has gone to Bunbury looking for you, but don't worry too much,' he said, as he observed my stricken face, 'I don't believe you should have been sent down there in the first place.'

That was it. No questions. No recriminations. A terrifying and unlawful thing had happened to me, but it did not occur to me to confide in my mother or expect understanding. I only expected blame because I put myself in that position and deserved what had happened. *So I told no one.*

Keeping quiet seemed the best way to avoid further trouble. It appeared at that time that I might be copying the evasive ways of those around me, but I found that secretiveness, whilst it might temporarily avoid trouble, was an uncomfortable, worrying state.

Amy arrived back the following afternoon. I braced myself for an onslaught that did not happen. What a strange situation! My mother often created such a fuss over nothing, leaving me bewildered as to what had brought about the anger. That time though, when I knew that I had really done wrong, very little was said. Neither my mother, nor Con, made any further mention of my abrupt departure from Bunbury. I had done such a foolish thing and I thanked my lucky stars that the result of my impulsive action had not had dreadful consequences for me. I had Con to thank for my trouble-free return to Perth and, for the fact that Amy did not punish me.

I did not return to Bunbury.

Chapter 9

Pick of the Bunch

Keeping with the theme of arriving home during the month of December, I soon found myself enveloped in the warm embrace of Con's family for the Christmas festivities. I wondered if they even knew that I had been in Bunbury for the past several months.

Amy liked to browse the city shops and one afternoon, as we walked along Hay Street together, she suddenly stopped and pointed to a card in a dress shop window. The ornately printed card invited applicants to apply for work during the school holidays. Without comment, or hesitation, Amy firmly guided me through the doorway into the elegant, hushed interior of the salon. Several women dressed in black and with their hair stylishly set in rigid, lacquered waves, stood attentively behind glass topped counters. Each woman looked at me enquiringly, and I hesitantly approached one who smiled at me and asked quietly, 'Are you here about a school holiday job?' I nodded mutely, and she directed me towards a woman, so plump that she almost touched the sides of the glass fronted cubicle in which she sat.

My nervousness lessened, as I studied her appearance and became intrigued by her multiple chins, and her cyclamen coloured, pursed,

Cupid's bow lips. She smiled a small smile, and asked me for name and my age and when I replied, she said, 'Very well. You have a pleasant voice and you look like a nice girl. Come back on Monday at nine o'clock and remember, you must wear stockings and your dress must be black.'

I thanked her breathlessly and hurried back past the elegant women.

When I re-joined Amy outside the shop, she hurried me along to Aherns to buy a black dress.

The school holiday period came and went and when nobody suggested that my time was up, I continued to work there. I revelled in the shared exhilaration as women and girls flocked to purchase their new gowns and sundresses for the festive season. I had discussed with my mother the possibility of returning to school and studying languages. Considering the huge influx of migrants to our shores, I had thought it a reasonable idea. Amy had replied, 'I have already spoken to your teachers, and they didn't think that you had the necessary ability for higher study.'

Given the fiasco of my time at the country high school, I believed, and accepted (perhaps erroneously) what I was told.

During my lunch hour, I usually ate a sandwich and then I enjoyed walking out from the shop, along Hay Street and down the Plaza Arcade to Murray Street, past Boans, along to Bairds and around the corner into William Street. I simply could not get enough of the sights and sounds of the city and the glorious sensation of being unwatched and unrestricted.

One hot February day as I strolled along Hay Street, I glanced up to see a familiar figure striding purposefully toward me. I instantly recognized Mr Ryder, my teacher from Thomas Street School. To my surprise, he shook my hand formally, saying at the same time, 'I am delighted to see you. What are you doing? It looks as if you are no longer at school. That's a shame; I had great hopes for you, as you were different from the others.'

How different? I wondered. When he paused to draw breath I pointed out the dress shop just along from where we stood, 'I work in there.'

He looked quite the stern school teacher as he replied, 'You are too bright to be working in a shop.' Then, maybe to soften what might be perceived as a criticism, he continued, 'I do think that you are looking very grown up and pretty though.'

There seemed no point in mentioning that I felt something of a failure for not continuing with study and for a few moments we spoke about the school where he taught before parting and going our separate ways. Walking back to work, I thought over his words. Dismayed at his remarks about me working in a shop, I told myself that I was happy enough. I enjoyed the respect and courtesy that I received and in many ways preferred it to school where I knew that, sadly, I was never going to be particularly comfortable. Now my life was interesting and busy. I was treated as a person of value and, although a junior, treated with respect.

'Good morning, Faye,' greeted me each morning from the women that I worked with.

There it was again, *Faye*. I still experienced a sense of belonging when I heard my name. I sometimes wondered if it was as unusual as I believed to have to live under a different name, or if I was just particularly sensitive about the nothingness of it.

Our rate of pay was what was then known as the basic wage and we earned one penny in the pound commission on sales. Juniors rarely earned any commission though, because we were not permitted to approach a customer if a senior staff member was available. In addition, they made sure that they were mostly available, often ushering a departing woman towards the door with unseemly haste so that they would be in position to greet the next customer as they entered.

In my new world of retail fashion and occasional fashion-house modelling for a manufacturing agent, the days passed by swiftly and happily. I did not mind that my feet and my back hurt from standing all day. I had known worse pain, in a far less enjoyable environment.

The year was 1954. People were optimistic and hopeful for the future, and the spirit of renewal flowed through all aspects of everyday living. Regular concerts were held on the lawns of the Esplanade beside the Swan River. Families assembled to have a good time, young and old mingling happily together. However, the best time for me was when the city came to life during the annual Flower Week. On a September spring morning, I stepped from the bus and knew immediately that it was Flower Week. The shops, the office buildings and the large, imposing foyer of the Commonwealth Bank in Forrest Place were alive with incredible floral displays and the air was redolent with the scent of boronia, which, with daffodils and all their glorious companions, sat amassed in containers along the streets. Our city was so much more then, than the visually-overloaded and audio-bellowing, demanding dinosaur that it was destined to become.

My boss, Miss Cohen, was a large Jewish woman and, because she had a large puffed up chest and a body shape which gradually tapered down to dainty little ankles and tiny feet, my mother named her Mighty Mouse.

Affordable housing became available and we moved from Havelock Street to Doubleview. I recall my sense of wonder, that for the *first time* in my life I had a bedroom. Until then, I had shared my sleeping place with an adult or slept on a roughly enclosed veranda, or worst of all, in a dormitory.

While my sense of wonder was having a bedroom of my own, Amy's was her Hills Hoist, a height adjustable rotary clothesline. A modern alternative to a long line of wire strung across the backyard and held aloft with a wooden pole, known as a clothes prop. How hilarious Con and I found it watching her grab a towel or sheet and go tearing around with it creating her own drying force on days when there was little wind to propel the thing.

At work, I met Nan, a young, fair-haired girl, newly arrived from Holland with her parents and her younger sister. We were both starting on a journey and a completely different life. Only I knew how different mine was. Over the next couple of years, we became firm friends.

I was sixteen and allowed to go to a dance with Nan on a Monday night. I lived for the weekly outing, barely concentrating at work all day waiting for five thirty so I could fly to the bus stop to catch the first available bus for the hour-long ride to Doubleview. Nan and I joined the Teen and Twenty Club, a dance and social club run by a local radio station, which took place each Monday at a restaurant and function centre called The Marelle.

The Marelle was in Hay Street, above Eziwalkin shoe shop and diagonally across from the town hall.

We drifted into a comfortable group with four boys, Les, Merve, Ted and John. We six went on outings together. Sometimes we fancied one or the other for a week or two, but mostly we remained as a group. Con laughed and teased me and called me heartless for being unkind to Ted when he rode his pushbike over the causeway from Victoria Park to our house in West Perth on several Saturday mornings to see me. I stood and talked to him at the front fence but it never occurred to me to invite him in.

The one that made my heart beat faster, though, was a little older than the rest of us. He was tall, with fair, curly hair and, of course, blue eyes. I learned that his name was Ron, that he told jokes and he laughed and clowned around a lot, and I thought him just splendid. He was friendly to me, but as one of the organisers of the club, he was friendly to everyone, so I was not too heartened by his pleasantness.

Soon though, we danced together, almost exclusively.

Amy came to town most days and met me during my lunch hour. Miss Cohen seemed to find it strange and once asked me why my mother was so often waiting for me outside the shop. Embarrassed, I answered that I didn't know. We usually shopped around a bit and then went to the Coles cafeteria to eat lunch. On one occasion, as Amy and I stood looking at the lunchtime display of pies, sandwiches, pieces of fruit and brightly coloured jellies in tiny glass bowls, a hauntingly familiar voice, saying, 'Fancy seeing you here' made my senses twang like a faulty guitar string, sending all thought of food scurrying from my mind. Amy and I were equally startled to see the unpleasant, challenging face of Stella standing beside us. I had nothing to say to her. Revulsion made me stride quickly away to sit at a distant table far away in a corner. Amy exchanged a few remarks with her and then, with her face flushed, re-joined me. I never asked what passed between them and, I never saw Stella again. I ate no lunch that day and, when I left work at the end of the day, I cautiously looked up and down Hay Street in case I saw her again.

One night at the dance, Ron mentioned casually, 'I won't be around for a while. I'm a butcher and I'm going to Wyndham, boning at the meat works for 16 weeks. It's a great opportunity and the earnings are huge,' he continued. 'Each year many want to go for the season, but few are chosen,' he added with a grin.

We were not going out together at that stage. We just spent the whole time each week at the club together, but I never thought he would up and go somewhere.

Sixteen weeks dragged by and I marked each day off on the calendar and waited expectantly for Ron to return. Time continued to slide by, yet there was no sign of Ron at the dance. I continued to have fun with the others, but something was missing. My mother greeted me at the front door one day when I came in from work and asked, 'That boy you know from the club, is his name Ron Bohling?'

She handed me the morning paper and pointed to a news item. The article reported that a vehicle had been involved in a major collision with a bus loaded with passengers and that the car driver, Ron Bohling, of Leederville, was in Royal Perth Hospital with serious, multiple injuries. I said that I intended to go and visit him, but my mother stated, 'No, you mustn't go to the hospital. You wouldn't want to look pushy nor cheap, would you?'

I could not defy her and visit him. I was not brave enough. Instead, I wrote a letter of commiseration and sent it to his address in Leederville. By the time I did that, he was already out of the hospital. He penned a shaky reply. He was pleased, he said, to hear from me. He was going down south for a couple of weeks and would see me when he returned. The weeks went by and still there was no sign of Ron and I accepted that, perhaps, I would not see him again. Then one evening I heard his laughing voice call my name as I danced past. I waved and smiled and the butterflies in my insides did little cartwheels. He seemed not to be dancing, though, and I wondered why and, specifically, why he was not dancing with me. The evening was about to wrap up when he limped awkwardly across the room towards me and the reason for his not dancing became clear. He put his arm around my waist, 'I've got a wonky leg, so dancing is out for a while.'

More severely hurt than I realised, he was left with a narrow scar across the top of his face and down over one eye and a persistent limp that plagued him, aching painfully, whenever he was tired or when the weather was cold. With his earnings from Wyndham, Ron had bought his dream car: a gleaming black FJ Holden. Two weeks later, it had been completely demolished in an accident from which he was fortunate to have survived.

The following Monday at the club Ron offered to take me home, but I had to decline because Con usually came to meet me so that I did not have the long walk alone in the dark. The regular bus driver Morrie, was a friendly, flirty sort of fellow and he usually dropped me at the corner of my street where Con waited for me.

I told Con that someone had asked to bring me home.

'Why didn't you let him?' he asked.

'I was so surprised I didn't know what to say to him.' I answered.

'Well, if he asks next week, go with him. If you're not on bus I'll know you're with him and I'll see you when you get in.'

I worried that Ron might not ask me again after having refused him the first time, but the following week just before I needed to leave to catch the last bus, Ron said, 'I have a couple of things to do first, but I'd like to drive you home if you're not going with anyone.'

As coolly as I was able, I replied, 'That would be fine. Thanks.'

Slightly overawed by the splendid black car, the replacement for the one lost in the accident, I sat in the passenger seat beside Ron. The car seemed to glide along Scarborough Beach Road, past the bus stop and around the corner. As the car turned, I saw Con. This caused me a moment of indecision. I did not wish to appear young and unsophisticated, having a parent meet me at the bus stop. Con did say if I was with Ron he would see me at home later, but Con waited for me week after week at the corner, leaving the comfort of his easy chair, no matter what the weather. I could not just sail past and leave him standing.

Hesitantly, I said, 'I feel a bit silly, but I just saw my stepfather. Could we go back and get him, please?'

Looking slightly bemused, Ron smiled, 'Of course. What's he doing there?'

'Well, he's waiting for me.'

Ron rapidly reversed back to the corner and stopped with a rather showy flourish. He jumped out in front of Con and, shaking his hand vigorously, said 'How're you going? Jump in.'

When we arrived at the house a few moments later my mother rapped on the window for me to go inside, which I promptly did, leaving and Ron and Con to sit in the car talking to each other for a further half hour or so.

That was how my relationship with Ron began. I was inside with my mother and the boy of my dreams was outside with my stepfather.

It was never going to be easy. Amy disliked me having friends. Ironically, after so many separations she now wanted me nearby all the time. Except for when Nan and I went to the Claremont Speedway on a Friday night with the four boys, or occasionally to a movie, I rarely went anywhere without Amy. However, she did appear to like Ron and treated him in a friendly manner. He was six years older than I was which put him in a more mature, responsible league. Amy was also impressed, I thought, by the fact that Ron's family owned a business and the fact that they all, including his mother, had their own cars.

I met many of Ron's friends over the ensuing months. The Wainwrights had lived opposite the Bohlings in a small cottage with their two sons, Robert and Stan. Ron and the Wainwright boys were inseparable as youngsters and they remained life-long friends.

I also met the Sue family, including four brothers and their two sisters. I experienced a 'remember when' feeling the first time I went to the Sue home. They lived in Aberdeen Street about five houses away from where I once lived as a child. It was the first time I had been back to the area since I was about seven years old. The Re Store stood unchanged, the second shop back from the corner, but Uncle Bordoni's was no longer the same. No enticing aromas or cheery greetings rang out any more. It had different owners and traded as a liquor store. The Sue family were a noisy, exuberant group of people. Their elderly Chinese parents smiled in a benign, enigmatic manner as they sat, side by side, in their matching cane chairs on a small, shrub enclosed back veranda. I sat uncomfortably trying to chat and join in. However, in the face of so high spiritedness, I felt out of place, and I hoped that Ron would not think that I was aloof or unsociable. After we left, all he said was, 'They're a rowdy lot, but you will get used to them. They're a great family.'

I did get used to them and they were a great family.

The weather remained unbearably hot, and on an idle, humid, Sunday afternoon, Ron called by and asked me if I wanted to go for a drive. I held my breath and, when Amy said that I could go for a while, I dashed through the front door and leapt into the car before she changed her mind.

Ron turned the car towards the city, 'We might go and see friends of mine, Ron and Laura Wray. They live in North Perth. Okay with you?'

Ron and Ron Wray were close friends, since they had worked together at the Wyndham Meat Works. We spent a pleasant, companionable afternoon, drinking tea and nibbling biscuits with Ron, his wife Laura, and their children Rhonda, and Joanne.

Sometime later, as we prepared to leave, Ron Wray said, 'Bring Faye along to tennis next week.'

Oh great! I had never even picked up a tennis racquet. Nevertheless, Ron insisted. So I started going to tennis with him and a group that he played with regularly. In the beginning, I played with little enthusiasm and less skill. But after Ron and I spent many Sunday mornings hitting the ball backwards and forwards against the brick wall of the Leederville Primary School, I did improve considerably and, over time, I grew to love the game. We were a group of eight, sometimes ten, like-minded friends and we regularly played tennis and had card nights together. The two Rons were as close as brothers who, sharing an unquenchable energy and zest for life, also shared a sense of the ridiculous, and their loud laughter echoed around the tennis courts as they smashed the ball about. Nor was it being overly romantic to say that we all did have such a wonderful, unforgettable time. We were so young and blissfully untroubled.

I had been working for a year and Christmas was drawing near.

Maude had invited us, my mother, Con and me, to Bunbury for the Christmas holidays. We left Perth on Boxing Day and planned to stay for two weeks. The train journey to Bunbury took about four hours back then and, on that particular journey, we sat stranded in the middle of the night for an additional two hours waiting until some hold up on the rail line cleared. Finally, the train moved cautiously forward and then rapidly picked up speed as we steamed our way through the inky darkness towards Bunbury.

Precisely at midnight, dear, ever patient Chris could be seen, looking anxious and stamping his feet to keep warm, or to keep awake, as the train drew in to the station. He greeted us warmly, at the same time bundling us hastily into the waiting car. I heard no conversation as I went to sleep almost immediately.

The following morning, I had no recollection of arriving at Maude's, or of going to bed. I went looking for my mother or Con before I made my way to the kitchen. I was not at all sure of how I would be greeted. I had not seen Maude since I had run away and I fully expected her to be cool towards me, or, if not noticeably cool, certainly reserved. However, I was welcomed and fussed over and nothing was mentioned about my previous abrupt departure. This led me to think that maybe Maude or my mother had realised that being dumped in a strange country school without any support might have presented some difficulty for me.

Our stay was enjoyable but not overly festive, because of Maude's devotion to the Jehovah's Witness' sect who did not celebrate Christmas or birthdays. I did enjoy spending time with Paul, though, and the day before I left to go home Paul and I went for a walk into the town centre. As we ambled along, contented in each other's company, Paul looked across the road and observed, 'There goes Effie from Egypt.' He then added, 'Everyone calls her that.' I looked over. I knew Effie. She *was* from Egypt and used to visit Maude's house for Jehovah's Witness meetings. I looked and blinked in astonishment as Paul collapsed to the pavement with laughter. Effie from Egypt was wearing my red-checked coat. I must have forgotten it when I left so suddenly to return to Perth.

Laughing hysterically, Paul gasped, 'At least it went to a good home!'

Before we returned to Perth Amy had confided to Maude that she had a lump in her left breast. Maude, upon hearing this and suspecting that the lump may have been there for some time before Amy mentioned it, was uncommonly concerned, stressing many times the seriousness of a breast lump and advising Amy to go to the doctor as soon as we returned to Perth. Amy, no doubt alarmed at Maude's sense of urgency, did go straight to the doctor and he referred her to a specialist who agreed to see her immediately. The doctor phoned her later the same afternoon and told her that she was booked into the Mount Hospital for immediate surgery. Without exception, any woman who went through that dreadful, out-of-her-control experience anxiously patted around her breast area as she awoke, to see if she could feel the outcome of her surgery. Amy did the same and handled the operation and the loss of her breast with a mixture of bravado on some days, laughing and talking gaily, and terror on others, when her mood made her behaviour difficult and contrary. To my amazement one day as I sat talking with her during a visit, Amy reached for her cigarettes: very casually, so as not to provoke any uninvited scrutiny or comment. Even in 1954 we knew that smoking was not healthy, although most had no idea of just how terribly dangerous it was.

In a much weakened state, Amy eventually left the hospital. Her surgery was followed by months of fear-inducing, painful radiology. Her recovery was slow and debilitating and she was alone a great deal of the time.

Con worked as a fitter and turner at Hume Steel, one of the main steel manufacturing companies in Western Australia during the 1950s. While Amy was still recovering, he came home one day with the news that the company had secured a long-term contract for a large enterprise in Geraldton. Con had grown up with all of his family in Geraldton. He had now been offered, or maybe he'd applied for, the opportunity to go there to work on the new project. Amy and Con's relationship was troubled and they were not getting along. I sensed that Con was worn out and fed up with all the aspects of the life he lived being married to Amy. The job in Geraldton required the workers to be away for several months at a time. He might have thought that their marriage would benefit by being apart for a while. I did not know if Con had more opportunity to come home, or if he opted to stay there during leave breaks, but we seldom saw him. He did return, though, to attend the Masonic Ball at the Embassy ballroom. Uncle Harry belonged to the Freemason's Lodge in Bunbury and he offered to sponsor me to be a debutante at their annual ball. For many weeks, I practised with the other girls as we swirled and twirled our way through the modern waltz. We learned to perfect the deep, low curtsy, to be given to the Governor of Western Australia. It was exciting and I loved the formality and elegance. I felt beautiful and confident in the long, white, soft tulle gown, embroidered with French Guipure lace inserts.

Con made a special effort to be at the ball and I treasured my signed souvenir program. Amongst the signatures was Con's message, *'To the pick of the bunch, from your loving dad.'* I was a long, long way from The Home of the Good Shepherd that night.

Soon after the ball, Amy decided to go to Geraldton for a holiday and further recuperation in the sunshine. There was no time limit set for the holiday and I expected that she would be away for several weeks, but only two weeks passed before Amy unexpectedly walked through the front door. Clearly, something major had happened. Amy told me tearfully and angrily. 'I had the days to myself to go shopping and look around the place while Con was at work, then in the evening we went out to dinner. We were fine,' she claimed defensively. Pausing to take a sip of tea and light a cigarette, she then continued, weeping at intervals, 'I wandered in to town one day while Con was working.' Her voice rose in agitation, 'I went to the damn newsagents. I just wanted to get the paper and some books to occupy the afternoon.'

Between bouts of anger and self-pity, the story continued to unfold. As she left the shop, Amy glanced in the window at some glossy photos of recent social events in the town, and recognised Con smiling, dressed in formal clothes with his arm around an extremely young girl. He did not pretend it was a casual photo taken randomly at a party. She told me that he freely admitted that he was seeing the girl and that was that. It was out of character for Con to behave in such a way. Nobody, excepting Amy, who was most vocal, quite knew what to say or do. It seemed that Con had reached a point of no return with nothing to discuss.

Ron was not overly sympathetic towards Amy. He helped her in practical ways. However, I think he believed that she had brought most of her woes upon herself.

One evening when she was unhappy about me going out, Amy spun around in the middle of a diatribe and said to Ron, 'You've always liked Con better than me.'

Ron thought for a moment, 'Yes. That's right.'

It was a difficult time. I went to the dance and to the movies, but Amy wanted me in so early, I sometimes wondered if it was worth going at all.

George and Clare, my mother's reputedly long-lost brother from England and his wife, lived in South Perth and they had invited Amy, Ron and me to dinner. When we finished the uninspired, but tasty, meal of mince and boiled vegetables, Ron and I escaped from the dinner table while Amy was regaling George and Clare with tales of a party she had attended.

We laughed at our own cleverness as we disappeared like naughty children across the front lawn and hastily walked the short distance along Hurlingham Terrace to the nearby Swan River. We walked across the soft lawn until we came to a park bench, then we sat close together. We had no need for words and sat in silence. Fairy-like lights reflected and twinkled across the water from the brightly-lit city buildings and street lamps and a yellow moon cast shimmering ripples across the river. The bright lights of the cars as they slowly wound around Riverside Drive added sparkle and created the illusion that if I leaned forward and stretched my fingers, I would touch something precious. With Ron's arm warmly around me, I sat peaceful and contented. We watched as a ferry glided smoothly by, carrying carefree people, laughing and enjoying themselves, and as the ferry drifted past, the memory of my trip on the ferry with my mother came to me. I pictured the woman, wearing a white apron over her floral dress standing in the doorway of the large, rambling house in South Perth, holding her ginger cat. I imagined the tremor through my body when the lions roared and I felt the heady anticipation at the thought of the exciting prospect of living there with my mother. A small lifetime of sadness had passed since that night. Many times tears threatened me at unexpected moments. I did not know if they were tears for the known past, or for the unknown future. At times when I was with Ron, I found the words almost spilling from my lips. I wanted to say to him. 'Things about me are not what they seem. I was in an unbelievable place for a while. I was in ....' I failed every time. I could not bear the thought of Ron looking at me with disbelief or even disdain and asking me questions for which I had no answer. It never occurred to me for a moment that I might be comforted and consoled. Accustomed as I was to blame and desertion, when there was no one blaming me for anything, I took it upon myself to be my own accuser. I waited too long. I was never to tell him.

We walked back to the house, not rapidly, as we had departed, but slowly, enjoying the peaceful, balmy evening air. I sat on the front porch and Ron called through the open front door. 'Goodnight folks, have to run, early start tomorrow. Thanks for the dinner.'

As he left, he kissed and hugged me, and arranged for us to meet in Hay Street on the following Saturday morning. He gave no explanation. I walked along to the Piccadilly Arcade where we had arranged to meet, wondering why he had left his dad alone in the shop and why he wanted to meet me in the city. My heart warmed when Ron walked towards me rapidly, with his endearingly familiar, lop-sided gait. Smiling, he took my hand and as we walked along I was about to ask where we were going, or what we were going to do, when suddenly he tugged at my arm and bundled me through the doorway of Mazzuchelli's jewellery store. There he explained to me that he would like us to be engaged on my eighteenth birthday. No words came from me. Ron led me slightly to one side and murmured in a soft voice. 'I think that you love your mother, but she scares me. I am worried that without Con to care for you, she will break us up, somehow.'

I knew his fears were justified because I shared them. The smiling assistant rolled out a small, soft, red velvet mat and placed many beautiful diamond rings before us. I chose a flat band of gold set with three equal sized diamonds. I was like any other young other girl. Somebody loved me and found me special and deserving.

Ron suggested that I not say anything to my mother for the time being, feeling sure that there would be an argument and hoping to find a way to avoid it. I was young for such a big step, and it seemed a hasty and even designing way for us to go about things. However, I had learned, and Ron was learning, that fear of Amy's reaction to events occasionally meant one needed to be less than straightforward.

On my eighteenth birthday, when Ron came for dinner he told Amy that he had something to show her. They went into the lounge room and he showed her the engagement ring. I think it pleased her that he paid her that small courtesy and dinner went surprisingly well. Over the next few days, though, I did feel once or twice that she was a bit annoyed with me for not saying anything to her previously, but she kept the peace. Meanwhile, I sat on the bus each morning, completely absorbed, twisting my hand with the diamond ring back and forth, so that I could see the sun's reflection casting dazzling rainbow patterns around the interior of the bus.

A week later, Amy amazed us both by suggesting that we have an engagement party. It was the last thing that I imagined she would want to do, although Amy was a party girl and things had been gloomy for quite some time. A party might shake off her blues. For many years, Ron's family had held family celebrations in the Masonic Hall, in West Leederville. So, we did too. It pleased me to celebrate there with the familial vibrations of previous good times surrounding us from the walls and rafters of the old building. A lively local band and plentiful amounts of good food and drink were all that we needed to ensure that a party was happening.

I seemed to have collected no photographs from the party, but in my mind, I saw clearly my green ballerina-length dress with minute black flowers patterned across the skirt. There stood my mother in her dramatic dark blue *Cheong Sam*-style dress, inspecting the tables laden with food and cakes. The memory of the aroma from a glass of red wine drifted toward me as Stan Wainwright leaned forward to kiss and congratulate me. Ron's mother, Madge, twirled expertly around the dance floor, her skirt billowing, while Ron's Aunty Hope pulled the bashful, reluctant Jack to his feet. I saw myself standing with Ron in the centre of the room as the band played *If you were the only girl in the world*. No photographs, but many memories.

Chapter 10

Who was Lorna?

Two weeks after the party, Amy had taken a large dose of some tablets. I came in from the garden to hear her gasping and coughing in the bedroom.

'Hurry, quickly, get me some water,' she whispered. I ran to the kitchen tap, filled a glass, and flew back to the bedroom, where I placed the glass firmly in her shaking hand.

She drank thirstily before sinking back on the pillow. 'Don't blame yourself darling, I just want to sleep.'

Blame myself for what, I wondered. I had no way of knowing that she had anything in her mouth. I did feel fear for her safety, though.

Therefore, I did what we all did in times of trouble. I phoned the police. A voice barked at me down the phone, telling me I was speaking to Sergeant Page. I blurted out. 'I think my mother's trying to kill herself.'

He replied. 'Phone an ambulance. At this stage I will treat your call as if it never happened. It's a criminal offence to make an attempt on your own life. It'll be better for your mother if you keep quiet.'

Within a few minutes, the ambulance wailed urgently along our street, bringing curious neighbours to their front door. The sirens were blaring again, as the ambulance carried Amy and me to the Royal Perth Hospital. I prayed. Please God, not this way, not here, not now. At the hospital, I was shocked at their treatment of her. I was surprised at the hectoring tone of the elderly nurse and the doctor was loud and unsympathetic. They made her sit up when she wanted to lie down and their attitude was severe.

A harried looking, young doctor told me to go home.

Childishly, I asked, 'May I stay with her? I don't think that nurse will look after her. I don't think she likes her.'

The doctor smiled wearily, 'Your mother will be looked after, so you go home.'

I went home and eventually fell into a fitful sleep, after praying that never again would I need to accompany a family member or anyone at all, in an ambulance with sirens screaming out in dramatic urgency as it dashed through the suburbs.

Before Amy left the hospital, the doctor came to speak to me, and he told me that that only a couple of the pills appeared to have been ingested and that they were several years old. However, he told me that she did seem to have several unresolved issues and that she was crying out for attention. He recommended she go to Niola, a small private hospital, in Cambridge Street, that dealt with psychiatric issues, for a short stay.

During her time at the hospital, Amy's doctor rang Con in Geraldton and suggested he come to Perth and see Amy in the hospital. Con did not come and Amy left the clinic, never to speak of the incident again. Attention seeking or not, she must have felt quite bereft and desperate. I wondered what caused her sadness, desperation, and seeming inability to form a permanent relationship with anyone, even with her own daughter. The intense secrecy that was our way of life meant that I knew little about my mother.

Unexpectedly, Amy began corresponding with Lorna, Blanche and Rose, her three sisters. On the other hand, were they her three aunts? Long, interesting letters arrived regularly from one or the other. I think that Amy looked forward to those letters and found a small sense of belonging through them. Lorna wrote in 1956 with the astonishing announcement that she was coming to Australia to live permanently. Amy veered from being happy at the prospect to wishing that Lorna would change her mind and not come. Lorna did not change her mind. Three months after the arrival of Lorna's letter, on a cold, blustery morning, Amy and I waited on the Fremantle Wharf at the primitive tin shed terminal that once welcomed voyagers to Western Australia. *The Orcades*, a magnificent, all-white, passenger liner had berthed, but two numbingly cold, uncomfortable hours passed before the scores of passengers poured down the gangplank and congregated in bewildered groups as they waited for directions. An older woman separated from the crowd and walked around anxiously scrutinising a small photo held in her hand. She came close to us, glanced repeatedly from Amy to the photo and back again to Amy.

Frowning deeply, she asked, 'Are you Amy? I'm looking for my sister, and you do look something like the person in this photo that she sent to me.' Before Amy could answer, the woman flung her arms wide, 'Yes, it is you. Oh, aye, this is grand.'

I had expected a pretty and fashionable person, like Amy. This person looked a lot like the old women from my childhood. Shrouded in a dark, heavy coat and an extremely unattractive hat, she held her large handbag protectively at her chest. Many hours were to pass before Lorna's massive amount of luggage was cleared through customs and then, finally, laden like beasts of burden, we were able to leave the terminal. We took her to our house in a taxi and Lorna expressed her surprise at the length of the distance we travelled. Lorna remarked many times during her stay that everything in Australia was so spread out and scattered and I think she found bus and train journeys more boring than interesting. She expressed herself quite differently from the English folk who had stayed at Mrs Campbell's house. They enjoyed the wide-open spaces and bright sunshine and embraced the changes. Lorna, however, found much about which to complain. She stayed with Amy, with the intention of looking around to find somewhere to live permanently. I remembered little about her, except for a few occasions when Ron and I drove her along the beaches and to Kings Park and Yanchep. We took her to Bunbury for the weekend, but I had the impression that she thought that wherever we went, it took too long to see too little and that seeing Maude was hardly worth the effort.

I recalled no in-depth conversations with her, going to shops, or doing any of the special things that one did when anyone was staying. She frequently spoke scathingly about Australia. Perhaps she had expected more from Amy, or had hoped for her to be different in some way and was disappointed. As the days passed, Lorna and Amy's tone of speaking to each other became increasingly sarcastic and waspish and the atmosphere became heavy and awkward. Lorna left the house one morning and we assumed that she had gone to look for somewhere to live. However, upon her return later in the day she announced rather forcefully.

'I have booked my passage to go back to England. This country is nothing like I expected and I want to go back home.'

Amy did not reply, and to my knowledge, little or no discussion took place regarding Lorna's abrupt decision. Fifteen weeks after Lorna's arrival, Amy and I were back on the Fremantle Wharf waving goodbye to her. I found it sad. Lorna must have come to Australia with expectations of some sort of family bonding, or at least a chance of living a new life in a new country. What bitterness and disillusionment prevented her from opening her eyes to the possibilities? I thought it probable that she was

Amy's mother and that she came here to look her over. If all went well Amy would be declared her long lost daughter and they would live happily ever after. It did not go well. She and Amy did not like each other, nor did she like Australia. I felt sympathy for Amy too. In spite of her criticisms of Lorna, she probably had hoped for something positive to evolve from their meeting. The code of *do not discuss, do not say anything* went on and on. They knew no other way. This woman, somehow related, came all the way from England and returned without ever gaining the insight and peace that open and frank discussion might have brought.

I often wondered. Who *was* Lorna?

Chapter 11

Halcyon Days

In the days, following Lorna's departure Amy was moody and morose. I came home from work one day to find that Amy was packing her clothes. I immediately thought that she was going to England. It appeared to be an unusually serious undertaking. The house was in shambles. Clothes, shoes, books and correspondence were strewn all over the house. I could not see my own bed under the huge pile of garments heaped upon it.

'Guess what darling,' Amy said animatedly, as I came into the room, 'I have decided to go to Melbourne and I have arranged for you to stay with George and Clare.'

The arrangements had already been made with all the efficiency of a military evacuation. Tenants had been found to sublet the house. I was to be dispatched to George and Clare. I wished she would not continue to make me feel a mongrel pup, needing food and a kennel.

Amy's train ticket sat prominently displayed on the dressing table. I rarely questioned Amy's decisions and I asked no questions about her plan. Later in the evening, I placed Amy's piles of clothes on to chairs around the house and climbed into my bed. My mind drifted as I lay there, half awake. I would have more freedom with George and Clare. They lived in South Perth, closer to work and to the city than Doubleview. It would also be closer for Ron to visit me. I was beginning to feel rather good about this new development.

After a few weeks of planning and frantic activity involving everyone, Amy was ready to depart on her great adventure. Going far away was good. She might even find peace in new surroundings. Apart from the fact of her going to Melbourne, I did not even know where Amy was going to be – not to which part of Melbourne, the city or suburbs, or how long she intended to be away. Amy wrote a letter about two weeks later and told me that she had secured a live-in position in a small residential hotel in Little Collins Street in the heart of Melbourne. From that time on, I received regular letters and cards from her telling of her job, which she enjoyed, and she told of the excellent social life to be had in swinging Melbourne, as opposed to Perth.

George and Clare were good natured and agreeable. It took me some time to realise that I need not constantly explain myself to them. Nothing extraordinary took place, but the days were noticeably without tension. Seven months drifted by and I became settled into not expecting the unexpected – until I received a letter from Amy and read, with some misgiving, that she was returning.

Amy travelled back by ship and, once again, I found myself in the early hours of the morning jumping up and down on the Fremantle wharf to keep warm while, at the same time, peering at the disembarking crowd, seeking a familiar face. She came slowly down the gangplank holding the arm of a uniformed purser. She looked fragile and bewildered as he left her side and returned to his duties. I moved to her and she clung to me tightly. 'Oh God darling, I'm seasick. I've never felt so disgusting in my entire life.' I led her to a seat while we waited for the porters to haul the luggage onto the conveyor belt.

A group of noisy passengers from the ship walked by and, seeing Amy, they shouted farewells and commiserations to her. The various voices echoed, 'It was great to meet you *Ame*. Gosh, you don't look too chipper this morning. Hey, great party last night. What time did *you* get to bed? Don't forget to keep in touch.'

My mother now looked embarrassed, as well as ill. Whatever the reason, or combination of reasons, she suffered badly for a couple of days.

When Amy recovered, she brightly informed me that there was something she wanted to discuss with me. Apprehensively I lowered myself on to a canvas garden chair and waited. I gazed at the strangely shaped, brightly coloured strelitzias that Clare proudly grew in the garden and wondered why Amy having something to discuss with me sounded like a death knell. Smiling broadly, Amy settled in her chair, lit a cigarette, and asked, 'How would you like to get married?'

I thought that was Ron's question.

Still beaming, Amy went on to explain that she wanted to return to Melbourne and if Ron and I were married, she could settle over there without worrying. When did my mother ever worry about me in the past? Why start now? I felt a flash of anger that Amy had placed Ron and me in the childish position of not making such a major decision at a time to suit us. How would Ron feel about getting married because the timing fitted in with Amy's plans? I phoned Ron, and asked him to come to South Perth that evening after dinner.

I didn't intend to say anything until I saw him, but as soon as he asked me, 'What's up,' I blurted out, 'she wants us to get married.'

Ron was beyond surprise at any of Amy's foibles. 'Okay, I'll be over tonight.'

What a different situation and how different Amy's attitude would be if I had done the unthinkable and become pregnant so that we needed to get married quickly to observe convention! I stopped at that thought. The idea of my mother's wrath made such eventuality an absolute impossibility.

Clare and I lingered at the kitchen table surrounded by the dishes and the then unappetising remnants of the leftover food from dinner. She was almost quivering with curiosity to find out what Amy had in mind. Neither of us was game enough to get into a discussion in case Amy heard us and got annoyed.

I whispered to Clare as we clattered the dishes noisily around in the sink. 'She wants Ron and me to get married, soon.'

Clare asked in a hushed, scared voice, 'Are you expecting?'

I replied, surprised at the question, 'Of course not.'

A car door slammed and I heard Ron's voice laughing and talking to Clare's son, Ronald. As I walked out a bit hesitantly to meet him, he gave a quizzical glance towards the house and we went in together. Amy kissed Ron enthusiastically, took his hand and drew him into the lounge. With the air of one about to announce a lottery win, and pausing to take a deep breath, Amy announced, 'I think it would it would be good if you and Faye got married before Christmas. It is September now so you should be able to arrange it. I want to go back to Melbourne and if you two were married, that would be good.'

Later, long into the night, Ron and I talked about marriage and we each asked the other if that was what we wanted – then, at that time. We agreed that the timing was inconvenient, but we also agreed that for future harmony, fitting in with Amy was the best thing to do. I did not dwell too closely upon the fact that although it was what I wanted, being Amy's daughter meant that choices had never figured largely in my life.

We chose the last Saturday in November for our wedding day.

From the bridal department at Aherns, I chose a material of rich, ivory-coloured brocade from which Ron's sister, Joyce, made my elegant wedding dress. She also made aquamarine coloured brocade bridesmaids dresses for herself and for Nan, my dear first friend from when I started work.

Ron and I married in a little Church of England church in Woolwich Street in West Leederville, a short walk from where Ron's grandparents lived. The Bunbury contingent arrived in full force, with Maude, Alf and Chris travelling to Perth with Harry, Dorothy and the two boys, Paul and John. Harry walked me down the aisle.

I missed Con. My mother rarely spoke about him unless in anger which, effectively, cut him out of my life. I would have been so honoured to have my friend and sometime saviour – the closest person to a father that I had known – at my wedding. Because of Amy's resentment of him, I was unable to invite Con, or any of his dear family to be there.

The reception dinner and party with our hundred guests went late into the night. I wanted the most wonderful day in my life to last forever. But the evening inevitably wound down and it was time to think of leaving. We left our family and friends, and ran up the stairs and took off towards our new life.

We stayed at an old-fashioned hotel close to the beach. Early summer sun warmed us during the day. During the night, the breeze carried across the waves and wafted through the open window lulling us into a deep, seemingly-dreamless sleep.

I felt nervous and strange about getting into bed with Ron. We were young and enthusiastic, but during our engagement, the dreaded penalty of *going too far*, or worse still, *going all the way*, loomed over me. And, of course, so did the fear that Amy, the party girl herself, would kill me if I brought disgrace upon her. Funny thing though, in spite of my nervousness,

I wore a beautiful, sheer nightgown – not a cover-up, convent-looking affair. My bond with Ron was full of humour and fun, and that night was too. Ron was sleeping when I awoke the next morning. I thought how young and carefree he looked, with his curly hair tousled over his forehead and with his face completely relaxed. I felt that I would love him forever. A fierce need to protect him swept through me, but I could not imagine why I felt that way.

On a blustery afternoon, the last day of our holiday, we made our way back to the car from the beach. As we walked we came across a cave-like opening and Ron suggested squeezing through the opening to see what was on the other side. I did not want to go and I told Ron that I hated closed in places.

With little enthusiasm, I took his hand and followed him into the narrow rock cavern. It turned out not to be bad at all, but as Ron laughed, 'come on, I'll look after you' we came through the opening at the other end and were confronted with enormous, black, threatening waves and slippery, slime covered rocks. Ron called to me not to move any further, but I continued to inch forward a little to get a closer look at the tempestuous sea. I slipped, and the hard rock jolted me and cracked my spine painfully. When I tried to regain my footing on the glassy surface, I thumped repeatedly on to my backside. Ron tried to reach out for me, but with nothing to grasp for support, every slight movement saw us slipping closer towards the water.

Eventually Ron managed to grab hold of my top and drag me backwards. After what seemed an eternity, we managed to use our heels as tenuous advantage and scoot backwards to a dryer part of the rocks. We scrambled to our feet and holding each other for support, we sought the warm haven of the car. Ron's mood was morose and angry, which was a mood I rarely ever saw in him. He remained upset and I eventually asked him what was wrong and he replied angrily, 'I yelled to you not to go any further today and you kept going. That sea was boiling and I'm not a strong swimmer. If you had gone in, it probably would've been the end of both of us.'

Astonished, I said, 'But you're always at the beach. I assumed that you are a good swimmer. When we go to the City Beach Surf Club dances the guys are always asking you to join the life-savers.'

Ron shook head, 'No, I'm not a strong swimmer at all.'

His words would prove prophetic in the future and turn my world upside down. We did not return to the beach the next morning. We left early to begin life together at Heytesbury Road in Subiaco.

Old house Newcastle Street 1939. (City of Perth History Centre Collection).

On my toy car, Kalgoorlie 1941.

My first Communion 1945.

The Marelle function centre in Hay Street where I met Ron in 1954 (State Library of Western Australia. Permission 099569PD).

My mother Amy 1955.

Amy, Faye and Con. Masonic Debutante Ball 1956.

Wedding day Ron and Faye 1957.

Ron, Faye and Lynette, Ledge Point 1959.

Mrs Ed. She gave us our tomorrow.

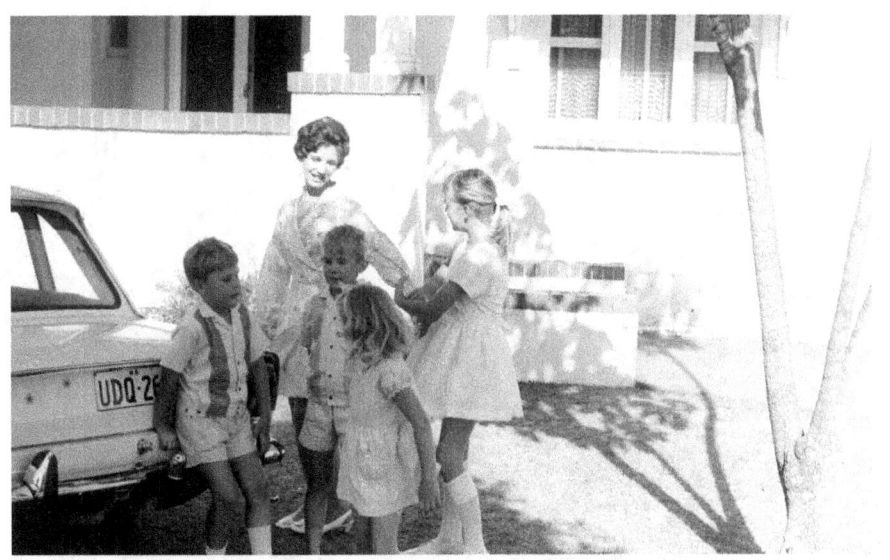

With the children at the front of the Essex Street house.

Colleen, Lynette, Faye (Lynette's wedding day).

Lynette with her husband Ron.

Glen with his sister Colleen.

John with his wife Leah.

Chapter 12

Heytesbury Road 1957

The village-like and friendly atmosphere of Subiaco in the late 1950s enfolded me as if in a warm embrace.

On the short bus ride into the city each Friday, I sat, enjoying the ride as the diesel operated bus wheezed along up past King's Park, around the corner and down St George's Terrace, eventually stopping outside Foy and Gibson's, one of the city's large department stores. Perth enjoyed several individual, department stores: Foy and Gibsons, Bon Marché, Boans and Aherns, Bairds, Moores, Economics and Sandovers. As well, exclusive shops abounded and I loved looking at the displays of extravagant hats in the window of Belle Gladstone's millinery shop on the corner of Plaza Arcade and in the Poppy Hat Shoppe further along Hay Street. People in town for lunch or shopping invariably met at Economics Corner opposite Wesley Church. On Saturday evenings, men and women sometimes stood forlornly on that corner, often glancing worriedly at their watches, or at the Town Hall clock up the street, waiting for the date that, for some reason or another, never turned up.

Our wedding celebrations were still fresh in our minds and we had barely become accustomed to living together when I suddenly started feeling odd and queasy at the most unexpected moments. It did not take me long to guess the reason. Dr Myles Clarke, Subiaco's local doctor, confirmed my thoughts, congratulated me and gave me an approximate date for my baby's arrival. I left the surgery and, instead of my usual wander up to the town part of Subiaco, I headed straight home, walking as quickly as possible to tell Ron the unexpected news. He smiled and looked mildly surprised.

'A little mother. Well, how about that?' It was apparent that, although a little taken aback, he was happy. Within a week, unbeknownst to me, Ron went shopping late one afternoon, and when he arrived back at dinnertime, there was a new cot perched resplendently on the back of Jack's utility.

Not at all sure of her reaction, I wrote, with some diffidence, to Amy to tell her about my forthcoming baby. She wrote back to congratulate us and seemed to be thrilled at the prospect of becoming a grandmother. Being young and attractive, Amy would, I thought, probably relish people saying in amazement, 'You, a grandmother? No!'

One day I went into the shop and Ron mentioned that I had just missed seeing one of their new customers, a woman not long arrived from England who had seen me in passing and said that she would like to meet me some time. I met her a couple of days later when a woman stopped me in the street and, letting go of her baby's pram handle, thrust her hand out to shake mine. I was surprised and at a slight disadvantage because women shaking hands was a European custom that had not yet caught on in Perth. In a well-modulated voice, she greeted me, 'Hello, we meet at last. My name is Elizabeth, Elizabeth Brett. Could you come to my house for morning tea on Wednesday, at ten thirty?'

Elizabeth did not seem the type of person who would appreciate me dithering, so quite crisply I answered, 'Yes, thank you. I would like to do that.'

Wednesday morning arrived and I walked the five doors along Heytesbury Road to the Brett house. That morning was the beginning of an enduring friendship with Elizabeth and her husband, John. I usually wandered along to Elizabeth's sometime during the day to sit on her back lawn with a cup of coffee, chatting as she pegged dozens of snow-white, baby napkins and clothing items on to the clothesline. Effortlessly, our friendship slowly developed into something special and irreplaceable.

Apart from being plagued with morning sickness that went on all day, I kept well and felt contented. Often, though, as I stood and ironed the many stiffly starched white shirts and short white coats that Ron wore for work in the butcher shop, I sometimes reflected that I should be good at ironing. After all, I'd had plenty of practice.

Amy returned and we shared an enjoyable time for the next few months. The thought of the approaching baby imbued us both with mellow and peaceful feelings.

After spending a few weeks with Ron and me, Amy found a little cottage to rent in Gloster Street, one street away from us, running parallel with Heytesbury Road. We saw each other almost daily and walked for miles together laughing and talking as we went. We never talked about the past.

As the months went by, I experienced many feelings of uncertainty. What was I going to do? I knew nothing about looking after babies. I may have held one for a few fleeting moments occasionally, but I certainly had no recollection of ever feeding a baby, or changing a nappy. I fretted and worried, but not for a single moment ever thought of Amy as a source of guidance.

One afternoon in the butcher shop as I deliberated the choices for dinner, Ron looked over at me, 'A girl was in here a minute ago. You just missed seeing her. I think she knows you.'

Immediately, I thought that the person who remembered me was someone from The Home of the Good Shepherd. I did not say anything. I could not think of what to say. I wanted to escape and hastily picked up the first thing I saw – some lamb chops and hurried back to the safety of the house. My throat constricted to the point of pain and I feared that once again my life was going to change and spiral out of my control.

Later in the afternoon, Madge called out through the back door to say. 'Ron tells me that Mrs Nicholls' daughter, Lynne, knows you.'

Striving to appear casual, I asked, 'Who is Mrs Nicholls?'

'Oh she's been a good customer here for years. Her husband is a watchmaker. He is such a nice man, very quiet. They live up the road on the corner of Redfern Street. Their daughter is expecting a baby, her first, I think.'

Ron chimed in, 'I think Lynne said that she went to Girdlestone at the same time as you did.'

I could have spared myself a great deal of anxiety if I had asked in the first place!

Unable to settle, though, and as Redfern Street was only on the next corner, I decided to go and see the girl. I quickly arrived at the front of a substantial, gracious, old-style Subiaco house and compared the number on the letterbox with the one Ron had given me. It was the right house and before I had time to change my mind I pushed the gate open and walked along a narrow red brick path, so edged with cottage garden flowers cascading over the edges and into the garden that the path was battling to retain its identity.

The doorbell barely tinkled when I rang it and I thought that I might be standing there for a long time, as the little bell could not possibly sound throughout the big house. Before I became too lost in my random musings, the door opened. The girl who smiled at me and invited me in was about as pregnant as I was. I recognised her, but had not previously known her, except to say hello in passing. Lynne led the way through a large entry hall and walked towards the back of the house and into the kitchen. We both felt a bit strange, as neither of us was socially adept. We had not had a lot of experience at breaking the ice in new situations. However, Lynne's manner, although shy, was warm and welcoming and soon the conversation flowed easily between us. I found that we had both married around the same time and that her husband was named Ron too. We were close in age and each about to have our first baby. How surprised Lynne would have been to know that earlier that day she had unwittingly caused me so much distress.

Thereafter we usually met once a week at each other's home for morning tea, followed by lunch and, if we spaced it right, we sometimes fitted in afternoon tea as well. We were just growing up and enjoying the novelty of doing whatever we cared to for a brief time before motherhood and responsibility caught up with us.

One day, when Amy had begun to visit Dr Clarke for any of her health issues that cropped up and we both had appointments to see him on the same day, we walked to the surgery together. I went in to see him first and then chatted to the doctor's nurse, Mrs Stockley, while I waited for Amy. Together we left the large, former-stately home, which now served as the doctor's surgery and residence, and turned right to go to the Subiaco shopping area.

Amy suddenly spoke, 'I have a lump in my other breast, and he, your doctor, says that I should have it removed.'

I took her hand in mine to express my support, careful not to say anything to upset her.

We walked in silence, until Amy said, 'Come on. Let's go and have morning tea. I'll worry about this later.'

Amy did go in to St John of God Hospital, but only consented to the removal of the lump, not the complete breast. After the surgery Amy saw an alternative health therapist, who told her that she had no cancer in her body and she decided not to have any follow up treatment with the hospital. All seemed well and the matter was relegated to the back of our minds.

Soon after lunch on the warm Friday, September afternoon, I clasped Ron's arm as I made my way awkwardly up the imposing marble steps that led to the admissions desk at St John of God Maternity Hospital. I planned to have my child and any future children at St John's. As a patient of another faith, I would be treated well. However, as a lapsed Catholic, particularly one who dared to marry in another church, I would not be considered married at all and my child would be condemned by that archaic word, *illegitimate*. It was simpler to claim Church of England as my faith. I wanted the best treatment without the imperious strictures of Catholicism. I had no way of knowing that fate had already decreed that at a future time, those same nuns were destined to sustain me with friendship and compassionate support.

The admission formalities were completed and Ron was summarily dismissed. I sat alone on the edge of a bed wondering if I was meant to get into it. I disliked sitting alone in any convent building, even a hospital. I heard slow footsteps outside the door and hoped that someone was coming who would tell me what to do. A well-built nun pushed a wheelchair through the doorway and, without speaking a word, bundled me into it. With little effort, we took off at a fast, dizzying pace along never-ending corridors. We careened around a corner and entered a brightly lit, stark, white room. I felt myself being hoisted out of the chair and on to a firm table. Whilst not exactly uncomfortable, I found the unyielding table and the blinding whiteness of my surroundings, chilly and unnerving. No baby seemed about to put in an appearance, so back to my room I returned.

Early the next morning one of the sisters came to take me back to the labour room. As she wheeled me along the corridor, more slowly than the other one had done the previous day, the nun leaned forward and whispered, 'Now listen to me dear. Some of the foreign women get frantic and they scream a lot. It is just their hysterical way of coping, so if you hear them, don't you worry or you will start screaming too.' She patted me in a motherly way and I determined that I would be very quiet. It took quite a bit of stamina to keep from weeping and wailing at anyone within hearing distance, but I remained stoically silent.

After all, no new baby should hear its mother's undignified screaming at first meeting.

September 26, 1958. Dr Clarke's mellifluous voice was telling me that I had a beautiful daughter. I looked at my little girl and my heart ached painfully with a love such as I had never known. My entire life had been waiting for that moment. *Welcome Lynette Sharon. I will cherish you forever.*

During the afternoon, while still in a distant state, I became aware of tumultuous cheering and I dreamily thought that I must be royalty. *Oh, listen to the cheering, the people know that my baby has been born and they are cheering for her. How wonderful.*

I lay there in a misty, emotional state and another tremendous roar rent the air as I nodded off to sleep. Sometime later I awoke to see Ron sitting looking at me. He hugged me tightly, 'It took me ages to park the car. The grand final of the football is on today, just over the road at Subiaco Oval. You can hear the crowd roaring for miles.'

Two years passed, seemingly quite swiftly, and the year was 1959. To celebrate my twenty first birthday, Amy, Ron, and I went to a concert at His Majesty's Theatre to hear to a popular visiting American pianist, Winifred Atwell. The show was loud, vibrant and a great night out. I paused and wondered how celebratory my birthday might have been had I not had Ron and my baby. We were in the same theatre that I went to with my mother not so many years before. We went there together, to see *Mother Wore Tights,* the day she took me to The Home of the Good Shepherd. Did Amy remember?

I met neighbours, and enjoyed becoming part of the community. Ron's Aunty, Anne Bohling, was a gracious lady who had been widowed at a young age and she and her attractive young daughter, Judith Anne, lived diagonally across the road from the butcher shop. Anne was a talented musician and she played and taught numerous musical instruments including the violin, mandolin, and the piano, with skill and precision. Regrettably, I never took the opportunity for my children to learn from her. I often crossed the road to her welcoming house though, with my small daughter walking importantly beside me, clutching a bone wrapped in white butcher's paper to give to their little dog. Lynette liked the village type social life, morning tea here or there, or being in the shop chatting to the customers.

I became adept at ignoring the ugly phantom of the past if it clawed and fought to intrude. We visited friends for dinner, to play cards and to play tennis. We were a happy group, and fortunate enough to know it.

New Year's Day of 1961 arrived with a burst of heat so intense that the city and suburbs were already sweltering before most people were up and out of bed. The first day of the year proved to be the harbinger of the summer months ahead. That year the small country town of Dwellingup, one hundred and forty kilometres south of Perth, was destroyed by out-of-control bush fires. High temperatures and searing winds roared furiously and decimated the district. Maximum havoc raged for forty one consecutive days before the fire gave up and was finally conquered, leaving a legacy that made sure few people in Western Australia would ever forget that summer.

My mother was to join us for lunch and I wandered listlessly around the already warm kitchen trying to decide what to prepare. Amy came through the door, holding Lynette's hand. Looking me over critically, she said, 'You look awful. What's the matter?'

Feeling a smile spread across my face, I told her that we were expecting another baby. I was twenty three years old and life was splendid.

However, I found little to smile about in the coming months though. The heat dragged on, and many nights I lay on a rug in the hallway with the front door open, trying to get cool. We had no lawn around the house, as the surrounding area was mainly concrete, so the house remained stifling, not cooling down, even in the evening.

Amy found a job that she enjoyed with a photographic studio. Initially her job was to set up appointments with families who had children. The photographer then followed and went to their homes to take the photos. Amy also learned to take the photos and was soon working for herself after the proprietor of the studio she worked for was sent to prison for eighteen months over a road fatality. Many years later, occasionally, and often in the most unlikely places, I would see old photos of small children or families and recognise the brightly coloured blue and pink hues of photos taken in that era – and if I looked closely, I sometimes saw Amy's studio name, *Faylyn*, in the bottom right hand corner.

One Sunday morning I awoke feeling sick and in a great deal of pain. Ron realised that all was not well with me and phoned Amy to see if she could come to our house. Amy was unable to come, because she had a date to go on a picnic with a fellow that she had met the night before at a dance. Unfortunately, there was no way of contacting him to let him know that she would not be there. If Ron thought her priorities were a bit skewed, he held his counsel. I later thought that it was a pity that Amy did keep her appointment with that man. He was an unpleasant, obsequious individual and, unfortunately, there was no joy at all in their three year relationship.

The pain became more severe and I feared for my baby. Ron phoned Dr Clarke and about ten minutes later, he strode purposefully through the bedroom door. He was dressed so casually in beige shorts and long socks, with a tan-coloured, cotton-knit shirt, that at first I did not recognise him. He looked carefree and years younger. He had phoned St John's and told them that I would probably be arriving soon. The cause of all my discomfort was Pyelitis, an extremely painful, inflammatory condition of the kidneys.

One memorable night in the hospital, I was not too sure of my destiny when I awoke to see a nun sitting at the foot of my bed praying earnestly and audibly. Oh Lord, I thought, she must be praying for the baby and me. As I was drifting off to sleep that night, she was back again. In a drowsy state, I asked, 'Sister? Am I really ill? Are you praying for my recovery?'

'Well dear,' she replied. 'Of course you are included in my prayers. However, I must say my daily devotions and they take a long time and, as I have to keep an eye on you, I might as well get my prayers out of the way at the same time.'

I was glad she did not say anything about killing two birds with one stone!

For the next few months, I was never to be completely free of the underlying nauseous feeling associated with a kidney ailment. In the close-knit community, friends and customers knew that our baby was due around August 19. As the days passed into late August, I was still waddling, blimp-like, around the place. People stopped me in the street to enquire. One woman said, 'Oh you still here? Poor Ron must be getting anxious.' *Did she really say, poor Ron?* On another occasion as I stood a short distance from the shop, a woman spoke enthusiastically about the joys, and the perils of childbirth. The familiar feeling from my childhood swept over me. I had been standing motionless for too long, and I knew that I was going to fall. The woman prattled on while I did an ungainly dive over a low fence into a Plumbago hedge. I heard her agitated voice from somewhere far distant. 'Oh good Lord, let me help you. You should be more careful, you might have hurt the baby. Here comes Ron. Thank goodness you're here Ron, we were talking and Faye just tumbled right over into the hedge.' Ron helped me up and urged the woman away. From that time on, my neighbour waved to me from across the road. It was wearying being so huge and *expectant*. I went to see Dr Clarke. Smiling, he commented that I was looking huge and needed to get a move on, because he was booked to take the family away on holiday and they would not be forgiving if he changed their plans.

I did not want a different doctor, so I walked the longest way home and sent positive hurry up thoughts to my reluctant child. At six o'clock, I stood in the kitchen feeling very uncomfortable and odd. Ron looked at me, 'What are you doing?'

I replied, 'I am going to have the baby.'

Ron bundled me into the car and hurled my bag of necessities on to the back seat. He drove at top speed through Subiaco on a journey that only took five minutes anyway.

September 1, 1961. My perfect son, Glen Ronald, lay in my arms, his eyes closed as if in bliss. I hugged him tightly and adored him. I wondered about how I could love another child as much as I loved Lynette. She was all the pure and beautiful things in my world. How could I share that love? The realisation came to me. Glen had his own unassailable share. It could not be taken away, transferred, or shared. It arrived with, and belonged wholly, to him.

Ron did not see his son until the next morning. He was not permitted anywhere near the birthing area. They were not too keen on fathers even remaining at the hospital for any length of time. My room, with its aroma of flowers and floor polish, reminded me of the visitor's rooms at The Home of the Good Shepherd, but this beautiful old building was a pleasant place. Early in the morning, beaming inanely, Ron tiptoed into my room and gently hugged me to his chest.

He told me that from inside the house on the previous night he had heard a tremendous bashing and clanging on the metal gate that led to the butcher shop and to the back door of our house. Ron went to investigate and there stood Dr Clarke with his arm raised ready to bang the gate again, but when he saw Ron, he said. 'Congratulations. You have a big, healthy son. Faye tells me you have decided to call him Glen Ronald. I wanted you to know that all is well before you went to bed.'

That doctor was a splendid man.

Glen quickly distinguished himself as a force to be reckoned with. Mostly, he was calm and happy, but there were signs that one day, in the not-too-distant future, he might possibly be rather determined about his wishes.

Ron was thinking about buying a butcher shop that was situated within a supermarket in the suburb of Midland. He decided with the owners that he would spend a couple of mornings a week there to check the potential and viability of the venture. Early one morning Ron and I shared our breakfast and the morning paper in easy silence, when with a quick glance at the clock; Ron suddenly jumped up, and was gone, waving goodbye to me as he sped away.

From the doorway, I waved until the car disappeared from sight. Beattie, the shop cat, a motley old black and white mother of countless kittens, was not a great beauty, but Beattie did not know that and cavorted, kitten-like, around my feet as I tried to close the door. Ron preferred the cat not to come into the house because of the baby so I plonked her by the shop door and told her that Jack would feed her later.

Lynette slept soundly and Glen was drowsing in his cot. It was only five o'clock and the morning was cold. I decided to go back to bed until the children woke up. I looked at my sleeping children and felt uneasy. A moment later the feeling had gone. I pulled up the covers and went to sleep.

Unable to move in any direction. I stood and watched in helpless horror as Ron's car glided towards the large bus. I heard the harsh screeching grind of metal smashing metal and I saw glass shattering to the ground in an elongated, silvery shower. The two vehicles collided with a thunderous crash. I called out and tried to run, but no sound or movement came from me. Ron looked at me imploringly, as he staggered from the car holding his injured, bleeding arm. My leaden limbs continued to hold me fast. Angela, the nurse at The Home of the Good Shepherd glared at me malevolently as she sidled past and disappeared behind the bus.

I awoke with a parched throat and a hammering heart and I knew that the images had been a bad dream, but that did not stop me from feeling sick with the memory. I got out of bed quickly, not wishing to go to sleep again in case the dream continued.

Around mid-morning, Elizabeth called through my open front door to say that she was going to the baby clinic and would call in and see me on her way back. The nightmare was on my mind and I found myself waiting for Elizabeth to return so I could tell her about it.

In her inimitable, practical way, she told me, 'Well, that was not very nice for you, but it was only a dream, so don't fuss yourself too much.'

I *did* feel fussed about it, though.

I rang Ron at the Midland shop, hoping that once I spoke to him I would relax. I dialled the number, waiting to hear Ron's familiar, bantering greeting. Instead, the apprentice's voice travelled cheerily along the line. I asked for Ron and the boy replied, 'He is not here, Faye, he should not be away long. He's just gone over the road to see the doctor.'

I asked, 'What's the matter? Is he sick? Did he cut himself?'

'No, he is not sick. He was cleaned up by a bus on the "mad mile" stretch this morning and he's got a crook arm.' (The 'mad mile' was a straight stretch of road approaching Guildford, where motorists were notorious for exceeding the speed limit.)

Ron had been involved in three accidents involving a bus since I had known him. There had been other accidents too, some minor, some more serious. Our friends teased Ron sometimes, telling him he was a walking accident. The image of Ron in the dream with a severed arm played on my mind, because it was clear that Ron had had the accident on the way to Midland while I slept for about twenty minutes after he left.

The conclusion was inescapable. I dreamt about the accident as it was happening.

I walked into Elizabeth's kitchen, 'You know that dream I told you about?' She nodded, 'Yes it really upset you.' I told her what had happened to Ron on the way to Midland, fully expecting her to say, 'Are you telling me that you dreamed something, and then it actually happened? Don't be such a goose.' Instead, she replied, 'Oh Faye that is strange. No wonder you're so upset.'

Ron paid little heed to my story of the dream. He just wished that the accident that caused damage to him and, more sadly in his view to his FJ Holden, had not happened.

I felt it a good thing that I told of the dream *before* I knew what had happened to Ron that morning, because the extreme uneasiness that I felt at that time validated fears that beset me in the future. Unfortunately, though, it gave me no wisdom or power to alter anything.

My second child, Glen, was approaching twelve months when I realised that we were going to increase our family again. Hesitantly, almost confessing, and wondering how he would feel about the added responsibility, I told Ron when he came in at lunchtime.

'That's great,' he said, flinging his arm around me. 'We will create a dynasty.' Without knowledge of the institution that I had been in, he did know something of Stella and of her cruel treatment towards me. He intuitively knew that he and my children gave me a place and a sense of belonging. As far as he was concerned, another baby was good news.

My father-in-law grinned happily. My mother-in-law pronounced in a worried tone, 'It is a lot of work for a young girl, with all those babies and nappies.'

My mother said, 'You are not very strong you know. You should not keep having children.'

She was telling *me* that I was not strong.

Chapter 13

A Bad House

To continue living in the house attached to the shop was no longer practical. It had been a wonderful starting point, but with the new baby's imminent arrival, it was time to move to something bigger, hopefully with lawn and a tree or two.

Ron did buy the butchering section in the Midland supermarket. Then we bought a house in Bayswater, half way between Subiaco and Midland. It was an old, timber, family type place. Not luxurious, but it did have the wonderful benefit of being large. The garden had been kept in a rambling, meandering way that I found appealing. For the first time I had a garden with roses, beautiful, old, well-nourished bushes that bloomed prolifically, and some large trees to sit beneath. However, to my surprise and intense disappointment, I discovered that Bayswater was a barren and lonely place compared to Subiaco. I found no pleasure at our new address. Subiaco was the first home with friends and neighbours that I had ever known. In Bayswater, there was no company, no Elizabeth, no Lynne Gregor, nor Aunty Anne just over the road. I tried to persuade myself that more room, lawn, trees, and roses were enough.

The Laundry Girl

Within weeks of our move, my feelings of uneasiness increased, and the house made me uncomfortable and a little afraid. At first, I put the strange feelings down to missing Subiaco, but I gradually, and unwillingly, became aware that the atmosphere was simply wrong. I was familiar with individuals who could project an aura of negativity or menace, but I thought that my imagination must have slipped into overdrive when I experienced such vibrations from a *house*. I never understood what was happening, except to say, *that house did not like me.*

In our bedroom, I experienced an air of disquiet and an indefinable, sense of another's presence whenever I walked in there. Not necessarily a person, but a tangible force. Late one night, so convinced was I that a presence had been in the room that I even looked under the bed, expecting to see the cat hiding there. Another night I was so convinced someone had been in our bedroom that I got out of bed and went into the children's rooms to see who was awake. They were both sound asleep. I returned to bed and moved closer to Ron's warmth for comfort. The mantle clock chimed four times with slow deliberation.

My apprehension increased. However, with my strange, Catholic, horribly-superstitious upbringing and the fact that I was conditioned to be afraid, I knew that it *was* possible that I was over-imaginative. Eventually though, I told Ron about these feelings. Surprisingly, he did not laugh or disbelieve me, but he saw no cause for concern.

Lynette started her school days with Yvonne – her friend who lived a few doors down from us. Together each morning they bounced along chattering busily, with their ponytails bobbing in unison with their footsteps.

On March 26, 1963, John Edward was born. He was the most beautiful and agreeable baby and his personality never changed. I gazed entranced into his sweet, baby-boy face, and into his bright eyes, which seemed to me to be unusually far seeing and wise for a newborn.

Despite our joy with our new son, my mother was most unhappy. She was spending a lot of time at our place, which Ron did not particularly care for because her influence was so negative. Although Amy loved the kids and they enjoyed her zany carry-on when she was in a good mood, all too frequently her moods were not good and she showed no patience at all.

Lynette loved *Noni* and her sense of humour and, because Lynette was amenable and quiet, Amy had more patience with her than with the boys. Amy and Glen drove each other to distraction. One afternoon Amy dealt with Glen in a way that to him might have been seen as unreasonable. She shouted at him. He then waited until she looked at him through the rear vision mirror and, steadily meeting her gaze, he pulled a large chunk of hair from his head. 'Don't you dare do that,' Amy screeched at him.

Calmly, and defiantly, he made eye contact again and, before I could stop him, he pulled out another large chunk of his hair. It must have hurt but it was clearly his misguided, childish way of saying, 'Don't you yell at me.' During those altercations Lynette looked bothered and tense and I suspected she was praying under her breath for her brother to be good. John gazed steadily into the distance as if he had never met Amy or Glen.

Somewhat uneasily, the days moved along. I tried, but I still did not feel comfortable in that house. I did not have time to brood though. My baby kept me busy, as did his brother. Lynette was already slipping seamlessly into the role of mother's helper and all-round-good girl. Glen's escapades kept us all on our toes. He regularly climbed on to the shed roof and, just as regularly, fell off, usually incurring some painful injury. He made himself violently ill on two occasions, by eating the berries that fell in vast quantities from the lilac tree. We could not keep up with the amount of berries that fell each day and made hasty arrangements to have the tree felled. On one occasion, Glen drank kerosene from a bottle that I had left sitting towards the back of the copper in the laundry. I was alerted to this when I heard him coughing in the back garden. It was a worrying time, and Ron and I took turns to sit with him as he spent the next three days in hospital. He recovered well, but he was quiet for a long time, preferring to be with Ron instead of me. I think he thought that I had failed to care for him properly leaving kerosene for him to find and drink, and decided that his dad was a better person to protect him. All of these things happened in an instant. Playing happily nearby one minute, the next, I would hear shrieks that meant he 'had done something again.'

It was a bleak time for Amy. Illness, anger and uncertainty were attempting to insinuate their destructive forces between Amy and the rest of her world. The lump in her breast, that she had previously ignored and no doubt out of fear had decided not to have treated, had returned and she went into St John's for an operation for the removal of her remaining breast. After the operation, Amy did follow up with radiology treatment and stayed with us during her recuperation, but the situation became increasingly hopeless. My mother did not want me to socialise or have anything to do with anyone outside the house. The unsettling, unseen presence remained. In those days most people didn't even say the word 'cancer' out loud. Feeling depressed was referred to as having a *touch of blues.* If the depression was really bad, you were hospitalised and sedated, not knowing, if, or when, you might be released. Discussion was not encouraged, and feelings and fears were mostly kept under wraps. What I did know though, was that I couldn't allow the course of my life to change again. I was no longer a child and there were too many other issues – and another important life – to consider at that time.

Ron laughingly said that we must have been aiming to create a dynasty when I told him that I was pregnant *again*. We were both happy, but I wondered how our respective families would react. My mother-in-law, once again, could see endless, sleepless nights and more nappies ahead for poor, young me. My father-in-law, grinning from ear to ear, decided it was time for a beer.

Amy's reaction was, 'Oh God', although later on she did say that she hoped that the baby would be a girl. During that pregnancy the kidney problem that I experienced when I was expecting Glen reoccurred and I felt terrible. Neither my body nor my spirit felt at ease. The atmosphere in our home became toxic.

Fortunately, my mother did behave quite reasonably when Ron was around alleviating some of the concern about what I would do if Ron asked her to leave. My mother represented a strong, powerful, controlling force in my life. She was the person who had abandoned me and many times had left me feeling let down by her behaviour towards me. Therefore, it was difficult for me to see her as weak or vulnerable, or needing support from anyone. With hindsight, I think that I failed my mother at that time. I was unable to console her. Of course, I looked after her and did everything that I could to make her comfortable. I was as gentle as possible when I patted lanoline onto the inflamed, tender skin and I helped her as she gingerly lifted her left arm above her head to keep her muscles supple, but I don't believe that I fully comprehended her suffering, or her fear. The night was stiflingly hot and I tossed and turned. The bedcovers wrapped around me irritatingly as Ron slumbered on by my side. Eventually I fell asleep, and I dreamt:

The forthcoming baby came into my dreams and I saw myself in unfamiliar surroundings. I was in a luxurious room and I knew, even though I had never been there before, that I was in the recently completed new maternity wing at St John of God Hospital. I heard hushed voices outside the slightly open door to my room. I heard one nun asking another why the door to my room was partially closed, because normally the doors were left open. The other nun replied, 'Oh that girl needs quietness and privacy she has a new baby but she doesn't have a husband.' 'Doesn't have a husband?' the first nun enquired in soft tones. "Where is he? What happened to him?' Another voice chimed in, 'Oh he's just gone.' I called loudly so they would hear me through the half-closed door, 'What are you talking about? I have a husband. He hasn't gone.'

A nun's head poked around the door. 'Don't you worry, dear. It will be all right.' And their footsteps echoed hollowly as they walked down the passage.

If I could only walk along Heytesbury Road and talk to Elizabeth and have her laugh at my fears and call me a silly goose. I could no longer do that.

Bury it deep, Faye, and never think about it. Ignore it and it will go away and just remain a nasty dream.

Chapter 14

Ledge Point 1964

Ron was an enthusiastic angler. He was enthusiastic about everything he did and was never satisfied with half measures. A fellow business owner from Midland had acquired a new boat and he invited Ron and a few of his other mates to try it out. They decided to go and stay at Ron's father's shanty at Ledge Point, which was, at the time, a largely undiscovered fishing area with a few shacks and beach houses dotted along the coastline north of Perth. The trip had originally been planned for the previous weekend, however, it had been postponed because I had been admitted to hospital for a couple of days with a reoccurrence of the kidney complaint. In spite of their disappointment, the men were surprisingly gracious about their cancelled getaway. Their trip subsequently took place on the Foundation Day long weekend, which in 1964, fell on Saturday, June 1st. I have often wondered if the eventual outcome might have differed had they kept to their original plan.

Preparing food for the fishing trip, I stood in the kitchen furiously beating eggs with my old-fashioned, hand beater. They finally doubled in volume and I added them to a spicy mixture to make Ron's favourite ginger cake.

The back door banged as Ron came in. He picked up John, deposited him in the high chair, and handed him a plastic Mickey Mouse cup filled with water, guiding his small hand towards his mouth. Ron and Glen had been fossicking around in the garden shed. They were now hot and hungry and looking for lunch. Ron sat with the boys and me at the table as we ate thick, fresh-bread sandwiches. Yvonne stayed for lunch and the little girls took theirs to the cubby house. I cherished this great time in our lives and in society generally. A time for work, hard work mostly, but also a time for play.

Because Glen was such a livewire, Ron decided to take him on the fishing trip, leaving me to recuperate with the 'quiet ones,' I phoned Dr Clarke to ask if it was okay for Glen to go away to the beach, because he was recovering from an ear infection. Dr Clarke agreed that it would be fine as long as he continued taking his antibiotic tablets. Madge and Jack were also going to Ledge Point for the weekend and, because his Nana and Grandpop were also going to be there, I felt no qualms about Glen going.

The air was storm-like and oppressive, the atmosphere draining and heavy and the children were out of sorts and cranky. Added to that, Amy was furious. She had been staying with the children and me during the time that I was unwell and while Ron was at work. When Amy heard that Ron was going fishing, in a fit of pique, she threw her clothes into a bag and declared that if Ron was going fishing, she did not see why she should remain, and off she went to Gerry's place. Gerry was her latest companion.

Saturday arrived and amid a flurry of activity, Ron rushed around getting ready to go on the trip. Warm clothes were needed, plus food, rod and reels, bait and then a bit more food. What a production. Glen was all set to go too, sitting expectantly in the car waiting for his dad to jump in. Ron lifted John from the high chair and hugged him tightly, 'Soon little man, you will be big enough to come with us. You won't always have to stay behind with the girls.'

Ledge Point 1964

They drove off waving like a pair of exuberant runaways and I waved back, smiling at their antics, but inexplicably, I felt extremely low.

I went into the house and mooched around aimlessly for a while, but as I passed the laundry door my heart missed a beat. Glen's tablets and his bright blue beanie were sitting on top of the washing machine. As they had left not long before, my first thought was to call a taxi and follow them, but then I realised that I would probably be following them all the way to Ledge Point. I then had the idea to call the main taxi company in town and ask that if any driver in the Wanneroo district, or beyond, saw a black FJ Holden, license number 92583 – would they stop the driver and send him back home. And, unbelievably, they did! Half-an-hour later, I stood on the driveway, waving the tablets and beanie as Ron's car screeched to a halt and he came running towards me, laughing. He seized the tablets, jammed the beanie on Glen's head and was ready to take off again. I felt foolish because suddenly I was crying bitterly for no apparent reason. Ron turned to go. 'Do you want me to stay?' he asked, as he came back and put his arms around me.

'No, of course not. I'm fine.' Then I said my last words to him. 'You go. Don't worry about us. We are fine. Have a good time and bring back some fish, or better still, some crayfish.' I remind myself so often that I did say, 'Have a good time and don't worry.'

The next morning I took Lynette and John out for the day.

It was late afternoon before we arrived back at the Bayswater station. The conductor leapt from his small cabin on to the platform, and lifted the pram up and over the large hooks from the back of the bus for me. Thanking him fervently, I staggered up the hill with Lynette helping me push the pram. It remains the same today. Lynette was always there to help me push whatever loads besieged me, only these days she offered me a gin and tonic as encouragement. Weariness and the strange feeling that I had felt earlier in day gave way to me being just plain tired. My children and I had our dinner and I then bathed them ready for bed. They slept soundly, not knowing that life as they knew it was over.

We owned a black, Labrador puppy, named Kelly. That night though – and it was the one and only time that it happened – she howled and whimpered for several hours. Many times, I got up to her, even giving her some warm milk and some of the children's milk arrowroot biscuits in an attempt to settle her. The air changed from heavy and oppressive and became chilly. I shivered as I fell back into bed and I welcomed the warmth of Kit, our big ginger cat, as he curled around my feet. The dog stopped barking around four o'clock. My unborn baby was safe and unaware. I slept sporadically and the long night passed from dark to light. The unsettled mood of the previous day returned with the early morning shadows.

The air chilled the house and I turned the heater on to warm the kitchen. I lifted John from his cot and deposited him alongside Lynette in her bed. He was such a placid, undemanding little person, content to lie beside Lynette, warm and cosy, while I prepared breakfast. The children ate most of their breakfast and toyed with the remainder, while I lingered over the Sunday paper with my coffee and toast. I did the usual morning things – washing the dishes and making the beds. Lynette stood on one side of her bed and together we pulled the covers up into some semblance of order. We then went to the outside laundry to put the washing into the machine and to feed the pets. The rest of the morning dragged on endlessly. The hands on the kitchen wall clock barely moved. *Hurry up*, I urged. *Move on. Get the day over.* What was I waiting for? Usually there were not enough minutes in the day to do all that was necessary. I put some toys out for John and persuaded Lynette to sit with him while she coloured in her book. However, she quickly tired of doing nothing interesting, and perhaps sensing my uneasiness she wanted to do something different and asked if she could go to play at Yvonne's house. Before she had a chance to leave though, there was a knock at the back door. I hoisted John up into my arms, feeling the familiar surge of melting love that I always felt when my baby wrapped his arms tightly around my neck.

I opened the door to see two people in police uniform looking in at me. One was a typical, old-style copper, big and genial, but he looked worried. The other was a woman, young and attractive. She looked capable and efficient, but also worried. They were both clearly uncomfortable and the silence lengthened awkwardly as we stood there in the doorway. My first thought was that they were there to warn people about a prowler in the district who still had not been caught. I glanced at the clock, and registered that it was just ten o'clock.

'Mrs Bohling, may we come in?' the male officer asked. I must have looked at him enquiringly, because he then said, 'I believe that some of your family are at Ledge Point. We need to come in to talk to you. There has been a tragedy up there.'

I felt the inescapable rush of dread that any person must feel when a policeman stands at their front door to tell them that they have bad news. Trapped, with no escape, I wanted to close the door. My only hope was to close the door and try to disassociate myself from the couple standing in front of me. Iciness around my heart let me know that there was no escape for me. I was forced to remain in their presence and hear what they had to say. The young police officer began to look flushed and seemed on the verge of tears. Detached and distant, as if all of this was nothing to do with me, I thought what an emotionally devastating duty it must have been for the police. They got up in the morning to go about their daily tasks, most of which were demanding, but none as demanding or harrowing as walking up to an unsuspecting person's front door to deliver a blow that would change an individual or an entire family forever. I was acutely aware that they were there to deliver such a blow.

The weak morning sun streamed in and the dog and cat both rushed out as I held the door open for the still waiting couple to come in. The young woman asked if she could take Lynette to another room to play with some of her toys. The world spun and I started to count. The old refrain was familiar and comforting. *Four, eight, twelve, sixteen ....* The hard, cold laminex chair chilled the back of my legs as I seated myself at our kitchen table. Counting silently and continuously, I felt remote and detached. I seemed to be looking at a jerky, amateur movie from high above, with me as the central figure. There I was, sitting with a policeman who was speaking earnestly. In the background of the screen, I was able to distinguish the playpen with John sitting engrossed with a tiny, red plastic car. I was able to see out of sight behind the screen where Lynette was sitting in her room, with the young police constable watching her sympathetically. The movie flickered from scene to scene and I heard the word, 'drowned'. God, this is awful, my father-in-law is dead. No! I'm wrong. It is not Jack. It is one of the other men. In quick succession, my mind tore through the names of everyone at Ledge Point. The policeman looked so concerned. I wanted to tell him not to worry. He leant towards me', and took both my hands in his. 'I need to know who to call to come and be with you. Who can I get in touch with?'

Who was missing? And why were those people so concerned for me? I had gone through all the possibilities, there was no one left. He could not mean that Ron was missing in the water, possibly drowned. Slowly I began to list in my head the names again of all the people who had gone to Ledge Point. *Then I knew.* I had not wanted to hear or understand. The movie flickered and dimmed, the world imploded, and I felt myself slide away into a quiet place. Then all too soon, the movie started up again and jerked me out of the quietness. They had not found him yet. In vain, I sought comfort from the notion that he could still be found alive. The policeman stayed with me and sent for my mother. The young female constable had taken Lynette and John along the road to Yvonne's mother.

In the garden, I sat and waited for my mother to return. Soon I heard her familiar footsteps hurrying along the side of the house. Her face contorted with anguish, and her appearance dishevelled, she flew across the lawn towards me. We rocked back and forth in each other's arms. She was, I knew, as disbelieving and as numb as I was. There seemed no provision in my consciousness that enabled me to accept the inevitability of the sudden death of the other half of my life. My reactions travelled slowly through a conduit of denial and disbelief. Eventually, the truth connected and the pain began. Ron's sister, Joyce, and her husband, Rod, arrived at the house soon after my mother. They waited with me – stunned, shaken, and heartbroken – for Joyce's parents to arrive. I rocked and howled in my mother's arms. *What am I to do? I don't know what to do.*

Sometime later across the lawn, they came to me: a pilgrimage of shock and grief. My devastated in-laws had arrived back from Ledge Point. My father-in-law looked harshly aged and unrecognisable in his agony and he shuffled slowly as if on fractured limbs. My mother-in-law's eyes were filled with disbelieving anguish: begging – imploring – me to tell her it was all a mistake. She clung to me, saying, over and over, 'I'm so sorry'.

Glen – tired, dishevelled and bewildered – stood near Kelly, our dog, just inside the gate. I gathered my child in my arms as my heart shattered.

Perth was a small place in 1964. Ron, his parents and his grandparents, had all grown up, living and working around Leederville and Subiaco. On that Foundation Day holiday weekend, the newspapers filled the front pages with photos and the story of the tragedy. The phone rang endlessly with people expressing their shock and disbelief that such a tragedy should happen to Ron. Stupidly, I wondered if he had eaten the ginger cake that I had made. I was never to make that cake again.

Ron Wray was grey-faced with shock, as haltingly he told me of a dream that his youngest daughter Joanne had had the previous night. Upset and crying, the child had woken her parents. She had had a disturbing dream about a man lost in the water. People were running along the beach looking for him and then she saw footsteps disappearing into the distance. The sight of the footsteps did not console her, though, because she could not see the person, only the footsteps.

Would it be too fanciful to think that as Ron left this world, he tried to connect to his best friend through the little girl?

I stared through the window, unable to tear my gaze away from the jagged fronds of the palm tree moving briskly backwards and forwards in the wind. The phone rang. I did not hurry to pick up the receiver. I did not care. It was not going to stop. I might as well pick it up. John Brett was on the phone to tell me that when the sisters at St John's heard the news of Ron, the bell was rung to call them to the chapel. Several of them left their beds to go and pray for Ron, for our children and for me. We were well known to the nuns of St John's through our friendship with the Brett's and after having had three babies born there. How different those nuns were from those cruel women of my childhood. I had affection for those women, but that did not alleviate the scorn and dislike that I will never cease to have for the others.

Gradually, the details of the night emerged. When the fishermen had not returned at the expected time, my father-in-law became worried. As the time lengthened, and with no sign of the boat or the men, the permanent residents and other weekend visitors joined them. Anxiously, they scanned the beach and strained to see through the dense blackness of the night as yet more people arrived with torches and lanterns. Vehicles arrived one after another and stood facing the ocean with their glimmering headlights switched on to high beam. They hoped to see some sign of the men and to act as a guiding light for them.

The three men had set out together many hours earlier. Several hours later, their battered boat washed up on the shore with only two of the three fishermen clinging desperately to its side. And the waiting group heard of the catastrophic events of the night. The night, they said, was calm, but extremely biting and cold. They told of how, as they headed back towards Ledge Point at around eight o'clock in the evening, the calm conditions changed with dramatic swiftness, and huge, mountainous waves swamped the dinghy, tossing the three men into the now tumultuous ocean. Fighting desperately, they all managed to struggle back into the dinghy, but waves that were more gigantic quickly followed, and the completely exhausted men were tossed into the seething water again. Two of them managed to cling to the upturned boat. They later stated that they battled for what they thought was about an hour-and-a-half. One man clung to the boat with one hand, and desperately tried to hold on to Ron with the other. They were all suffering from cold and cramps. They held on to Ron for as long as they were able because they knew that he was not a strong swimmer. Tragically, as it happened, none of them was strong swimmers. Another massive wave took Ron away and the easterly wind carried him out to sea. The boat rolled several times and, after some four hours in the water, the current carried the dinghy and the two survivors to shore. At first light, eight boats searched as far as five miles out to sea in the hope of sighting Ron. A chartered, twin-engine aircraft with three police constables as observers, searched a twelve square mile area, all to no avail.

The tragedy upon tragedy was that as distraught people searched the shore and water for signs of Ron, they had his little son beside them.

Over the next forty eight hours, I heard, and read, the differing reports of the events. I imagined when Ron told me that his friend had a new boat that it was what I called a proper boat. I pictured something thirty or forty feet long, with a cabin, and rails. That was not so. I learned they had been caught unprepared against the elements in a twelve foot dinghy. I did not know if I blamed anyone for the accident. It seemed unfair if I did. But I do know that when my mother told me that the owner of the dinghy was at the front door to see me, I told her to send him away. Four days later Ron still had not been found.

Jack Sue rang and scalding tears fell when I heard his voice and remembered meeting the Sue family and the happy times we had all shared in his parent's Aberdeen Street house. Jack was a well-known and highly decorated World War Two veteran and, returning from the war, became a professional deep-sea diver. He quietly offered to go, dive, and search the area for Ron. He avoided saying too much because of the dreadful implications, but the inevitability attached to the suggestion still startled me. Perhaps I thought that I would drift forever in a limbo-like state, never knowing where Ron was. For me, though, a more likely thought was that Ron would appear unexpectedly in the doorway one day, and then we could all go back to being the way we were. I still had faint trust that he might be found injured, but alive, in the sand dunes or washed up along the coast somewhere.

I thanked Jack and agreed to the idea, asking him what he planned to do.

He suggested that we wait another three days, making it seven days from when the accident had occurred. He told me that, from his experience, it was most likely that when the tide turned after seven days, Ron would be found. That is exactly what happened. Early in the evening of the seventh day, there was a knock at the front door. My mother hurried to open it. My mother opened the door and I caught a glimpse of the big policeman whom I had seen the previous week. This time he was alone. I was quite taken aback to hear him and my mother talking animatedly.

The burly police officer, Bill Bazely, from the Bayswater police station, who had looked so troubled on my behalf, used to be one of the regulars at Uncle Bordonis. He hugged me, 'I can't believe this. I used to bounce you on my knee when you were just a little girl.' Still holding me tightly, he whispered that Ron had been found earlier that day.

Ron Wray came to our house on many of those sombre evenings. His company brought comfort, especially for the children during that surreal, waiting period. I cannot recall him being there on the night when Bill Bazely brought his message, but he later told me that he was there and, at Amy's request, he was the one to phone Ron's sister. He phoned hoping to speak to Joyce's husband, Rod, but Joyce picked up the phone and when she heard Ron's voice, without him saying anything further, she knew that he was about to confirm that she had lost her brother, her only sibling. With despair, I accepted that the hope and waiting was over. Ron would not come home to us again. Finally, I would have to talk to our children. Thus far, I had sheltered them from the exact truth, but with all the unusual activity and distress, their own inner voices would begin to worry them soon.

I gathered them to me and we curled around each other on my bed. I told them that: 'There is a lovely place where some really special people go. It is called heaven. It has the most beautiful gardens. No houses, everybody lives in the gardens. Millions of butterflies fly all over the place, and there are so many colours, even colours we did not know about. There are fairies, angels and ladybirds that hide under the flower petals, then jump out and make everyone laugh. There are rainbows, roses and so much glorious colour. But it is only for the most special people, and your daddy was so special that he was able to go there. You know that we have been very sad, and we really want him here with us, but he is in a wonderful place and he does not want us to be sad. He wants us to look after each other for him, forever. He will want us to be happy again, and he wants us to talk to him each day.'

The links that were to bind us forever were forged as we wept. I did not know what else to say. I tried to create a beautiful, unfearful place for our children. I did not wish to speak of a God whom they might realise was not always just and merciful.

The funeral day wept with desolate, damp tears, and a cold wind blew as a large sombre group of people stood beneath black and occasionally coloured umbrellas.

Our children did not attend the cemetery.

As Ron's cortege appeared in the forecourt, and as we were about to enter the cemetery, the ship's company of a naval officer, who had just been buried, was about to disperse. They quickly reassembled and formed a guard of honour as we drove by. It seemed appropriate that Ron received respect from strangers as well as from his friends. He was such an all-round, good person. The tribute was unforgettable. My mother sat beside me holding tightly to my hand. And I felt so proud to have been part of Ron's life.

Anguish harshly etched into his face, and blind to the surroundings, Jack stood beside his daughter and his son-in-law. The three were bowed low with grief. My mother-in-law was unable to attend the funeral. She was in hospital with a mental and physical collapse. Countless people attended the funeral, people that I knew well and many whom I had not met before. At the graveside, there were mutual friends of Ron and myself. Nan, my girlhood friend was there, and she wept as she hugged me to her. Elizabeth and John stood alongside our family. Many of the people who came to mourn and comfort (we did not have the agreeable expression of 'celebrating' a person's life back then: we went to mourn) had attended our wedding a mere seven years previously. When I turned to leave the unproductive, sandy patch of earth, Canon Halley, the minister who had officiated firstly at our wedding and now at Ron's funeral, came towards me. Benevolently, he put his arm around my shoulder and murmured 'Now, you're only a young girl. You'll need someone to take care of you and the babies so don't stay on your own too long.' I felt such scorn for the insensitive old man. I thought he must be mad. What was he thinking? Why say such a thing to me at that time? I continued to stare at him unable to think of any response. As the silence lengthened, he removed his arm from me, did a *harrumph* sort of noise and wandered off. I recalled nothing of leaving the cemetery.

Friends and relatives were crowded into our house. I felt hemmed in by their presence and their voices racketed around in my head. I wanted them to go away. I knew that they were there to respect Ron's memory and support us, but I feared that at any moment I was going to scream. *Ron is dead. He won't ever come back. Drinking tea, eating cake and laughing is not appropriate. Can't you all see? I don't know what to do without him. You need to go away so I can think.* Across the room, my mother carried a tray with cups of tea. George and Clare stood together talking to Yvonne's mother, Alice. Suddenly, George's hearty, braying laugh bounced off the walls. *Not now George, not now. Please just keep quiet.* Then I did what I had to do. I propelled myself out of the chair, out through the front door, and raced down the street. I felt immensely powerful and I would have done anything, gone anywhere, to get away.

Joyce, lost in her own sadness, took a moment to register what I had done, before rushing after me. Many years later, she told me that she despaired of ever catching me that day as I charged mindlessly away. Soon, though, I ran out of steam. Then we walked along companionably and, as I calmed down, we talked quietly and returned to the house. The guests departed and, to the best of my knowledge, nobody held my behaviour that day against me.

My mother moved in with me and helped us a great deal, but the harmony between us had an uneasy edge. I still remained afraid of her ability to ride roughshod over me. Clearly though, she had been shocked and possibly frightened by Ron's sudden death at such a young age.

The children and my mother had gone to the shops together and before they left, Amy and I had had some futile disagreement that left me feeling angry. In their absence, pent up emotions burst from me. Suddenly I screamed in frustration at the God of my childhood who, in the past, never listened to my pleas anyway. I howled as I paced up and down the side veranda with our little dog pacing anxiously with me. I asked God why he took Ron away from me. Why did he leave me with a mother who would not allow me to raise my children in the way I needed to. 'Why, God. Why did you do that?'

There were many things that hurt to look at. Ron was defined in many ways by his possessions. Some things he owned were intrinsically *him*, some created sweet memories and others were so unbearable that I could not look at them. I could not bear to see Glen waiting at the gate to see Ron's car come around the corner. Or to see him sitting down beside it thinking that if the car was there, Daddy could not be too far away. As a result, I decided to part with Ron's beloved Holden.

Would I ever, I wondered, lose the feeling that another human being would never really know the true *me* again? Ron had been there in my life for ten years – since I was sixteen. Was there another person in the world who would instinctively know what I meant when I made an obscure comment? Would anybody ever again give me the benefit of the doubt over some remark or issue? Would the people in my now-so-different world know when I was joking without me having to explain?

The pink blossom of the almond tree contrasted starkly against its branches and the greying sky. My baby stirred gently. Something else stirred even more gently within me. So gently, that I almost missed it. It was hope. The appearance of the blossom told me that spring and the spirit of renewal was returning and that the wintry days would soon be behind us. However, renewal and spring had not arrived just yet, and the last thing in the world I expected was to walk into the eye of a proverbial storm.

Amy had just answered the telephone and, as she banged the telephone receiver down, I was confronted with her angry, accusing face. Her voice pitched high with annoyance, she snapped, 'I just took a message from somebody called Jean. I know that Con married a woman of that name. She knew you and she asked after Lynette. Tell me! Have you been seeing Con and his new wife?'

That was the last thing I wanted to discuss. Of course, it was true, although it was far from my mind at that time. Ron and I had met up with Con again when Lynette was about two years old. Ron saw Con unexpectedly in the street one day and, after catching up on all the latest news, Con urged him to bring me to visit him and his wife. I needed no second invitation. The following Saturday afternoon, I walked with Ron and Lynette along a fern edged path to Con's front door. Con greeted and hugged me emotionally as Jean smiled broadly and welcomed us into the home that they shared in North Perth. As she urged me to join her for a cup of tea and homemade, sponge cake, she plied an enthralled Lynette with large dishes of ice cream: vanilla, strawberry, chocolate, lime – anything she fancied. Jean worked in the office of Peter's Ice Cream factory and her refrigerator held large churns of variously flavoured ice cream. At that time shops sold nothing larger than small blocks of ice cream, about half the size of a house brick, so this was indeed a treat. Lynette looked forward to going there to visit, obviously relishing the easy-going and no-fuss atmosphere of Jean and Con's home, as well as the ice cream. When I first walked into their lounge room I was thrilled to see shining brightly, on the mantelpiece, a silver shaving mug that I had given to Con years before.

However, my thoughts were dragged back to the present as Amy stood before me, seething expectantly.

I could not be bothered pretending. 'Yes, we've been visiting them for ages.'

Then, in a quiet, deeply wounded tone, Amy replied, 'Well, I feel very upset, to be betrayed by my own daughter.'

Within weeks of that phone call, Con and Jean left Western Australia to live in Tasmania and we eventually lost touch. I did not know what happened, but something went sadly wrong. Was it something that Amy had said to her on the phone? Or was it that, in spite of Jean's ready acceptance of me previously, she became concerned that, when Ron died, Con's relationship with us might ultimately turn out to be a millstone around his neck? I never knew.

I wanted to run as hard and as fast as I was able, to escape from my life. It was not the first time in my life that I had wanted to run fast and escape. In retrospect, I now accept that I was overwhelmed and possibly depressed. The children and I gradually returned to a strange sense of normality. I laughed, teased and carried on as usual as much as I possibly could. By laughing and being brave for them, I also helped myself.

Amy called down the passage to tell me that 'Sue somebody' was on the phone. I took the phone and smiled when I realised that the caller was Ken Sue. Ken was the brother of Jackie Sue, and he owned a driving school. He had phoned to offer to send one of his instructors to teach me to drive. I accepted his practical thoughtfulness gratefully. To my amazement though, when the instructor walked up the path it was none other than Morrie, the bus driver from the Doubleview bus that I used to catch home from the dance. I was so happy to see him and felt more at ease to be learning to drive from someone who I already knew. However, in spite of knowing Morrie, and in spite of his undoubted teaching ability, I took an embarrassingly, unbelievable length of time to learn to drive. I came in from a lesson one day ready to give up. I felt upset and dispirited, convinced that I would never master driving. It was simply too much. My mother had been off-colour for a few days but, perhaps thinking to cheer me up when I walked in, she dramatically whipped her dress up and said, 'Take a look at this,' It was a strange sight. Her body was covered in a rash and we had no idea what it was. The doctor came the next morning and told Amy that she had Chicken Pox. Amy was very ill as the disease swept through her system. It invaded her eyes, nostrils and ears, and covered every inch of her body. The following day the doctor had her admitted to The Infectious Diseases Hospital. When I phoned the hospital the next morning, the hospital matron was quite explicit when she told me that I was *not* to visit. However, about an hour later someone from the hospital phoned back and said that I *should* come to the hospital that afternoon. The person gave me no reason and, not sure what to do, I phoned John Brett. He offered to come and get the children and me. We took the children to stay with Madge, and then continued on to the hospital. Its appearance had changed little since my prolonged stay there as a child. Together we approached the reception desk, and I waited as John conversed with the ward sister. Shortly afterwards, enveloped in murky coloured, green gowns and, with uncomfortable masks on our faces, we were admitted into Amy's room for a short time. Obviously she was ill, but as we chatted she appeared lucid and conversational. She was amiable towards John, and surprisingly, enquired after Elizabeth. That was a rarity, as generally my mother resented my friendship with them. She also asked me if I was coping with the accounts and bookwork for the butcher shop. A nurse soon came in and said that we were not to stay any longer. Unable to kiss her through the mask, I hugged her lightly and left the hospital, expecting that Amy would come home in a day or so.

Unbeknownst to me, John had indicated to Madge that Amy was not as safe as I thought and, knowing that a call may come from the hospital anytime, he suggested to Madge that the children should stay with her overnight and that I would sleep at his place. Madge agreed, and the children stayed with Madge and Jack, while I slept at the home of my friends. After dinner, just as they were putting their children to bed, the doorbell peeled loudly and John's heavy tread hurried along the hallway. As he opened the door, I heard a male voice. More heavy footsteps echoed along the passage, and John walked in with Gerry, my mother's friend.

He was upset and clearly intoxicated. He launched into the room, sobbing loudly, and threw himself awkwardly across me. He ended up with half of his body draped across my lap and the rest of him balancing precariously on the edge of the lounge chair. Unimpressed by his behaviour, Elizabeth urged him away and suggested that he have a cup of coffee and calm down. That awful man had gone to see Amy and the hospital staff must have thought that he was her husband. They asked him if they should get the priest and he told me that he agreed, because Amy had once told him that she had been raised Catholic. Gerry told us that when the priest approached her, Amy became hysterical. The priest arriving to administer Extreme Unction might have been of comfort to some people, but not to Amy. It was more likely to frighten her to death because that ritual was part of the last rites of the church given to a Catholic person at the time of imminent death. As I understood it, it was a last forgiveness process, absolving the person from sin before they died. To a true believer it would be comforting to know that they might yet scrape into heaven. Amy was not a true believer and she was terrified of death. She never even used the words 'dead', or 'dying', preferring the euphemisms of 'passed away', 'lost', 'gone', or even that they had 'expired'. The arrival of the priest would have told her loud and clear. *You are dying.* I was angry with him. Gerry was somebody Amy went out with, argued with, and stayed with for her own needy reasons. Nothing more. Yet, he had taken the unconscionable liberty of making that last decision of her life.

Some hours later, I awoke and became aware of John and Elizabeth standing beside me. In the dimly lit room, the hands on the brass clock on the mantelpiece showed that it was almost midnight. Elizabeth looked quaint with a bright, multi-hued granny rug wrapped around her. John, in his sleepwear appeared nothing like the imposing figure that he portrayed when he cut a swathe through staff and visitors alike as he went about his administrative work at the hospital. He spoke softly, 'Faye, the hospital just phoned.' He did not need to say any more. I knew that my mother was dead. I had only talked with her a few hours ago and, at that time, I had not the slightest idea that she was going to die. Elizabeth and John sat with me for a short time. I drank the hot, milky drink that materialised in my hand. Did I taste brandy? And then I went back to sleep. To this day I find it hard to admit, and harder to believe, that I went back to sleep and slept until morning. My mother had just died. And I went to sleep. I voiced my shame to Elizabeth, 'How could I do that? How could I possibly go to sleep?'

She replied, 'You could not cope anymore, that's why.'

Ledge Point 1964

In Elizabeth's garden, I sat with memories of my mother. For some reason the image of a midnight blue bottle that sat for years on her dressing table came to my mind. The bottle contained Bourjois Evening in Paris perfume. I wondered if the old unopened bottle was a sentimental keepsake from an admirer, perhaps from the war years.

She died alone. In fear. I wished she had been spared that. I had had no opportunity to tell her that we were all right, to tell her that I forgave her, or to ask her to forgive me for the times that I let her down. I did not have the chance to tell her that when all was said and done, I was sure I loved her. Yet – was I really sure that I truly loved the person who abandoned me, the person whose self-serving actions had left me tormented with self-doubt and anxiety for the rest of my life?

What strange combinations resulted in the person that people called Amy?

No other person was ever able to reduce me to falling down on the floor with laughter as Amy had done, either by some outrageous comment about a person's appearance, or a risqué remark that frequently left me wondering if she realised what she had just said. She was a party girl who enjoyed a good time. Nevertheless, she could be prudish in her judgement of other people, ascribing a different standard for them from the one she set for herself. She was also often unreasonably touchy and guarded in conversation, as if afraid someone might ask an awkward question. And even as an adult, I was afraid of her and of her unpredictable, unforgiving temper. I usually capitulated in any confrontation, not just with Amy, with anyone at all.

Amy was born under the star sign of Pisces, and I had once read an astrologers summation of the Pisces characteristics. It was such an apt description of Amy, that I remembered feeling a glimmer of understanding and some sadness, when I recalled words to the effect that a Pisces female who had suffered harsh treatment at an early age, might become contrary and miserable, always struggling furiously and seeing herself everywhere as she tried to escape – never realising that the inward turning of her endless self-involvement and pity toward herself was the real poison. The astrologer said that the Piscean would suffer from misconceived illusions which would hide the truth from her and blind her to the reality that her own behaviour might destroy her and, sometimes, the people around her. The more I thought of Amy, the more I realised that that summation fitted her to a T.

I walked aimlessly along Heytesbury Road towards Jack's butcher shop. As I passed our old house, I paused and remembered; just remembered. I made a promise to Ron and his children and to myself, that the love and freedom of spirit that the children were born with would be nurtured. I wanted the best for them and felt that I was capable of fierce retribution towards anyone who ever hurt them.

I pushed the heavy door inward. Jack looked up and cried out when he saw me, 'Oh Christ! How much more are you supposed to take? This is terrible!'

Although his tears were for me, they were also for his own recent, terrible grief. We stood in the sawdust in the butcher shop that, until recently, would have been ringing with laughter as Ron teased and jollied one of his favourite customers. We hugged each other and wept, each holding the other for strength while we sought to console and find consolation at the same time.

That poor man. His life was irrevocably changed forever. Once again, I slipped away into a strange, quiet, white silence.

Because the hospital found Amy's case bewildering the Coroner asked for an autopsy. It appeared that she died of a viral pneumonia, with bilateral carcinoma of the breast being a contributing factor. The pneumonia was caused as a result of her Chicken Pox by a virus, which was commonly found in India, but the chances of getting it in Australia were one in several million!

I have little recall of my mother's funeral. Who was there, or even of the priest who officiated, I recalled nothing. I did see a couple of black crows flying overhead, cawing mournfully, and I remembered my mother telling me when she was a little girl that the sound of crows had made her feel sad. The twenty or so solemn faces at the graveside were nothing more to me than a shimmering blur. Many years later, my cousin Paul, who had loved Amy unconditionally, told me that on that day he had never felt so bereft. I apparently looked at him and gave him no acknowledgement. How terrible for him. He had no way of knowing that, although I appeared to be there, I was not.

Lynette, Glen and John had the foundation of their lives painfully shaken again within weeks. How was it possible that in two unrelated incidents they lost both their father and their grandmother with such cruel swiftness? My three children were never again to laugh and speak with them. My unborn child was never to hold his hand and walk beside her own father. Or know her complicated grandmother.

Once again, I told them of a beautiful place for especially loved people. It was difficult, and wrong to be having this heart-breaking conversation with them again. The agonised, grief stricken scream that erupted from my beautiful little five year old daughter was to remain in my mind forever.

The sadness was becoming habitual and the devastating occurrence of sudden death in our midst was becoming horribly familiar. I prayed that the shock of the sudden, devastating losses would not make them feel threatened and insecure. I implored and bargained, with an unknown, hopefully benevolent deity, to keep my unborn baby strong and healthy.

Chapter 15

We Need a Tomorrow

The month was September, and Dr Clarke suggested that the children and I should have someone stay with us until November when the baby was due to be born. With some reservation, I thought that company would probably be good for the children and for me too, but I had no idea who could possibly fill such a role.

Ron's sister, Joyce, solved my dilemma. Her voice echoed down the phone line, 'Faye! If you still need a kind person to stay with you, I know a wonderful lady from my church. Her name is Mrs Edwards, and she might be able to come.'

Joyce's enthusiasm was contagious, and I found myself asking her to speak on my behalf to Mrs Edwards. Joyce phoned again a few days later and we agreed that she would take me to meet Mrs Ed, as she was universally known. Even so, remembering my own experiences with previously unknown people who supposedly were to care for me, I went to meet Mrs Ed with trepidation. I felt hesitant about my family and, more than ever, I was afraid of anyone being unkind towards them at this time in their lives.

I need not have worried. The day I met Mrs Ed, I met a true saint. Not a *goody, goody saint*, but a truly splendid person. A little, round woman stood to greet us, putting her sewing aside as we entered through the doorway of her cottage. She barely reached my shoulder and she looked exactly like the sort of person who should live in a cottage with flowers around the door. Her greying hair was pulled back into a small bun and little round glasses sat perched on her nose. Her face held a gentle expression gentle and wreathed into soft lines when she smiled. Her voice had a discernible lilt which, I learned, came from her upbringing in India as a young girl. The comfortable feeling that cocooned me as I listened to her restful, slightly singsong voice seemed familiar, as if I had known her for a long time. 'Well my girl,' she said suddenly. 'I will come on Friday and stay for two weeks, if that will help you.' I felt as if I had passed some sort of test with flying colours. My soul warmed and responded to her nurturing spirit. Her company, even for just two weeks would be appreciated. Two weeks turned into months. Many times, I was to hear her say 'Well my girl I should be getting back to the cottage.'

However, other than for a night or two here or there, she stayed with us. Sometimes when she spoke of going, Glen would plead, 'Oh Mamma Ed, don't go yet.'

Her reply would be 'Well, my boy, I can't stay here forever, but perhaps just a little bit longer.'

She involved the kids in activities, cutting out pictures and pasting them in books and they squeezed countless lemons for her to make lemonade. In the warmth of the afternoon, they sat with her just outside the back door, shelling (and eating) peas for dinner. They were special, companionable times together – something to be forever grateful for.

Mrs Ed's husband had died many years previously, and one evening when she was recounting to me her feelings at the time of his death, she shared something that astonished and, ultimately, helped me. I had not mentioned it to her, or to anyone else, but a distressing dream kept recurring, in which Ron had returned many years in the future. He went looking for his car and clothing and his tools. He also went looking for his children. In the dream as he frantically tore through the house looking for things, I ran behind trying to tell him how many years had passed by. That the children were not babies anymore and that they were all at school now. Then he would stop looking and our life would be as it always had. The dream never varied and, although not nightmarish, I awoke from it unsettled and despondent. The presence of Ron was so real, as dreams could be, and waking up to the knowledge that he had not returned to me was terrible. Mrs Ed talked of her husband's death in India. 'I was so shocked,' she told me. 'He only went into hospital with high blood pressure. High blood pressure! That's all! And he was a young man. Who dies of high blood pressure? My girl, I had never heard of such a thing.'

I had the feeling that her husband had cared for her deeply and protected her from life's day-to-day worries. She took his sudden, unexpected death as deserting her, leaving her with two children to raise and educate alone. We settled in our chairs and our conversation resumed.

'What I didn't like at all,' Mrs Ed went on to say, 'was a dream that I had for a long time after my husband's death. I used to dream that he came home from the hospital in an ambulance and went looking for his possessions to take back to the hospital with him. He got so cross when I admitted that I had given his clothes away, and demanded to know what he was supposed to wear.' She continued, 'It was terrible, but since then I have heard that it is not an unusual dream for someone to have when they have lost someone close.'

Mrs Ed became a beneficial influence in our lives. I had huge respect for her intelligence and for her fervent belief in education. We adored her and welcomed her back over the years whenever she returned to visit us. Even when the family grew up, her first question whenever I saw her was 'How are the children? And how's my little Johnny?'

'Little Johnny's over six feet tall, and doing fine,' I used to tell her. Mrs Edwards died on December 26, 2003. She was 101 years old.

Above all else, she showed me the way to our tomorrow.

Chapter 16

My Colleen

It was Friday November 13, 1964, and slight, repetitive twinges had kept me awake and alert during the previous night. Mrs Ed phoned Madge the next morning and she rang Dr Clarke. He advised me to take the children to their Nana and then go to St John's.

Mrs Ed did not drive a vehicle, and one of her church members arrived to take her to her cottage. Madge arrived and piled us into her black Humber Snipe, and we took off for her place at a leisurely pace, dispatching children along the way.

My poor father-in-law – the least superstitious of men – was heard in the butcher shop lamenting: 'Oh no, not Friday the thirteenth I don't want it born on Friday the thirteenth.'

Memories of the previous occasions when I had entered the other, old maternity wing swept over me agonisingly when I arrived at the hospital with Madge. The appearance of the new facility was attractive and modern, but it felt cold and foreign. Strangely, as I anxiously held Madge's small, work-worn hand, when we approached the reception desk, I wanted my mother with me.

It was early in the afternoon when I first glimpsed my little Colleen. I trembled with the force of my love for her and I squeezed her to my heart so tightly that her face turned scarlet and she cried with her new baby wail. Tears flowed from the adults too, and love filled the room. In a voice gruff with emotion Dr Clarke said, 'Well done. You have a beautiful, healthy, baby girl. Ron would be so proud of you both.'

As I gazed at my baby, the tears stopped. There might be more tears, but not today. Now that I had my baby safe and sound, I had more certainty that all would be well.

Ron! Amy! A little Colleen! We have our tomorrow.

The sisters were elated and gave us a card welcoming 'Darling little Colleen Anne.'

Friends welcomed the news that Colleen had arrived safely. The sisters joked that that there couldn't be any flowers left in Perth. So many bouquets came for us that each day I gave the sisters some of the lovely arrangements to take to the chapel. A *Daily News* reporter came and wanted to feature us in that day's paper. When I asked her the reason why, she replied that people would be interested to know how we were getting on after what had happened to my husband. But I could not allow it. The woman understood when I explained to her. People who knew and cared about us already knew how we were. I told her that if my daughter was ever to appear in a newspaper, it was not to be because of a tragedy. I was uncomfortable with public out-pouring of grief.

I remembered the dream that I had had all those months previously, before Ron died. Without any embellishment or drama, I had watched with an uneasy sense of inevitability as the dream unfolded. I had never been in the new wing of St John's. My other children had been born in the old maternity section, but when I observed the room and the layout, it was familiar and recognisable in all detail. Other than in my dream I had not been there before. The whispering nuns in my dream said that I did not have my husband.

Unbelievably, six months later, I did not.

It was time to leave the sheltered calm of the hospital, and I was alarmed at the thought of returning to the house in Bayswater. The place housed something evil and I did not want my baby and my other children there.

George Smith was a minister of religion, and a friend of Aunty Anne Bohling's. Lynette sometimes went to the local Sunday school, where he preached. We became friendly and in the close-knit community that automatically meant the young minister took a friendly, non-intrusive interest in us all. He visited me in the hospital and as we chatted, I found myself telling him of my fears and of my dream.

The sisters brought Colleen in for him to inspect and admire. 'Do you mind if I say a prayer for you both for blessings and peace in your future life?' I nodded yes. 'Will you join me?' I agreed. We prayed to his God for a few minutes. He then departed, reappearing about an hour later, saying as he came through the door, 'I have an idea I want to put to you.' He knew, he said, a family, whose teenage daughter was unmarried and pregnant which, in 1964, was still unacceptable. The pregnant girl's family had several younger children, and ideally, they wanted her out the way for the entire pregnancy. The baby was to be given up for adoption and no one in the family ever needed to know. As far as I can recall, that is pretty much how it happened. George Smith's suggestion to me was that perhaps the girl, whose name was Cheryl, could come and stay with me. I would have someone to accompany me on my return to the house, and to help me with the children. Cheryl would have a comfortable home until her baby was born in about six months' time.

I thought it sounded like a win-win situation, and I agreed to meet Cheryl, so George Smith returned some time later with a short, rather dumpy girl, with an awkward manner. Her most outstanding feature was her long, shining reddish hair. Here into my life came a young person with nowhere to go. Although they thought that they were so civilised, her family had ostracised her. How curious that I should turn out to be her salvation. The minister introduced us, and then left us alone to see how we felt about each other and his proposition. By the time he returned, Cheryl and I felt confident enough with each other to agree to give it a trial.

I was desperate to put the overwhelming fear aside and go to my children. It is astonishing to remember that at that time a child could not visit its mother in a maternity hospital. With Cheryl for company, maybe we would be all right.

A favourite nun was Sister Lucilla. She did everything on the run, seeming to spread sunshine and laughter with her happy disposition and occasional irreverent remarks. During my prior stays in the hospital, we became friendly. I remember one day she tippy-toed into my room pulled up a chair and sat down. She then leaned back comfortably and rested her feet upon the end of the bed. 'Ssh,' she breathed, 'I'm exhausted. I'm hiding for ten minutes.'

She was off-duty when the time came for me to leave the hospital. I hadn't thought that I would see Sister Lucilla again before I left, but I should have known better. She burst into my room carrying Colleen, with a happy smile on her face. 'I'm here to take you both to the car.'

I have a set of rosary beads that once belonged to Sister Lucilla, which I treasure, not for their religious significance, but because they belonged to a woman whom I held in great esteem and for whom I had considerable affection.

Surrounded by well-wishers I stepped into Madge's waiting car and waved them goodbye. I stayed with Madge and Jack for a week before returning to Bayswater. My heart ached for Madge as she cared for us, and for Jack, when I saw him gazing wistfully into Colleen's cot. My recollections of returning to the Bayswater house and our first few days there are not particularly clear. Cheryl and I arrived at the house at the same time in different cars: Cheryl, with George Smith and I, with Madge. I crossed the threshold and I felt swamped with fright and aloneness.

Any previous feelings of optimism and of being able to cope with the future deserted me and I wanted to escape.

Cheryl, to me at that moment, was an alien stranger. I did not want her. I wanted the impossible. I wanted my children's father.

The evening passed in a chaotic, busy blur of kitchen activity, unpacking clothes and bathing children. And then we ate a simple meal of, I think, soup that Laura had made for us, and some sandwiches.

One after the other, the children were placed in their beds and, within minutes, they were all sleeping soundly. Cheryl and I talked in a desultory fashion for a short time until I showed her to her room, and took Colleen and went to my own bedroom.

In the forthcoming weeks, Cheryl and I did grow closer, and I appreciated her more each day, aware that without her, physically and emotionally, I might have become stuck in a bad place. It was the worst time of all. I wondered how she felt and coped with that first strange night, because I had no comfort to offer her, and looking back, I feel that I was barely courteous.

The next morning Lynette appeared at the breakfast table pale and weepy, with an enormously swollen face. She had the mumps. It proved to be beneficial in a way, in helping Cheryl and me find our feet around each other. Cheryl occupied Glen and John by reading for them and playing games with them, thus enabling me to devote time to the little girls. Lynette's face was swollen and although she did not complain, I knew she was in a lot of pain. Dr Clarke left pain medication for her, and she beamed crookedly at him when he told her she was a brave little girl. I think her joy at being back with me, and the buckets of fortitude that she seemed blessed with, partly overcame her discomfort. By the time Lynette was well, Cheryl and I had settled into a pattern and, because we had been so busy, we escaped the initial awkwardness of two strangers who didn't know what to expect of each other. Our lives formed a haphazard pattern.

Not necessarily the life we wanted, just the life we had.

Christmas drew near no matter how hard I willed it to go away. I was filled with dismay at the thought of how we were ever going to get through the day that we all had previously shared with two other very vibrant people. I had visions of the children crying all day for their Daddy and their Noni. I told myself, *act normally, Faye ... remember, you can do it, you know how to do it ... you just act normally and don't tell anyone how desperate you feel.*

Therefore, I bought presents and special food treats, I decorated the tree and I took Lynette, Glen and John to see Father Christmas.

On Christmas morning, we awoke to hear a most unexpected sound. It was the raucous jingle of the Mr.Whippy tune as the ice cream van crawled slowly past. Glen raced outside with Cheryl, convinced that Father Christmas had sent the Mr Whippy van especially to our house. They weren't to be denied such a wonderful treat. Ice cream before breakfast! Christmas was off to a good start. The morning passed swiftly as the children discovered their gifts, and played far more happily than I had dared hope. Cheryl left the house early to meet her parents. The children and I spent the day at Madge and Jack's house in Leederville. People came and went at intervals throughout the day, leaving little opportunity to brood. We all kept a tight rein on our emotions. As dusk fell, I took my family home.

Shortly after Christmas, I received a phone call from Morrie, the instructor from the Ken Sue driving school. He had been 'drinking and thinking,' as he put it. Because of Amy's death, my driving lessons had

My Colleen

been put on the back burner. Besides, my confidence to tackle anything different had plummeted to zero. Anyway, Morrie had decided in his drinking and thinking state, that I should get my license, and get it now. He would be at my place the following morning to recommence lessons. It was fortunate that Cheryl was still with us, so I was free to go. After a few lessons Morrie decided, 'Let's go for it, and apply for your license. If we wait until you feel confident, it will never happen.' So with a dry throat and quaking legs I found myself being dragged kicking and screaming, metaphorically, towards the licensing centre. Stiff and tense, I huddled in the corner of the driver's seat and waited for the police licensing inspector to come and join me in the car. Another typical burly copper, much like Bill Bazely, soon joined me. 'Now take it nice and easy, and let's see what you can do. Indicate, and then pull out slowly, slowly now.' So far, so good, I thought as I crept along. The instructor smiled kindly, 'When you reach the corner, I want you to indicate and turn left.'

Yes, I thought, I can do that. *But I didn't.* I hurtled into the middle of the busy Midland intersection, and put the indicator on to turn right. We sat stranded in the middle of the road, like a beached whale, waiting to get around. With a bemused look, the examiner asked, 'Why did you do that? I said turn left to make it easier for you.' Trembling, I eventually completed the turn, and as I bit back tears, he told me to head back. When we returned to the station, he leapt from the car and with not a word to me went inside. I just sat there feeling useless and disappointed. That's it, no license. Suddenly though, Morrie bolted through the heavy doors at the top of the steps, and jumped down them two at a time until he reached the car. He pulled me out, dragged me up the steps behind him and through the door where the beaming police officer handed me my driver's license. Hugs all around, and then I was on my way, tightly clutching my prized piece of paper. I believe that that license was a huge, charitable gift. They knew that I wasn't going to be silly, I just needed practice, and more practice. I arrived home triumphantly and we had cake to celebrate.

Always, always celebrate the good things!

Cheryl was gaining weight rapidly and I thought that George Smith had intervened just in time if her pregnancy was to be kept secret from her brothers and sisters. She waddled towards me and handed me the mail from the letterbox. Amongst the pile was a letter from the Midland Shire Council. The letter congratulated me on the safe arrival of Colleen, and went on to say that at their recent meeting the councillors all stood and observed a minute's silence to respect Ron's memory.

They were kind words from an unexpected source.

When Colleen was a few months old, it was with stunned disbelief and shock one morning that I read in the morning paper that Morrie, my friendly driving instructor, had died. Morrie was only in his late thirties. He had small children and he was such a livewire. What could possibly have happened to him? I rang Ken Sue, and he told me that Morrie had had a heart complaint since birth. He needed to look after his health, but it seemed that he had adopted the philosophy of, I'm here for a good time, and if it's not for a long time, so be it. What a wretched time it seemed. Death was still forever skulking around. Ron died aged thirty one, my mother aged forty five, and Morrie was in his thirties. To add more misery, in the weeks following Ron's accident, the sixteen year old apprentice from the butcher shop was killed in a road accident. I was twenty seven and if I let my thoughts take hold, I could have become obsessed with death and dying.

I was to learn that grief had to pass through the four seasons. One spring. One summer. One autumn. One winter. One of everything that fell within the year following the cause of the sadness. The second time, around things became easier.

Chapter 17

Essex St Wembley 1965

As 1964 drew to a close, it ended a year locked in my memory for all time. For countless others it was it was possibly a year of little consequence – twelve months of their lives in which nothing outstanding or memorable took place.

The law was that every deceased estate was subject to a government probate tax. Ron's estate was no exception, and all of our finances, including the shop accounts, were untouchable until the probate details were finalised. The long drawn-out process meant that assets were frozen, (solid) and inaccessible, leaving me with no access to the business bank account, which was our only source of income. Fortunately, the shop takings for the week prior to the accident had not been taken to the bank and Ron had also kept a sizeable amount of cash in the house. That money, and a compassionate bank manager, meant I was able to keep the business afloat. I was not eligible for government assistance until after probate was completed and my status regarding entitlement was decided. With no income except for the most minimal amount left from the shop proceeds after I had paid the salary of a butcher, and with four small children to care for, I wondered what more proof of my status the government needed. Probate usually took at least a year, in some cases two or three years before being finalised.

Uncomfortable in my own skin, I was afraid ... all the time. However, when anybody enquired how we were getting on, I answered. 'We're fine, everything will be all right.' If I said it often enough, surely it would be so. I reverted easily to my old way of *don't tell anyone*. In hindsight, there was perhaps no need for this show of bravado and extreme independence, but I knew no other way.

From Dorrie, my mother-in-law's twin sister, I learned that there was a house for sale on Essex Street in Wembley, a leafy, older suburb with substantial, well-kept streets and gardens. As a child, I used to gaze from the trolley bus window and think how I would like to live on one of those safe looking, well-kept streets.

The house, at number 74, was next door to Mrs Chaplin, a friend of my in-laws, whom I already knew. Persuaded by Dorrie, I went to see Mrs Chaplin and she took me to meet her neighbours. I walked through the perfectly kept rooms and visualized us living there. When I walked into the garden and saw a wall lined with beautiful hydrangeas, ready to bloom fully in a couple of months, I imagined sunny times ahead There were ferns and geraniums, and an almond tree with grey, sturdy branches showing just a glimpse of pink blossom, with the promise of green leaves and almonds soon to follow.

I wanted to live in that house with my children and I spoke with Mr Lemonis, an intimidating man who was the solicitor for Ron's estate. I told him about the Wembley house, and I felt encouraged when he told me that he would do whatever he could to help. Several weeks passed by, before Mr Lemonis rang one afternoon and explained that the probate department had agreed to release enough funds from Ron's insurance to pay a ten per cent deposit on the house, as well as an assurance to the owners that the balance of money would be paid directly to them when probate was finalised in approximately three months' time. I had no idea if such a brilliantly simple arrangement would suit the owners. They were agreeable and the arrangement went well.

It seemed that almost every time that I felt abandoned, and was afraid, a rainbow of kindness encouragingly swept over my children and me.

An estate agent handled the sale of the house and I tried never to drive through or think about Bayswater again.

Furniture and a mountain of boxes were loaded on to the removal truck. Teddy bears and dolls were grasped in small arms and Kit, our big ginger cat, glared furiously with indignation as John and Glen held him tightly in a stranglehold in the back seat of the car.

We moved into Essex Street in August, 1965. Each anniversary of that date saw us having a celebration dinner. Always, always celebrate the good times.

I walked into our peaceful new home to the scent of freshly cut flowers arranged in a tall *jardinière* standing in the entry. In the lounge room and bedrooms, the soft aroma of a flowery furniture polish lingered. I knew no demons lurked there, only the harmonious spirit of the previous owners.

I worked through the night, while my children slept soundly and safely.

The months flew by and it was almost Christmas time. Lynette had been attending Wembley Primary school for the last term of the year, so that after the holidays she wouldn't be starting the new school year as a stranger.

On warm evenings, I drove to nearby City Beach, with the children, firstly picking up fish and chips to eat at the beach, and then to spend an hour or so driving through the suburbs to the Subiaco and Claremont Council gardens – a simple but memorable outing, to see the brightly-lit, decorated, Christmas trees.

The holiday season passed swiftly and Lynette continued her schooling at the Wembley primary school. She seemed to be happy there and quickly resumed the friendships she had made in the previous term. The teachers at the school were a unique and caring group, special to the school and to our family. Lynette quoted Miss Pougnault, her Grade Three teacher, endlessly. Miss Pougnault was kind, she was funny, and she wore great clothes. Frequently, as she walked through the door after school, Lynette greeted me with, 'Guess what Miss Pougnault did today.'

I looked forward to meeting that paragon. One Friday afternoon I stood at the gate of the little school, while I waited for Lynette to appear from her classroom. Why, I wondered, did my kids seem to appear only after all the others had gone and the place was practically deserted?

She appeared at last, all smiles, talking animatedly to a tall, slim, striking young woman. 'Mummy, this is my teacher. Her name is Miss Pougnault.' Teacher and mother, we each observed the other with interest and exchanged pleasantries before Anne said that she had to dash to the library before it was closed.

I liked Lynette's Miss Pougnault. She drove a Citroën sedan and my kids watched and waited expectantly as it majestically rose slowly from its lowered position, before she drove away.

That year, Glen started school at Wembley too. School was not his favourite place, not then, not ever. However, he did have the good fortune to become friends with the school gardener, a man named Harry Laidler. Glen gravitated naturally to that mild, unruffled fellow who worked with the earth. They ate lunch together and Glen trotted around with him until it was time to go back to class. Harry approached my car one day as I waited for the kids to come out from school (last again) and introduced himself. That meeting began a long friendship between my family and Harry, and with his wife, Norma. We had some splendid holidays with them at the Murchison River after Harry and Norma moved back there some time later. Visiting the Murchison district, and experiencing the dry, hot days and cold, biting evenings, was reminiscent of my childhood in Kalgoorlie. Harry took us to the historic Woolleen Station, and Norma packed sandwiches and homemade cake before they drove us hundreds of kilometres to see carpets of amazing, startling red and black Sturt Peas stretching far into the distance. We slept in a caravan surrounded by everlastings, bright pink, mauve and purple, mixed with yellow and delicate white, which all grew abundantly in stunning contrast against the rich, red Murchison soil. What a splendid and rewarding friendship our family enjoyed with Harry and Norma. Remembering our trips to the Murchison district led me to think that in today's society such a friendship probably would never have had the opportunity to grow and flourish. Society was changing rapidly and I found it easy to imagine that in the not too distant future no school would be permitted to stand by and tolerate a small boy pottering around in the garden shed and eating his lunch with a male staff person, preferring his company to that of kids his own age. Harry, I thought, would probably lose his job and the school principal may possibly refer Glen for counselling!

With the help of my next-door neighbour, Colleen had slowly overcome her dread of letting me out of her sight. One day as Colleen cried heart brokenly because she could not see me down the bottom of the garden, Mrs Chaplin came in to see what the trouble was. Alarmed to see Colleen so badly upset Mrs Chaplin suggested that I take Colleen into her house regularly and leave her. Starting with just five minutes before I returned, and then gradually increasing the time to fifteen or twenty minutes. It took considerable time but eventually my little girl realised that I always came back and her crying whenever I was out of her sight stopped.

The neighbours all took a kindly and practical interest in the young widow who had settled in their midst 'with all those little children.' The neighbours on the other side of our house were another middle-aged couple. My children often went next door to 'Mr Bill' as they called him. He fixed bikes and mended punctures for them. He allowed them to hammer bits of wood together and he even, on occasion, removed splinters from their fingers or feet.

The September school holidays were almost over and we had taken an early picnic lunch to nearby Lake Monger. We settled ourselves in a shady spot close to the old-fashioned-tyre-on a-rope-swings. Lulled by the gentle waves rippling across the lake we ate our sandwiches and cake, sharing our bounty with messy little ducks and cross, imperious-looking swans. The intense sun suddenly shone into my eyes, and as I turned sharply to avoid the glare, I glanced upwards. Through the tall trees, I saw glimpses of the threatening outline of the building of The Home of Good Shepherd. We lived close to the convent and I drove around the lake on most days, however, because the building was set high above, and screened by trees, it was not visible to the passing traffic below, and I never gave it a thought. Momentarily though, knowing that I was directly beneath that frightening place, my spirits dropped, as I recalled standing in the dormitory at night time, gazing through a barred window at the twinkling lights as my silent tears fell.

I was diligent in taking the children regularly to visit their grandparents. I wanted Ron's children to be familiar with, and hopefully, to love, their father's parents. We left the lake and I drove to fulfil a promise, which was to visit Nana and Grandpop. Madge and I sat companionably at the kitchen table drinking tea and talking about nothing in particular, while the boys spent an hour or so investigating every square inch of Grandpop's shed. Lynette and Colleen usually read or coloured in picture books.

My friendship with John and Elizabeth had remained constant and for my thirtieth birthday, in 1968, I celebrated with them at a trendy, new restaurant in Fremantle, called the Tum-Tum Tree.

For Christmas in 1968, I wanted for my children something different from what other kids were having and something *completely* different from my own Christmas when I was ten, in 1948. As I drove along Gnangara Road one afternoon, I saw a wooden sign tacked to a tree, and it read: 'Pony hire for kids' parties.'

I immediately swung off the road and followed a bushy track until I came to some stables. I met and convinced the somewhat bewildered owner of the ponies that although I did not have a huge back yard or a paddock, I did want a pony surprise for my children. As so often happened in those days, the stable owner recognised the name, Bohling, and the tragedy associated with it. That was it. Nothing was too much trouble for that kind man and the week before Christmas, a docile little pony sauntered around our back garden accompanied by her new foal. John was most unhappy when the bigger pony made a sudden (I thought playful move) towards him. John didn't think it playful at all and went tearing back towards the house.

I went to the ballet with Elizabeth and learned to appreciate the beauty of movement to music. I relaxed in coffee shops with rice paper lampshades and psychedelic posters decorating the walls. I listened to the mellow strains of Tijuana Brass and Acker Bilk, and I enjoyed Bob Dylan and Cat Stevens. My espresso coffee came in a tiny cup. I toyed with waxy, stalactite shapes formed by candles as they dripped down the sides of round wine bottles, which were often used at that time as a statement of understated *chic*. I was gratified for those opportunities to be interested in life outside my own four walls. I was also grateful that I had some fine-minded friends. Their interest and invitations encouraged me to grow.

Our life was contented, but of course, there were some not-so-good times. The four children occasionally suffered from childhood infections, accidents and injuries that on a few occasions were potentially serious. Overall, though, they were healthy and happy. I reprimanded my children and I was firm. I did not threaten idly. If I declared some action would bear a consequence, then they knew that it would. I tried hard not to lose my temper, or be unreasonable because I was feeling burdened or worried. That was not their fault. I also had a notion that if I lost control of myself, peace would be difficult to regain. Being born under the sign of Aries, I could be unexpectedly fiery and hasty, even slapping backsides sometimes. But even when annoyed, I could mostly see a humorous side to our issues. I knew the isolation of being alone with an adult who was angry and not speaking to me, and I never wanted my children to go through that. I made a daily, conscious effort not to emulate my own mother in any way. I had no wish to disrespect her, and acknowledged that we did have our good times, but the thought that I might be like her in any way as a parent was frightening. I had read that people who were ill-treated and abused as children often repeated the behaviour towards their own children. I vowed, however, that I would *never* not be speaking to my children, or even be cool with them for any length of time. *I* simply could not stand it. I kept my promise. Years later, when Lynette was a teenager, and we had a minor confrontation over some issue, she said, 'I may not always like your decisions, but you are always fair.'

That was my gold medal day. When my daughter let me know, I had broken the cycle of abuse.

Chapter 18

Earthquake

Thus far, my life had seemed to rocket along generated by events totally out of my control, not necessarily earth shattering to others, but of huge import to me. Then an event of wider effect happened – the day of the earthquake.

The day started ordinarily enough with no omen or forewarning that, later in the day, our city and, on a lesser scale, my life would be rocked again. This time it was by a truly earth-shattering event that affected many people and, as a direct result of the damaging, destructive phenomenon, I met my second husband.

The newsreader gazed solemnly into the camera and spoke in measured tones. He informed us that the small country town of Meckering, one hundred and forty kilometres east of Perth, with a local population of just over two hundred, had been hit by an earthquake at eleven o'clock that morning. Measuring 6.9 on the Richter scale, the centre of the 'quake caused massive damage, decimating the town. It also caused considerable damage to a small area along the Perth coastal plain and to widespread sections of the Perth metropolitan area.

My own house in Wembley sustained some damage in the form of large cracks in the walls of the lounge and dining room. Other large cracks appeared in three of the rooms, and the insurance company promised to send an assessor as soon as possible to inspect the damage. I was pleasantly surprised at their promptness when, the following week, a tall, business-like man stepped from his car at the front gate and stood for a moment adjusting his tie, then checked the number on the letterbox against the manila folder that he held in his hand. I saw all this as I stepped through the side gate and called out as he started to walk up the steps to the front door: 'I'm over here in the garden.' He looked a little disconcerted as if the last thing he expected was a disembodied greeting from somewhere in the garden. In an abrupt, manner he enquired, 'Is your husband in? I've come to look at your damaged walls.'

I explained briefly that I was the homeowner. He introduced himself. 'I'm Sid Osborn, the insurance assessor.' His demeanour was pleasant and efficient. He wandered around making observations and taking notes. As he took his leave he told me he would let me know when the repairs would be done, warning me that it might be a few weeks, owing to the large amount of claims flooding into their office as the result of the earthquake. Over the next two weeks he phoned several times, keeping me updated on the progress of my claim. The walls were duly fixed satisfactorily and I had no further contact with the insurance company over the issue.

During that time, I started to suffer relapses of an inflammatory, intestinal disorder that had troubled me since childhood. Afraid that I had cancer and that I would soon die and leave my children all alone I often woke in the middle of the night in physical pain, my body sweating, as I gasped for breath and visualised my own funeral. Coincidence arrived via the morning paper. A large article appeared about an organisation called Birthright, which called itself: 'the civilian counterpart of Legacy.' Birthright helped the children of civilian widows. Their members included, among others, company managers, lawyers and civil servants. The men involved played a male mentor role to fatherless children, taking them on occasional outings with Birthright members' own families, especially fishing and football outings for boys. The calibre of the volunteers usually ensured that they had the expertise to offer advice to families with the day-to-day problems that saw many widows confused and worried. I phoned for information and was encouraged, after speaking with the secretary, to agree to go on a list until a volunteer became available to come and visit us. After making the call, I felt that I had done something positive and taken a step to providing an independent source of support for the children if ever they should need it.

Fine and sunny weekends usually found us in the garden. On one particular Saturday, the two girls played together in an outside, small room near the back door that had become their playroom, while the boys trundled around on their bikes and I tidied up the garden, not too enthusiastically, but doing enough to keep it looking good for the moment. I walked up the back steps and into the kitchen with Glen right behind me. I really needed coffee. Above the sound of Glen fossicking around in the food cupboard and the kettle boiling busily, I heard the front door rattle. Looking from the hallway, I saw a tall man's silhouette through the pearly, glass pane. I opened the door to see a vaguely familiar face.

'How strange to meet again,' he said, and as he spoke, I remembered him. Several months had passed, but I recognised his voice. 'It's Mr Osborn, isn't it?'

'Yes, but call me Sid. I'm here from Birthright.'

My mind went blank. I could not make a connection between the insurance company and Birthright. Of course, another few minutes' conversation revealed that he represented both. I invited him into the kitchen and offered him a cup of coffee, he accepted, and we drank our coffee and chatted companionably for a few minutes. After a while we agreed that Sid would call around every two or three weeks to visit and, if everyone was comfortable, the children, mainly the boys, could go out somewhere with him for a while. The visits went well and the children looked forward to seeing Mr Osborn.

Gradually, a pattern emerged and Sid became a more frequent visitor. He appeared to be a reserved, reticent man, but as the weeks went by, he appeared eager to share his life experiences. I listened to his story and felt sympathy for him. He told me about his upbringing in poor circumstances. He had been the youngest child in the family, with two brothers and a sister. He described how their situation deteriorated after his father walked out of the house one morning to go to work leaving his door key on the table and never returning.

There seemed some resentment in him as he intimated that fate had singled him out and denied him opportunities when, at the age of sixteen, he caught the measles, resulting in a condition known as bronchiectasis. He grimly told me that after months of treatment the doctors told him that they were going to remove his left lung on the following Monday morning. He was seventeen. When I asked him one day if he ever had been married, he reacted abruptly, saying, 'No I am a single man.' Gazing off into the distance, Sid told me that he was forty three and that he had never formed a close relationship with another person. He attributed this to being isolated when young because of the operation. He explained that he hated the three years of daily hospital visits and he longed to get away from England. He settled in New Zealand, where he lived for thirteen years before the cold climate there began to affect his remaining lung.

Western Australia seemed to have the climate that he needed to maintain reasonable health, so he moved there. I learned more about Sid as the weeks went by. I respected that he worked hard as a young man to improve his status, achieving considerable success in the insurance industry. He had an appreciation and knowledge of art and music and it occurred to me one day that perhaps he had put all his time into pursuing singular interests that expected nothing from him in return. I did not think at all about Sid between his visits. Mostly, he phoned every couple of weeks, late on Friday afternoons, to see if it suited to visit for a while on the weekend. Christmas was near, placing me in a quandary about whether to include Sid in our celebrations, I eventually decided not to. That led me to conclude that I did not really need Birthright. I was not sure what I expected when I first contacted them, but it did not include having such a regular family visitor, I had thought more of an occasional outing for Glen and John. People sometimes commented to me, how nice it would be if I met someone to be a father to the children and a companion for me. I did not want to share my children's lives, or mine, with anyone. We were fine the way we were. Besides, they had a father – he just was not there.

One day just before Christmas, Sid called in on his way back from Donnybrook with a large box of beautiful, bright green Granny Smith apples. I simply told him that the contact with us was too frequent. We had, I told him, some family and numerous friends, and I did not want too many different people in and out of their lives. I did not want them looking forward to seeing someone who eventually would not be there. I probably chose my words poorly because Sid stood up abruptly and left. The image of the shattered, devastated look on his face, as if all the bad news in the world had suddenly hit him, stayed with me.

The following Friday morning, in my mail was a letter from Sid. A small part of the letter read: *'I thought I was getting close to you, and the kids seem to like me. I am fond of you, and I would like to take care of you and your children. I am lonely, and although I might cough and splutter a bit along the way, I am in reasonable health. I figure that I am good for about twenty years.'*

Prophetic words indeed. Sid died nineteen years later. However, all the right words were there in that letter.

Look after you. Need you. I have led a lonely life. I need your warmth. I want to find peace. In addition, scrawled in the far lower left corner of the page, *PS I love you.* I knew that the postscript was an afterthought of what Sid thought I expected to see. I felt wretched at what I perceived to be my previous harshness and lack of understanding, so I phoned him. He came to visit on the weekend, and a few short weeks later, I had gone from telling him to go away, to agreeing to marry him.

Lynette, with her optimistic heart was happy for me. Glen, I do believe at the tender age of eight, probably thought it was not a bad idea. Colleen, as the baby, largely ignored the whole matter and mostly continued to politely ignore him ever after.

Only my quiet, far-seeing little John queried in a puzzled voice, 'But why do you have to marry him?' I suggested to Sid that we wait until the next school holidays in May, but Sid chose an earlier date in March. When I commented, 'There's really no great hurry,' he replied, 'if we don't do it soon, we never will.' With the fast moving tide of goodwill and enthusiasm surrounding us, and thinking that my son had just made a cute, kid-like comment, I was swept along. I ignored the loud clanging of warning bells, which, at the time, threatened to deafen me. However, I did believe that Sid, having no former wife or children, was a good thing, as there would be no previous family complications.

At thirty two years old, I gave up a pleasant, reasonably uncomplicated life, stepped into the unknown and married Sid a few months later.

The day was bright and clear. Optimistically, as I slid the modern, ankle-length, cream, crepe gown over my shoulders and tugged the heavy gold lace trim into place, I hoped that the sunshine presented an auspicious beginning, on the day Sid and I were to be married. Our wedding party was held in the garden of Joyce and Rod's home. I wanted a party where the children could run around and have fun, not a reception in a formal setting and Joyce and Rod's relaxed and casual, large, leafy garden was familiar to the children. I also wanted them to know that, although someone new had entered the picture, primarily they belonged to the Bohling family. Their surname would never be changed.

Friends, some new ones from the Wembley district and from the children's school came to our wedding, but mostly they were the same group of people that have been there for nearly all of the significant occasions throughout my life, whether happy or otherwise. Sid seemed not to mind that our guest list was heavily balanced towards my family and friends. He invited just two families and a few of his work colleagues. My memory was of a good day, with warmth and good wishes.

I listened nonplussed when, a few months after our marriage, Sid mentioned that he felt a fresh start would be good for us all. 'I don't feel entirely comfortable living in your house. I sometimes feel like an intruder,' he said, almost sulkily. I did not know it then, but I was soon to realise that no matter how hard anyone around him tried, Sid always felt like an intruder, or felt someone was intruding and invading his space. Sid had a small, old, rather-rundown house, but in a fast selling area, and he suggested that if we sold both our houses we could build a new, much larger home to accommodate the changes that, in his opinion, we needed. When Sid broached the subject again, I told him that I was not keen on the idea of moving. 'I chose this area so carefully, and it's good for so many reasons, especially being close to the school and to Madge and Jack.

Sid had ready answers. 'I think you take your responsibility to Madge and Jack too seriously. As long as you take the kids to visit their grandparents, where we live won't matter.' With feelings of disquiet, I allowed myself to be reeled in, bit by bit, and agreed to leave our almost perfect location. The move took us to a two-acre property, about forty kilometres southeast of Perth. On a slightly overcast, damp day, we drove away from the city, and set off on our seemingly idyllic quest. We found our way to the two-acre block of land after intense map scrutinising and many wrong turns. We clambered out of the car ignoring the bog underfoot as we wandered around. The boys tore around in and out of the muddy, loamy soil. The drizzle stopped and the sun shone briefly, both warm and brilliant. Surely a good omen, I thought. An expanding image formed in my mind. It drew a picture of me and of my family as we entertained by the flowing stream that ran along the tree-lined edge of the property. It was easy to envisage friends travelling to the foothills for barbecues and picnics. With no traffic concerns, I imagined the kids riding on bikes and a dog romping, and perhaps a horse grazing contentedly, nearby. Oh yes! I could see it all.

In many ways the outer suburban lifestyle and our newly built house did suit my young family, giving them freedom to roam unfettered, but after the initial excitement of moving, an uneasy feeling settled upon me. The feeling now was different from the dread and anxiety of the Bayswater house. Wembley had been part of our family in the same way that Subiaco had been. We knew everyone, we were part of the community, and I now had strong misgivings about the wisdom of my decision to move away.

Visitors came maybe once or twice, but after establishing exactly where we lived, and seeing the new house, the visits became less frequent. The weather was too hot, too cold, or too wet to come to what was perceived as such a distant place. It was also difficult to find, as it involved crossing a bridge over the small part of the river and the road map was less than clear. Friends and acquaintances had the notion, perhaps understandably, but mistakenly, that because I had a new life with another person, the friendship between us would change. Not wishing to be intrusive, quite sadly, in some instances, my friends became diffident around Sid and backed away. I recalled regretfully that when we lived in Wembley, few days went by without a welcome friend or neighbour calling in. No more Miss Pougnault dropping in after school. Elizabeth and John both had the notion that any journey so far south of the causeway required 'a cut lunch and a water bag.' Of course I still saw my friends, but not with the same casual and familiar frequency.

My vision of picnics by the stream never happened. We rarely sat by the stream. It was still, either fetid and muddy, or rapidly flowing and not a safe place. We never acquired a horse but we did have a donkey for a short time. Each time a shelter was built for him, he did not rest until he destroyed it. We would see him frantically tearing around the paddock with pieces of plastic, wood, or whatever else we had used to construct the shelter dangling from his mouth. His temper was ferocious and the kids were scared of him, afraid to go in the paddock because he chased them with clearly evil intentions. He had to go. I wondered how I ended up with a manic donkey.

My new husband and I lived like a reasonably compatible brother and sister. Each time we moved house, our sleeping arrangements changed. In our first home we shared a double bed. In the second house we had large single beds. The next house saw us move into separate bedrooms. Not quite realising how unusual the detached, non-sexual situation was, in an odd way I found it acceptable. It meant that my children were safe to come and find me whenever they needed to. Because of the lack of physical intimacy, there was no danger that I would ever be found by them in a situation that made them, or me, feel awkward or embarrassed. Naturally, if I had been in love with my husband, or he with me, I would have thought differently.

Sid had been made the manager of the Western Australian branch of a large Swedish insurance company, which meant frequent entertaining of overseas and eastern states business associates of the firm. I enjoyed entertaining and I basked, a little self-consciously, in the fulsome, complimentary remarks as the guests took their departure.

Sid started going on short holidays and weekends away alone. It was all quite casual. At the dinner table Sid, gazing at his plate, might say, mid-mouthful, 'I think I will take a run down south on Saturday, perhaps stay overnight, and return on Sunday.'

I would ask, 'Where will you stay?' In a vague, contemplative manner he would reply, 'I don't know really. I might just camp out in the car.' Because he had always lived alone I tried to understand that he wanted to go somewhere and be by himself for a while. I am sure that he found living with five other individuals quite overpowering.

The local doctor told me that the almost constant headaches that I was experiencing were undoubtedly migraine and he prescribed strong painkillers, which had no effect, and anti-depressants, which I did not take. There was not a pill in the world that could alter my existence. A little over a year passed, and possibly, for the first time, I allowed myself to consider the fact that my situation was not what I had expected. I did not understand life with Sid and found the variance in his day-to-day attitude difficult to understand. Sid sometimes withdrew from all around him, displaying unbelievable coldness and detachment. He would then act as if nothing untoward had happened, and suggest that we go somewhere nice for dinner, so I pushed negative thoughts away and went out to dinner.

It occurred to me that if we sold the house and moved back north of the river, closer to the familiar people and area that I missed; perhaps my health and emotions might repair. The last thing I wanted was for my children to realise how empty I found my life. I regretted that I had altered their lives irrevocably and I was too embarrassed to reveal to any of my friends that I was unhappy. So what did I do? *I told no one.* Eventually, though, I did approach Sid and I told him that I would like us to consider selling the house and moving. He proved most amenable to the idea, as he had previously been quite nomadic and had never stayed long in one place anyway. I did not know how to tell the children about the move because, although I sometimes did not succeed, I tried to maintain stability and the least amount of disruption to their lives, so I was hesitant to mention moving to them. Lynette, being the eldest and in high school, was a concern. I decided to sound her out and see her reaction. I sat on her bed with her one afternoon after school, 'Darling, you know that when a decision is made within a family, it for the benefit of us all, don't you?'

Her clear blue eyes widened and she gazed back at me apprehensively. I thought that she knew about moving and was not happy about it. Taking a deep breath, I ploughed ahead. 'Lynette, I haven't been well lately and I think it is partly because I don't like it here. It is too far away. We spend half our time on the highway getting to where we need to go. I am missing Wembley and I am quite lonely, not especially lonely for people, but lonely inside myself.' Finally, I said in a rush, 'So we might be selling this house and going back closer to where we were before.' Lynette looked surprised, and then relieved. 'That's okay. I don't mind moving. I thought you were going to put me into a boarding school.' We both fell about laughing with relief and I asked her how she could possibly have had such a notion, she replied, 'Sometimes when you are a bit annoyed, you say that, boarding school for a while would do you good, young lady.'

Glen and John seemed okay about the move, but later on though, they were to become less happy about being shunted around. Colleen, seemingly, would happily go wherever her Mummy went.

I found that, in Sid's and my less-than-perfect relationship, a common goal had a uniting effect. In that instance, it was selling the house and planning what type of home, and where to build that restored much of Sid's former good humour. The decision to sell was made easily, but actually selling was not so easy and it took over twelve months to find a buyer.

Sid was changing. His mostly kind, tolerant attitude towards the children started to slip. He seldom displayed temper or anger. His moods were more subtle, but inclined to be cold, and when anyone other than me entered a room, usually the kitchen, Sid often didn't respond to their greeting or look up at them. With a casually studied attitude, he would pick up the drink, food, or book in front of him and leave the room without speaking a word, leaving an open-mouthed, puzzled child wondering what they had done wrong. John later likened Sid's behaviour to a light being switched off abruptly whenever he entered a room.

When I asked Sid the reason for this cutting and unreasonable behaviour, he answered, 'I don't mind you around me, but at times I find the kids too intrusive, and they're *always* there. I wish it was just you and me more often.'

I opened my mouth to reply and had difficulty finding the words. Finally I said, 'We were a family of five happy and contented people when we met you. We welcomed you. You could have joined us and made six. But you will never, ever, divide us into two plus four.' He did not reply, and left the room. I wondered why he thought that anything that he had to offer me in our unusual alliance would ever be enough to compromise my relationship with my children. The blinding headaches continued to cause me agony and, accompanied by nausea and vision disturbance, they became increasingly frequent and would send me to bed for days at a time. Medication or meditation did not help. Migraine laid me out cold until it had run its cruel cycle. Desperately I sought to understand, and hopefully accept the enigma I found myself living with. I made an appointment and went to visit Dr Clarke. Recollections of the previous times that I had sat in this waiting room before, and after my four children were born edged into my mind. However, before I had time to get too introspective I found myself wrapped in a warm, motherly hug. The lady doing the hugging was Mrs Stockley, the nurse in the practice for many years and we knew each other well and talked on the phone sometimes.

I followed Dr Clarke into the surgery. I spoke to him, not as a patient but as to someone who had known me for a long time, someone who had supported me through the most joyous times and through the cruellest time of my life. Although I did mention the migraine headaches, what I really wanted to know was, why my marriage was so unusual, or was it so unusual at all?

He frowned and spoke very directly. 'You have allowed yourself to be placed in an untenable position. You do not have a marriage, you have an arrangement, but the terms of the arrangement were not put before you to accept or reject. The situation is wrong and you should get out of it as quickly as you can.' He went on to say, 'I feel angry that the other person in the picture got exactly what he wanted, an attractive wife and a ready-made family of delightful kids. Also, he has the accolades of the people thinking him a splendid fellow because he has taken on such a commitment.'

I listened, but I had mixed feelings. Sid may have acted selfishly, but at that time, I chose to believe that he, himself, was naïve, rather than calculating. Perhaps he thought that marriage and family life would chase away his demons. A person from a different, more normal background from my own would undoubtedly have reacted differently to Sid. I had no doubt from what he told me, that any women he met prior to me would have been very negative towards him. Therefore, he must have seen my children and me as a ray of light and a step towards what he saw as normality. It made me feel better though, just to hear Dr Clarke tell me that our marriage was unusual. It meant to me that if I felt angry or resentful at times, I had a right to feel that way.

A Welsh couple with four teenage children eventually bought our house. We bought a corner block of land in Trigg, two kilometres from West Coast Highway. It was close to the beach for the kids, close to schools and not nearly so far away from my familiar haunts.

We poured over plans, changing our minds several times over, although my mind did not change as often as the plans actually did. My specific requests and suggestions were frequently over-ridden and Sid argued endlessly with the designers. It proved to be a difficult time to be building a house. Bricklayers were at a premium and could be selective about their choice of work. We rented a house close to our block for twelve months, thinking that it would be ample time for our home to be completed. The twelve months came and went. The lease expired on the rental house and the owners wanted the place back. We had to find another rental property because, at that stage, the completion of our house was nothing more than a distant dream. I drove hundreds of kilometres over many months to keep the children at one school rather than move them mid-term.

We were gaining something of a reputation amongst friends and acquaintances for the number of times we moved house over the years. John Brett jokingly assured Sid, one day, 'Wherever you move to, do not worry, we will hunt you down and find you again.' In response, Sid smiled a little uncertainly.

The imposing, red-brick house was finally ready for us to move into and none of us was yet so jaded from moving around that we did not find the well-designed, new house exciting. There was much work to do to establish a garden. Glen and John were strong twelve and ten year old boys and, because they were accustomed to helping and willingly doing things for me, Sid sometimes forgot that although strong, they were still only young boys and he expected far more than was reasonable of them. He looked on, overseeing, as they moved heavy limestone rocks and planted lawn and shrubs. The boys soon became fed up and I was less than impressed to see my sons used so badly. They had a friend, Nathan, who lived nearby, and one day I suggested to Sid. 'The boys are going to Nathan's this weekend. There is still a lot to do in the garden, but it is taking so long to get anywhere, and because your health stops you from doing heavy work, I think we need to look for a local handyman to help.'

Looking a little disappointed at the loss of his hard workers, Sid sighed, 'Oh! All right then.'

There were some all right times, though. Like the evening when Sid came in from work and announced with a bit of a flourish, 'The Swedes have invited all of the State Managers and their wives to Sydney for a week. It's going to be a gala occasion.' He went on with enthusiasm, 'There will be business meetings, of course, but also celebrations to mark their successful venture into the Australian market.'

I had never been to Sydney, I had never been out of the state and so before I became too dazzled by the prospect, I asked Sid, 'Are you sure that wives are invited as well?'

'Yes! Yes, of course I am sure,' he replied as he poured himself a glass of wine.

I had not anticipated fear of being on a plane and I was not afraid when sitting comfortably in my seat, but I became panicked at the thought of closing the door, when midway through our flight, I went to enter the tiny toilet. People were standing around, waiting their turn, and I let them go ahead of me. A flight attendant looked at me quizzically and asked if I was okay. I told her I was afraid to close the door.

'No worries' she said brightly. 'You go in, and I'll hold the door from the outside for you.'

Perhaps flight attendants saw many people like me.

I returned to my seat and as I squeezed past Sid, he asked, 'Where on earth did you get to?'

Sydney held me enchanted. And has done so ever since. Our hotel looked directly towards the Sydney Harbour Bridge and each evening when we returned, feeling as if I could reach out and touch it, I stood and gazed at the bridge, fascinated by its magnificence. With the other visiting wives, some Swedish and some Australian, I spent time exploring The Rocks area, which lay in the shadow of the Harbour Bridge. The area held a wondrous fascination for me and I took every opportunity to visit and wander along the cobbled stone laneways, alone, or with the others. Restored warehouses used in the 1850s by traders and whalers brought the past close. I imagined rough, sea-faring men exuding the pungent smell of raw liquor, tunelessly bellowing *Yo Ho Ho and a bottle of rum*, while they lolled in the alleys. I stood on the steps of the magnificent Opera House, on Bennelong Point, and I remembered the recent bad feeling and vilification displayed by people of little vision directed towards Joen Utzon, the architect responsible for the design.

From Sydney we travelled to New Zealand. To Sid, New Zealand was home in a way that England never had been and he had yearned for some time to go back there on a holiday.

We travelled around for a total of four weeks – far too long for me to be away from my children. In fact, the idea of going to New Zealand never attracted me. However, a sense of fairness prompted me to realise that after the wonderful time I had enjoyed in Sydney, I probably owed it to Sid to continue the holiday and spend time with him in New Zealand. For some reason, I sensed resentment and I did not hit it off with Sid's New Zealand acquaintances, with whom we spent more time than I was comfortable with. Maybe they thought I had deprived the world of an eligible bachelor and saddled him with four kids.

My children and I had not been apart before and this had been for such a long time. I missed them and, more importantly, worried that they might be missing me. When we returned, I went straight to pick up my family from their various locations; Glen met me with a complicated story about knocking himself out. Grandpop had tied a rock to a fishing line while teaching him how to cast. The rod apparently spun around, and the rock hit Glen in the head. John had had a good time with his cousins in spite of somehow managing to swallow a goldfish. They all had missed me but I did not get the feeling that they had been unhappy. Sid had no idea how much I had missed the children, and when he told friends about the wonderful time that *he thought that I'd had*, I nodded in agreement, because Sydney had been wonderful.

Chapter 19

No Rose Garden

Anne Pougnault was then teaching at a different school, however we had remained friends and I met her for coffee late one afternoon at a nearby shopping centre. During our conversation, Anne mentioned to me that her mother, Jessie, ran a program on behalf of the Cerebral Palsy Association and they needed volunteers, people who were able to give some time helping with the collection and handling of donations.

The association welcomed my offer of voluntary help and, when I later applied for a paid position to work as a fundraiser and entrant coordinator for the Cerebral Palsy Association's Miss Australia Quest, Jessie enthusiastically supported my application. I appreciated her confidence in me but did not expect my application to be successful. For some years, I had only worked at short-term jobs to earn extra money for birthday and Christmas presents. I once even worked in a fruit shop for about six weeks, where the fresh, earthy smell of fruit and vegetables reminded me of long ago days in Kalgoorlie. I enjoyed that job and each time I weighed tomatoes or apples to the exact ounce at my first attempt, my feeling of triumph knew no bounds.

A phone call came from the Cerebral Palsy Association a few days after I posted my application and a woman's pleasant voice invited me to attend an interview the following morning. By the time I left the majestic old Mount Lawley house – one of many buildings used by the association – I was ready to begin work the following week.

Soon I knew most of the residents by name and watched their tenacity with admiration as they hauled themselves from place to place. They sometimes ate their meals in a most untidy fashion, but took no assistance if they could manage alone. The afflicted adults saddened me because many of them, although unable to function physically, were mentally unimpaired and had full realisation that this was their life and that it was not going to change. Remarkably, though, few were sad or moody – frustrated, maybe, and angry sometimes, but usually only for a brief time. A couple of the young men, aged in their twenties, were like twenty year-olds everywhere. They were cheeky and flirtatious, practically throwing themselves out of their wheel chairs, convulsing with laughter as they told the most outrageous jokes, often about people with afflictions. I could laugh with them at their jokes, but never felt comfortable repeating them to other people. I embraced the cause of cerebral-palsied people and, in doing so I opened myself to friendships and laughter with some sadness and some definitely wild and unusual happenings. It was a challenge and I had stepped a long way out of my comfort zone.

No longer did I hide under a red-checked coat.

To find a more diverse collection of women working for a common cause would be difficult. Some were the life and soul of the party. They relished the glamour of being associated with a beauty, albeit a fundraising, quest. There were a couple of school ma'am types who did a marvellous job convincing young girls that they had a good life and owed it to their lucky stars that they were healthy, therefore, they should show their appreciation of their good life and get off their backsides and work for a cause such as ours. It was a heavy-handed approach but some girls responded to that. Some of my co-workers were nightclub and event attendees. They knew all the movers, shakers and moneyed people around town. All had their place in appealing to different sections of the community to become quest entrants and raise money. It was essentially selling, selling the idea of raising funds in return for rewards and prestige. The quest had its critics, particularly people who believed that society should look after the handicapped without expecting reward. However, over nearly fifty years, the quest demonstrated that it worked well, because incentive and recognition did inspire people to raise money.

Filled with optimism I drove along to my first assignment, surveying the scenery and the livestock as I passed from Perth through all the country towns that make up the South West region. Like that of my co-workers in the other districts of the state, my task was to stop at every town, large and small, where I was to seek the assistance of local business people who, generally, knew that I was coming. We hoped that they would have suggestions as to who might be a suitable entrant. Mostly we were welcomed and treated courteously, but sometimes one walked unsuspectingly into a hornet's nest, especially if visiting a particular town for the first time and not being aware of the local politics. *Our girl didn't win last year.* Although I drove hundreds of kilometres, my first trip to the country started out particularly unpromisingly. Too nervous to stop, I kept driving and, vowing to myself as I drove through each town that I would definitely stop at the next one. I ended up that first day in Augusta – some four hundred kilometres from Perth – without stopping once on the way.

I booked in and stayed overnight at the local motel, hoping that the next day I would have more courage. I tossed and wriggled restlessly throughout the long night and as I lay awake, agitated, I decided that in the morning I would drive straight back to Perth, and resign.

Finally, the sun lightened the room and I heard birds chirping in the bottlebrush shrubs surrounding the car park. Nearby truck drivers revved and roared their motors before moving on. The generator outside the window that had run noisily all night shuddered violently and slowly stopped.

I finished breakfast and waited at the deserted reception desk to pay the account. As I waited, I found myself thinking that I had spent my honeymoon, a lifetime ago, in a similar type of coastal establishment.

The motel manager appeared from the dining room, attempting to restrain a frenzied puppy, while carefully holding his full coffee mug aloft. 'Sorry love. Just grabbing a bite before I get busy. Where are you headed? Are you working, or taking a break away from the kids?'

With all the aplomb I could muster, I told him that I represented the Miss Australia Quest.

'Oh, we often have a girl in that. Go up to the school and talk to the secretary. She's a good sort, and she'll help you.'

Not wanting to return to Perth, defeated, now that daylight had arrived, I set off for the school. The secretary was indeed 'a good sort'. Affable and helpful, she recommended several girls, one of whom was intrigued with the idea of joining the quest. Buoyed with confidence I stopped at each town on the return trip and the next day sailed back triumphantly into the office waving a sheaf of completed entry forms.

In those pre-satellite G.P.S. days, the way we travelled around – women alone, miles from anywhere, perhaps lost at night, trying to find a farm, or a hall where a function was to be held – was sometimes raised as a negative aspect of our job by the staff. But conversely, the trip from the country for the entrants provided them with even more challenges when the winners from city and country districts moved into Perth's Sheraton Hotel for the final selection process. The judging of the quest entrants was an event fraught with occasional drama and difficulty. The week included store appearances by the entrants to promote the major sponsors. There were also formal cocktail parties and dinners. I accompanied the entrants when they met the state Premier, the state sponsors and other leading business and social identities. It was a hectic time for the young women and some enjoyed the fuss, while others were clearly uneasy with the crowds and social duties and would not have minded going home.

I met dignitaries and, occasionally, some not-so-dignified people in my quaintly-worded role as 'chaperone'. Every six years a different state hosted the national judging to choose Miss Australia. What a production!

One morning I found myself scampering breathlessly down London Court and along St George's Terrace, beside a burly, gun-carrying detective. We were going to collect the Miss Australia crown from the vault at the bank that provided the crown and sponsored the Quest. The following day, the airport waiting area was abuzz as we arrived *en masse* to await the arrival of the State Finalists and Charity Queens from the other states and territories. Visitors to the airport crowded around, eager to see who was arriving and what was happening. Soon the girls descended upon us amid a flurry of colour and an aromatic invasion of flowery perfumes. Laughter and chattering resonated through the terminal as the girls met officials and each other and cameras flashed. We then tumbled into the new vehicles provided by the major sponsor and our motorcade, led by a police escort of impressive, slow-moving motorcycles driven by off-duty, police officers, flowed importantly on to the highway. Regardless of whether the finalists were impressed, or not, as cars slowed down to make way for us, *I felt positively regal.*

Sid occasionally accompanied me to various dinners and fundraising events. He never minded me travelling to the country alone, nor moving into the hotel at judging time. Sid did not mind what I did. We were pleasant and courteous and everything in his world was just peachy. He trusted me implicitly, with good reason. I enjoyed the social life associated with my job and I had a good time. I liked the prestige and I met some outstanding people, male and female, but wanted no other involvement, because, deep inside, I was still the little girl who did not want to be bad. Besides, I was also afraid that any change might take me to a worse, even less comfortable place, because long ago I learned that change for me was not necessarily auspicious.

Sid took the boys fishing sometimes, driving them to the coast, but he did not fish with them. I discovered that when the boys came home from a trip to Mandurah. They arrived upset and pale, and they both went straight to their bedrooms. I followed them down the passage and said, 'What's the matter, John?'

Angrily, John answered, 'Mum, he left us all night on the jetty by ourselves.'

Sitting on John's bed with both boys, I listened with anger rising as they told me that they had stayed alone on the freezing cold, dark and deserted Mandurah jetty until after three o'clock in the morning. They recounted how John became sick, shivering uncontrollably with cold and fright and of Glen taking off his outer clothing to try to keep him warm. They were not dressed warmly. They had been taken there about six o'clock and were to be picked up at about eight o'clock. Sid had returned a little before eight, but when they asked to stay a bit longer, he did not insist that they leave with him then. Instead, he agreed, apparently quite cheerfully, to come back in a while. He returned in the early hours of the morning. Their father had drowned. How could Sid be so foolish? The thought of my sons alone and scared, late at night, in a deserted, uninhabited place, surrounded by deep water, dealt one of the many increasing blows to my relationship with Sid and threatened any friendship we might have. I confronted him angrily and told him what I thought of such unthinking, irresponsible behaviour towards my two young sons. He agreed that what the boys told me was correct, beyond that I don't remember any other response from him. I suspect he had gone to sleep, or else he simply forgot about them. He probably felt bad about it, and meant the boys no harm. He was simply being himself. *That was the last fishing trip.*

Lynette had put her excellent school results to good use and was working at the National Bank, in St Georges Terrace.

Around that time, Lynette's childhood friend Yvonne was about sixteen when she and her cousin disappeared from a local suburban hotel one Sunday afternoon. Many of the kids went to listen to the popular band of the day and it seemed not too many questions about their age were asked. Shockingly, neither Yvonne nor her cousin were seen, or, to my knowledge, heard of again. I often thought of Yvonne and when I did, I wished that we, my daughter, who played and went to school with Yvonne, and I, knew what had happened to our freckle-faced little neighbour from all those years ago.

Both boys left school at a young age. Neither of them liked, or had ever enjoyed school, so when the time came, I agreed to them leaving, but only if they secured a job, ideally an apprenticeship. They both towered over me, causing me to look upwards to meet their eyes and as they each had a healthy dose of determination, I felt it better for them to use those attributes working and being productive, rather than remain in the classroom, idle and bored, distracting and annoying teachers, and perhaps ending up in trouble.

With both father and grandfather as butchers, the boys' connections within the meat industry provided opportunities for both of them. The work was hard and the hours long. Butchering was an extremely arduous trade requiring strength and stamina. Glen and John later gave up their trades as butchers and moved to other fields of work, but as their Nana and Grandpop frequently used to say, 'At least they'll have a trade to fall back on.'

Jack Bohling, aged seventy one, passed away in 1977. Sadly, Glen was in the shed with his Grandpop when Jack suffered a stroke, which resulted in his death a week later. How sad for my son that once again, at such a young age, he was so close to a tragedy involving a loved family member.

Country travel with my job was taking me away from Colleen too often. Lynette had accepted a transfer with the bank to Port Hedland and, although Colleen said little, I knew that she missed her big sister. I became increasingly concerned that Colleen might feel lonely, or insecure, without Lynette, when I was not around. After some thought, I decided that I needed to be home and I left the quest for a time. I enjoyed fashion and knew that I had some flair when it came to buying and selling. After discussing the practicalities of such a move with Sid, I opened a boutique in Grantham Street in Wembley, which I ran successfully for three years, but Sid was getting restless for change. Sid sang my praises long and loud regarding my business acumen, but he also treated me like a child and questioned all my decisions.

John came to the dinner table one evening and remarked that our nearby neighbour was selling his house. After dinner, Sid went to his room and emerged some hours later with facts and figures set out explaining the benefits of selling *our* house, *and the boutique*. Like an edict from the Pope, the decision was made.

Moving and relocating again was the last thing that I wanted. However, Sid felt that as he had agreed to leave Kelmscott to suit me, I should see his point of view this time.

I live with the knowledge that I was wrong and, at that time, I did fail my family. They were not happy about all the moving around, but they were my children and I felt that as long as we were together that was what mattered most. I am indeed fortunate that their resentment of the situation did not become resentment towards me. I allowed myself to be coerced into accepting decisions that should have involved discussion with my children, instead of presenting the decision as *a fait accompli*. I never stood firm and insisted, 'No, we are not moving again.'

Although the standard of the houses remained high, each time we moved there was one less bedroom. I eventually concluded that Sid meant one less bedroom was designed to ensure one less person lived under our roof. We had moved house, and now my business was about to go too. A welcome distraction came via Elizabeth. She was planning to go to England for a lengthy holiday, and needed someone to do her job temporarily during her absence and she asked me if I would fill in for her. Elizabeth worked for Dr Tom Dadour, a member of the Federal Parliament who was also a well-known general practitioner in Subiaco. I did not have the expertise under normal circumstances to be employed as a parliamentary secretary, but Elizabeth's boss was a man that I knew and it seemed that he preferred trustworthiness and confidentiality to skill in the short term. He asked me if I took shorthand and I told him that I did not, but he suggested that if he spoke slowly, and I wrote quickly, we might get by. We did get by quite well.

Around that time, Glen told me he wanted to go to Port Hedland to where Lynette was living. With a frozen, rock solid lump in the region of my heart, I said good bye to him. We went to a coffee shop to have lunch before he set off alone on the long, solitary drive up north. My heart was too full to say a lot as I attempted to eat a toasted sandwich. He was very quiet, too, and when we could delay no longer, he got into his car and drove swiftly away. Although waving good-bye to any of my family made me fearful, I waved until he was out of sight.

Many times, I thought of leaving Sid, because I felt that he had driven Glen away and maybe Lynette, too. I was despondent, and soon after Glen left, when Sid suggested going somewhere nice for dinner, I yelled at him. 'You can afford to be magnanimous now that two of my children have gone.' That was the worst time in our marriage. I began living the *'don't tell anyone*' scene again. Make believe that selling the shop is a good business move. Act as happy and successful and, of course, happily married. I was not happy and two of my children were far away.

Overpowered and defeated, I remembered how as a child I waited to tell my mother how badly Stella treated me, certain that once I told her she would take me away and everything would be all right. Waiting to tell someone how I felt never worked for me before and it was not going to work then. The anxieties that had been part of my life escalated to what the doctor told me were serious panic attacks. Panic attacks were an apt description, as the inability to breathe had me gasping and afraid, terrified of fainting as black spots leapt and merged to a foggy mass before my eyes.

One day as we sat in the front garden, I told Sid that I really needed to talk about the problems within our marriage. Calm and unruffled, he replied, 'I don't have a problem with our marriage, dear. If you have a problem, you must deal with it as you see fit. You must understand that I am an emotional cripple. I don't mean to be cold and hurtful. It is just the way I am,' he continued. I wondered if his manner was what was called 'passive aggressive' because of his deliberately acting calm and reasonable, as if his situation was quite acceptable and any problems were entirely due to the misconceived view of the other person.

Angrily, I replied, 'You say you are an emotional cripple. If you were physically crippled, would you expect me to get in a wheel chair and ride around with you? Because that's what is happening, we are all leading our lives in an unsatisfactory manner to accommodate your idiosyncrasies.'

The lyrics of a popular song drifted from the radio of a passing vehicle. I heard Loretta Lynn's country twang. *I beg your pardon. I never promised you a rose garden.*

Well, lady, I thought. I *never* expected a rose garden.

Usually after any dispute, I was immediately sorry and forgiving towards Sid. However, on this occasion I could only think of my young son and of how desperately I wanted him home.

My outburst might have shocked him and maybe I hurt his feelings. I never knew, because he did the thing that astrologers say is typical of people born under the sign of the Crab. He disappeared into his shell and remained there for a good long time.

I lived with a compulsive changer. Nothing was permanent. Not houses, not furniture, nothing was special, or worth keeping. Always, he always sought change. The minute property values rose, no matter how settled we all were, he swung into the now familiar mode of what we could buy or build if we capitalised and sold right then.

Sid walked into the kitchen one day and started talking, 'I think this house has been a mistake. Everything is going wrong. How do you feel about selling it? We will start afresh, and build something new, and I promise that I will listen and involve you more this time.'

As he spoke two particular instances sprang to mind about things that had gone *very* wrong. The first involved Sid asking me to look for the floor covering for the kitchen.

'It's your kitchen, I'll leave the choice entirely up to you,' Sid had said benevolently. He had added, 'Besides, I'm too busy at the moment to deal with it.'

I chose three types of floor covering, three different prices, and patterns. Then I left to go down south with Colleen to spend three days in an old beach cottage, which a friend had loaned us. On the second morning of our stay, I heard the telephone inside the cottage ringing insistently. Colleen dashed inside, and hastily picked up the receiver, and handed it straight to me.

I heard Sid's voice, saying happily, 'I've got the floor covering. It will be laid first thing in the morning, all nice and ready for you when you come home.' I asked him which one he had chosen. Sid hesitated for a moment, cleared his throat, and said, 'Well actually, dear, none of the ones that you mentioned. I found one you must have overlooked. I know you will like it.'

I hadn't overlooked anything! Colleen and I had walked the streets of Perth, and the suburbs, looking for something different, but the floor covering chosen by Sid had been bought and cut to our kitchen's measurements, and was about to be laid before I even got home. No words came from me and I replaced the receiver. Colleen muttered something that I didn't quite hear.

Together, Sid and I had chosen the bench tops and cupboards for the kitchen. The cupboards were to be rich, dark blue, highlighted with deep cream handles and surrounding trim. I hurried home from work on the day the builders finally left, and flew eagerly through the house to see my lovely new kitchen. Transfixed, I gazed in horror at the brilliant, harsh, electric blue benches and cupboards. They had done the whole kitchen in the wrong colour! Not knowing what to do in the face of such a catastrophic mistake I phoned Sid's office. His brisk, business voice answered. I took a deep breath, 'You will need to talk to the cabinet maker, I practically yelled at him. The kitchen cupboards are the wrong colour. They're nothing like the colour we chose.' Unstoppable now, I rushed on, 'All this time waiting, and it looks ghastly.'

Sid said he was about to leave the office, and would be home shortly. I went to replace the receiver, when I heard his voice still talking. I put the phone back to my ear in time to hear him say, 'Exactly what colour are the benches?' I began going on again about the hideous mistake, when Sid interrupted, 'Well, come to think of it, I do remember suggesting to the tradesman that perhaps the dark blue was a bit heavy, and maybe we could lighten the shade up a bit. But there must be a mistake, because I know you would like the shade I picked out, dear, it's really nice. I'll see you as soon as I get home.'

I didn't need to wait for him to come home. I knew that the colour that I had to live with was *his* preference.

The house was a miserable mess and I felt my life was rapidly turning into a mess with it. Whatever camaraderie Sid and I had ever shared was now almost non-existent. I found it difficult to sit across the table from him, so I took to doing what he had done for so many years. I removed myself mentally and physically from his presence as often as I could. The dreams of my childhood taunted me. I stayed awake all night reading, and sometimes Sid would look in thinking that I had gone to sleep and left my light on. Reading then, as in my childhood, was my salvation. I loved riveting mysteries, which of course, kept me awake. However, soothing, positive words or beautiful scenes, impacted peacefully on my spirit in a way no sleeping pill ever could.

I couldn't reconcile the person that Sid had become with the one who had taken my children out when they were younger, and I felt that if he did not have a loving relationship towards my children, he had a least should have a friendly, supportive roll towards them. My son leaving home weighed heavily on my conscience. I should have done more to protect him. Glen, without me realising it, had been subtly removed.

Wherever I had lived, I always found comfort in the garden. My Buddha statue sat, benign and serene, in his home under the frangipani tree. His gentle look calmed me. I reflected that knowing *him* as a child might have changed my life considerably. I bent to pick up my book and go inside. Gingerly I eased my back up from the low garden chair and as I straightened, John came around the corner of the garage and I remembered that it was his half-day off.

'How's it going, Mum?' he asked, as he dropped his workbag on to the lawn.

He came over to kiss me hello and, and as he put his arm around me, I clung to his strong, comforting warmth, and prayed for life to make redress and be good to my gentle, respectful son.

'John, I'm worried about Glen. I miss him. We all miss him. Glen thought that Sid was his friend, and I don't know what went wrong.' With the same steady, far-seeing gaze, that John had from the time he was born, he very patiently said, 'Mum, Sid is a man who can tolerate kittens and puppies when they are tiny, but when they grow up into cats and dogs, he gives them away.'

What a simple, surprisingly accurate analogy from such a young person. I lowered myself back into the chair and sat a while longer in the sunshine with my son before he left to go the nearby stables to tend to Slade, his much-loved horse. John had been active in the Perth Pony Club since he was fourteen. The discipline and formality of the show ring suited both the boy and the horse and together they proudly collected their prize ribbons.

John had recently experienced loss and sadness. His boss, Bill Green, had been a long-time friend of the Bohling family. He was good to John, and taught him the trade of butchering with a mixture of old fashioned discipline and grandfatherly good humour and John held him in particularly high esteem. One day, Mr Green had gone into the ceiling above the shop premises to check the electrical wiring. A considerable time elapsed, and when John called, and no answer was forthcoming, he went up the ladder into the cramped ceiling space. In the dark, enclosed space, John saw that his boss had collapsed. John held his kindly mentor in his arms as he passed away. Mr Green had suffered a brain aneurism. John remained quiet and withdrawn for a long time.

Sid frequently went away on short trips, and these increased at that time as he padlocked himself tightly into his protective shell. Meanwhile, I was not exactly jumping for joy myself.

I began to ponder Sid's suggestion of moving and starting again. Maybe a new house would start us off afresh, just to get back to being friendly. Not feeling anger and spite whenever I looked at him would be an improvement, I thought.

A corner block of land, which backed on to a tree-lined well-kept park, in the small older suburb of Gwelup, immediately drew me. Close to the city, the district had an unusual rural atmosphere with market gardens dotted here and there. Down the road from us a picturesque school stood small and safe looking, surrounded by verdant gardens and tall trees. I no longer had children at school, but I still liked the look of it.

Glen had been back in Perth for some time and was renting a quaint cottage attached to a market garden. The house was situated, story-book-like, in the centre of a cabbage patch that stretched from the front door around to back door and across to the fence line. However, the rent was nominal and, as Glen was only about five minutes away from us, he did not find the surrounding cabbages that bad.

Colleen worked nearby as a pharmacy assistant and I had returned to the Miss Australia Quest, working full time, while Lynette had returned to Perth. I loved having her close by. After living, and working in Port Hedland for a few years and, for no specific reason, Lynette decided that she wanted to spread her wings and enjoy city life again. Lynette stayed with us for a short time and then moved to an apartment in Subiaco. We spent a great deal of time together, and she and Colleen accompanied me to Miss Australia Quest functions and, occasionally, we went to the theatre, or out for dinner. It was a delightful time.

I had maintained, throughout my story that I had never mentioned to a soul that I had been in The Home of the Good Shepherd. That was not entirely correct. I did tell Lynette. However, not in any detail, nor did I name the place. It was during her stay in Perth, and we were out together for dinner one evening. We were so relaxed and contented in each other's company that talking came easily, and the need to reveal the facts of *me*, never far from the surface, swept over me. I felt wonderfully close to my daughter and it was as we sipped our wine, and tucked into pasta *marinara*, that that feeling of dishonesty by hiding my entire childhood behind a veil of secrecy consumed me. I did not like being secretive, but the reasons for my silence was twofold: firstly, shame and fear and, secondly, as my family grew, I never wanted to tell them anything that might upset them. I gazed around at the other diners and saw young couples, some accompanied by those who appeared to be family and friends. One or two older men ate alone and they looked comfortable, as if they dined there regularly, perhaps in preference to their own kitchen, and a tin of soup.

I took a gulp of wine and heard myself saying, 'Lynette, there are things about me that nobody knows. I have said that I was brought up in a boarding school, which is true, up to a point. I did go to St Brigid's day school, but I spent only a short time at the boarding school. Where I did spend a long time, however, was in a place so awful that I have always kept it secret, but I didn't want to die without anyone knowing, because it was part of my life. Not, of course,' I hastily added, 'that I am thinking of dying any time soon.'

A condensed version of my time in The Home of the Good Shepherd followed. I told Lynette that I had to work hard day after day, even though I was only young and should have been at school. I may have added more detail, I could not recall. I had no idea what reaction I expected from my daughter, but unintentionally, I almost upset a pleasant dinner. Momentarily tears shone in her eyes. I sat quietly and, when Lynette recovered from her dismay, we had another glass of wine and continued to enjoy the evening. We never discussed the subject again. It remained unspoken knowledge between us but, thereafter, she never let me help her by doing her ironing.

Lynette returned to Port Hedland to run her own travel agency. I clung to her on the day that she left, remembering the grief that I experienced the first time she went away and I dreaded the thought of the emptiness ahead.

As she turned from me to pick up her bag, she looked into my eyes and said, 'Three kilometres, or three thousand, distance will never divide us. We are closer than many mothers and daughters who live around the corner from each other.' My brain knew that was right, but I had some difficulty convincing my heart.

I spent ten years at the Cerebral Palsy Association as a fundraiser and promoter of the Miss Australia Quest. I embraced the cause of cerebral-palsied people and, in doing so, I opened myself to friendships and laughter with some sadness and some definitely wild and unusual happenings. It was a challenge and I had stepped a long way out of my comfort zone. However, because I was respected, I learned to expect respect and not regard myself unworthy of attention.

Nevertheless, nothing lasted forever and the winds of social change were gathering. I appreciated having had such a rewarding time with the organization and to having a treasure trove of memories to keep and look back on.

I remembered Dame Leonie Kramer, who was a national finals judge in Perth in 1979, asking me if I enjoyed my job, and then listening attentively and with interest to my reply.

She heard about how I learned a lot about roses from a kind and friendly Premier John Tonkin, whose own rose garden, in East Fremantle, was renowned for its splendour. And about how I would never forget the night of high drama and the need for secrecy as plain-clothed police walked the corridors, so as not to create a panic, when the quest finals at the Sheraton were placed in jeopardy because of a rumour of a bomb threat. The memories flooded back to me years later. Danny La Rue, the famous English female impersonator, happened to be in Perth at the time of the national judging and the Miss Australia Quest secured him to perform at their television presentation. I stood beside him, chatting back stage at the Perth Concert Hall as he awaited his cue call. I was surprised at how extremely pumped up and nervous he appeared to be. He paced restlessly, perspiring profusely under the heavy make-up. Tightly corseted, he wore a spectacular gown and a lavishly-styled, blonde wig. I thought I had misheard when he turned to me, and asked breathily, 'Darling, come over here. How do I look? Do I look all right?' Before I had time to respond, he rapidly moved away from me with little running steps and dashed across to the centre of the stage. *He was on.* He had heard the cue. I had not. On another occasion, John Farnham, here for one of our presentations, turned around after a rehearsal and asked us how *we* thought the rehearsal had gone. Then there was Barry Crocker, a consummate gentleman, wistfully seeking out anyone who would bring him cappuccino at regular intervals. And a young Richard Wilkins hosted a finals evening at the newly opened Lord Forrest Hotel, in Bunbury.

Yes, I had enjoyed my job, Dame Leonie.

Early one warm morning, I moeched sleepily into the kitchen and was startled to see my youngest daughter, just out of the shower, with her hair wrapped up in a snowy white towel, sitting at the table. She looked so young, about twelve years old. How could she be 19 already? I switched the electric kettle on, 'Hello, what are you doing up so early? It is very humid. Couldn't you sleep?' Astonishment swept over me when she told me that she and her equally young boyfriend wanted to get married. One thing that I was not expecting to hear when I awoke that day was that my baby wanted to get married. My surprise was countered by her determination that this was what both she and her boyfriend wanted. So we planned a beautiful church wedding for a beautiful girl. Her simple chiffon and lace dress perfectly reflected her youth and vulnerability. Flowers entwined wreath-like around her long, blonde, curly hair. Treasured old, and a sprinkling of new, friends celebrated with us.

Wine flowed, and quietly and briefly, my tears did too *There was someone important absent from our daughter's wedding day. Her father would have been so proud to know her.*

It seemed that suddenly, in the twinkling of an eye, I became Nana Faye. Not Grandma, nor Granny, or Nana. I did not wish to lose my identity again!

My first grandchild arrived, small and exquisite. Her tiny fingers wrapped around mine and, as she gazed steadily into my eyes she moved into my heart forever. The sublime feeling of being related to my granddaughter let me know that no matter how many crushing things happen in a lifetime, there remained beauty and many glorious gifts. I skipped away from the office at any opportunity and dashed out to spend time with Michelle Faye. She shared my name. What an honour! And Colleen did not even know the importance of that to me.

Lynette had arrived from Port Hedland to prepare for *her* wedding, and my elegant, wonderful Libran girl planned everything to perfection. She was so beautiful on her wedding day. The sun shone brilliantly, belying the coldness of the wind. Sid was in gracious and hospitable mode, dispensing drinks and making small talk as family and friends gathered expectantly in our flower filled lounge room.

When my family were laughing and happy, and enjoying themselves, easy and relaxed together was the time I loved best. With my heart filled with memories, I walked forward to kiss my daughter as she emerged from the limousine that brought her to our home. A gown of exquisite Chantilly Lace draped itself elegantly over her slight figure. She wore delicate flowers in her fair hair and carried red roses. How serene and beautiful she was on that day, when she married Ron Stone, who stood, handsome, stylish and proud, at her side. Warmth enfolded me, and a distant voice whispered. *Don't be sad, Faye. Be proud of our beautiful treasure.*

Change was looming, but for the moment, things were amenable. Sid had found a level within the family that suited him – pleasant, but detached and cool. He still occasionally accompanied me to a Quest function, but his preference was for just the two of us to go out to dinner, or better still go somewhere by himself. He often went away alone and he went to concerts and recitals. Sometimes, on a whim, I went alone to a film or a show that I particularly wanted to see. Once seated inside the venue, even the barn like Perth Entertainment Centre, hearing the wonderful music from Aker Bilk, and seeing the extraordinary dancing of the Alvin Ailey dance company, or seeing Liza Minnelli in concert, I quickly overcame the embarrassing feeling that perhaps to onlookers I appeared as a lonely, isolated individual. I treasured those experiences, better seen alone than not seen at all. All this calm detachment was working well until the day Sid told me that he was going to retire in six months, and set up a consultancy business, working from home.

Just like that, no discussion, no warning, nothing. Speechless, on that occasion I was the one to leave the room abruptly. I had thought we were on a steady track and I had not visualised any changes in the immediate future.

Some changes were joyful and good though. I had a second granddaughter to treasure, a most beautiful child, with deep, sapphire-blue eyes. Clare Sharon arrived with her own parcel of love. Not for anyone else to share, just for her and me.

I had left the office early one afternoon. I needed time to prepare dinner for the family and get myself ready before I left to attend a fund raising concert that evening. I parked my car in the garage and jumped out fumbling frantically for my keys as I heard the phone jangling insistently inside. Thinking that the office was chasing me for something, I hastily seized the receiver from its stand. Sid's voice came happily through the phone line. 'I've been trying to find you for ages. Guess what! The firm is sending me to England for three weeks to chase up some ideas. I'm to leave at the end of next week.' Sid had only been back to England twice since leaving about thirty years previously, so he was understandably delighted when the opportunity to return unexpectedly presented itself. He vaguely mentioned me going too, but with barely a week's notice, and with the final Quest judging coming up, it was not possible.

At that time too, Elizabeth had been ill for some weeks. She was not a robust person, as she suffered from a congenital heart complaint that had caused the death at an early age of other members of her family. I decided to take flowers to her before leaving Perth to attend a fund raising function in Kellerberrin with the reigning Miss Western Australia, Lesley Cock.

Elizabeth looked so fragile, and I found myself saying, 'I love you, you know, and I appreciate your goodness and understanding towards me, Elizabeth.'

Then that warm, but extremely reserved woman, not at all given to flowery utterances said, 'I know, and I love you too.'

Just as a mother or a sister might, she forgave my faults and loved me anyway. Soon I had to leave, because time was pressing for me. I stood to take my leave and I repeated back to her something that she had said to me so often in the past. 'Never mind. It will soon be spring.'

The town's entrant and her committee welcomed us. They were thrilled to have Miss Western Australia complete with robes, crown, and sceptre in their town for a function. A popular rock band of the time had been hired at massive expense for the evening. I quailed inwardly when the fund-raising committee told me of the cost as I could not see how they could possibly cover expenses, or make money out of the evening. However, I had not allowed for the popularity of the band or for the lack of opportunity for the younger folk in country towns to see such a show. They came from hundreds of kilometres away. The screaming band rocked on into the night and, as my head throbbed with the vibration, I pondered the strange situations that my job sometimes placed me in. A woman from the committee stood in front of me, shouting over the din. Unable to make herself heard she beckoned me outside.

'Someone from your office rang our number and left a message for you to ring Katherine as soon as you are able.' The band continued to scream in the background. The cool, evening air brushed my face and lifted my hair back. My heart was breaking. I only knew one Katherine ... she was Elizabeth's daughter. She would only call me late at night when I was in the middle of nowhere for one reason.

I went with the woman to her house to use the phone. Katherine's sad little voice echoed hollowly down the phone line. 'Faye, Mummy's dead.'

It was August the 24, 1985, twenty eight years after that first firm hand shake and invitation to morning tea. I walked away from the phone, and returned outside to the cool air. I thought of Elizabeth, and I recalled how she had phoned me every year on the first day of June. It seemed just a casual call, for no apparent reason, until I saw the pattern. The first day of June was the first day of winter, and was the anniversary of another year without Ron. All of those years, without fanfare, or comment, she remembered, and quietly offered solace.

John wished only for himself and their children to attend Elizabeth's funeral, a decision that nobody, family or friends, were fully able to understand, because it denied Katherine, Hilary, Nicholas and Sarah, the love and comfort of people who had been in their lives from the time of their birth. It distanced and separated them at a time when they most needed support. Many years later Elizabeth's children invited a group of her close friends to attend a lakeside get together. They planted a tree in her memory. As her children pushed the soil firmly around the roots of the sapling, the air was filled with peace as many of the people who had known her finally paid tribute to Elizabeth's memory.

Sid returned from England. I could not talk to him about Elizabeth, possibly because I believed he did not understand the depth of our friendship.

Some days later, he asked, 'How's Elizabeth?'

'She died last week,' I replied with unintentional abruptness.

'Why didn't you tell me?' he asked, frowning.

'I didn't want you not to care.' I replied.

He answered quietly, as he hugged me awkwardly, 'I do care.'

Chapter 20

With Dignity

Within six months and true to his word, Sid retired. He appeared to enjoy not having the restrictions of dressing in a suit, adhering to a schedule and having to travel to the city each day. He still seemed to enjoy driving off now and then for two or three day breaks. Unfortunately, though, his idea of working from home never eventuated. His health deteriorated quickly and whereas previously his diary showed pages filled with business, as well as medical appointments, those pages now increasingly marked only times to visit his doctor and the hospital.

With a strong feeling of inevitability, I watched as Sid's immune system and overall health declined with unprecedented speed. He gasped and fought for breath as more frequent chest and lung infections assailed him. He developed arthritis and, after having come to terms with that affliction, his doctor then told him that he needed angioplasty surgery for a heart condition. Strangely, although life was grim for him at times, in between bouts of pain and breathlessness, he remained much the same as usual. He still went to concerts and we went on long drives together and out to dinner. He was no more, nor less, sociable. He rarely complained and I gained great respect for him and his dignified, valiant way of coping with his situation.

One morning, Sid folded the newspaper he was reading as he sat at the kitchen table and purposefully placed it to one side. 'I wonder what you think about this,' and he described the unusual bladder symptoms that he was experiencing.

Without hesitation, I told him, 'Sid, go to your doctor. Don't wait two or three weeks for your next appointment at the hospital, phone, and try to get an appointment today.' He did, and then, after countless hours of sitting around in various hospital departments and undergoing many tests and then anxiously awaiting the results, he was told that he had bladder cancer.

Through the operations and chemotherapy, through the sickness and pain, Sid remained optimistic and confident that he would defeat the illness. Perhaps if his health had not been so seriously compromised in other areas, he may have done so.

Still he craved those solitary journeys. The World Trade Fair, an annual international event, was being held in Australia in 1988, and Sid decided that he wanted to drive north to Darwin and across the top end of Australia and go to Queensland to attend, and he decided to go, *alone*. With his failing health, I considered it a risky thing for him to do. He probably sensed though, that the opportunity for such adventures was running out. He was away for a total of three weeks and soon after his return, he was admitted back into hospital. He remained in hospital for six weeks, and I visited daily with one or two exceptions when sheer exhaustion forced me to go home straight from work. We did not talk much, and I sometimes felt very alone as I sat there keeping him company. Sid lay drowsing one evening and I sat with my chair turned towards the window enabling me to gaze out at the trees. I had thought the soft footsteps that entered the room were those of a nurse, but when I looked up, it was my daughter.

Colleen's soft voice whispered in my ear, 'I've come to visit you, visiting the patient.'

A week of intense soul-searching eventually saw me make the tough decision to leave The Miss Australia Quest as the pressure of that lifestyle of work, together with my personal commitments, became increasingly difficult. Thus I moved on from one of the best experiences of my life. However, I had to make the practical decision. I took a less demanding, but equally rewarding position, promoting and fundraising for The Autistic Children's Association.

One warm, early spring afternoon, I sat reading as Sid slept. As sometimes happened, he awoke, and immediately started speaking, 'Has it all been bad for you? Being married to me?' I hesitated. I had no wish to be dishonest with a dying man and I had no anger or animosity to express at that time. What could I say? Then I remembered that we always had a good time when we went away together on holiday. Sid, more travelled than I, enjoyed being the experienced one, pointing out things of interest and, as he did, we became just two people seeing and enjoying different experiences together.

Without addressing the question directly, I answered, truthfully, 'Didn't we have some great holidays?' For an hour or two, we relived those times and places, at ease with each other. As we talked, Sid's voice became nostalgic, his eyes closed, and he drifted off in to a deep, drug-induced sleep. I picked up my handbag and book and left the room. The corridors were quiet. I passed no visitors, nor staff, as I walked towards the elevators. I waited for some time for the right elevator to arrive as I assiduously avoided the one used to transport the evil, over-cooked, cabbage smell of hospital food.

Colleen greeted me at home some days later, as I took Clare from her arms and she ushered Michelle ahead of her into the kitchen. 'I am going back to hospital soon. Do you have time for a cup of coffee?'

To my surprise she shuddered quite noticeably, and hastily said, 'No, thanks.'

I laughed and looking into her eyes for a clue and said, 'Women often have that reaction to coffee when they are at first pregnant.'

She replied, looking as if she were a little surprised, 'I am.'

I did not feel worn out anymore. The gloom lifted and the prospect of a new life for us to love shone brightly around us. When Simone Anne, Colleen's newest, lovely, baby girl entered our lives, she filled a niche in my heart that had been waiting for her and I saw acceptance and love for me in her eyes.

The doctor taking care of Sid caught up with me in the foyer of the hospital as I scurried through the rapidly closing automatic doors. He asked, 'Have you just come from work? Come with me to the coffee shop for ten minutes before you go upstairs to visit.' I accepted thankfully, welcoming the thought of hot coffee. Seated, waiting for our cappuccino and without preamble, he said, 'Sid won't get any better and I think he would be more comfortable at the hospice. I've spoken to him, and he thinks that he would like that, but he would like to come back home for a week or two first.'

I readily agreed, but I had no idea of the intensity of the care involved. The assistance that the hospital staff discussed as being available to us was, in reality, minimal. I took time off from work, but I felt inept and out of my depth, especially when measuring the morphine for Sid to take, afraid I would give him either too much and overdose him, or not give enough to dull the pain.

I mentioned that to the doctor, who with a bit of a smile, replied, 'Faye, it's not a cure, it's for pain relief and comfort, so a bit more or less for next few weeks won't really be cause for great concern.'

I thought that a bit casual, but Sid only remained at home for another four days, so I had no need to address the issue again. Despite having oxygen in his bedroom, whenever he became breathless he panicked and, one morning, after an uncomfortable and painful night, Sid decided that he was ready to go to the hospice. I dialled his doctor's number and handed Sid the phone. Even at that stage, he would not wish for another person to make those arrangements on his behalf. He spoke to his doctor who agreed to send an ambulance to take him back to the hospital.

Overnight, Sid deteriorated and a staff member called me to go to him in the early hours of the morning. When I entered the room Sid was awake and for someone so ill, he was extremely vocal and incredibly angry, blaspheming and using language that I had never heard from him before. He had just been told in front of several student doctors that he was dying, and that he was to remain in the hospital and not go to the hospice. He'd been looking forward to what he perceived as balmy, peaceful days, surrounded by gardens and serenity, before quietly, when he was ready, going to a well-earned perpetual rest. Now it was all over and he was bluntly told that his time was limited to not much more than hours. Did he need to be told so directly, with a group of students standing by? It was an invasive and insensitive attitude towards a dying person. On Sid's behalf, I resented their intrusion and I let it show. As I silently met the gaze of each of the students in turn, they swiftly left the room.

Not knowing if the vigil might be many hours, or few, I left the hospital for a short time to go home. I placed a large supply of dry food for *Middy*, my big, black cat, and batted him away before he affectionately sank his teeth into my stocking. I returned to the hospital to find that Sid was heavily sedated and non-responsive. Thoughts of my mother dying alone and afraid rendered me incapable of leaving his bedside.

A large hand rested familiarly, but gently on my shoulder, and without looking up, I knew that the hand belonged to Glen. He had good reason to be resentful of his stepfather, but stayed with me for the remainder of Sid's life. We talked some of the time during the long evening, and some of the time we sat with our own thoughts. Murmuring softly to each other across the bed, at one point we were discussing a vehicle that Glen was having difficulty fixing. Suddenly above the sound of the gently hissing respirator, Sid's voice clearly asked. 'Why didn't you just hire a white ute?'

Glen and I gaped at each other in amazement. We'd thought as Sid lay breathing irregularly and laboriously that he was beyond the power of hearing, or speech. That was his only comment before he lapsed back into apparent unconsciousness. It was midnight when the night nurse suggested that we go home and sleep, saying that she would ring if Sid's condition changed. I phoned at one o'clock. The night nurse told me that all was well, and I drifted into an uneasy, restless sleep. The telephone jangled near my pillow. The time showed ten minutes to four.

'Sid is distressed. You should come now,' I heard the doctor say.

The day was long and uncomfortable, as my son and I sat in silence. There was nothing to talk about, as we had exhausted all conversation during the previous night. However, although my mind was weary, it travelled back over the years that I had spent with Sid. I wondered how two such unlikely people had spent just on twenty years together. I believed that even if he had not found life perfect, Sid had found a reasonable compromise. I had my children and mostly that was enough.

My thoughts continued, as I shifted comfortably in the chair, and I thought of people that I knew, friends and acquaintances, and of how argumentative and, seemingly, unhappy their relationships were. I remembered women coming to the office each morning, angry, speaking disparagingly of their husbands, or partners, and crying bitterly as they told of the latest transgression. Why did they remain? Did they stay because they needed a hedge against long, lonely nights? I wondered if like animals in the wild, human beings sought to huddle after dark, drawing comfort from the body heat, and the noisy snuffles of one and another, to let them know that they are not completely alone. I guessed they all had their reasons.

Morning became afternoon and my introspective thoughts drifted away. I began to feel stiff and restless, my back ached unceasingly and I became unaccountably cold. In spite of leaving the room to go outside and stand in the weak, afternoon sun, I remained chilled. Back inside the sterile, bright, white room, Sid's rasping breath was the only sound in the frigid silence, and I continued to shiver. Quietly, Glen said, 'Go and see your grandchildren for half an hour. They will make you feel better, and the drive in the car will warm you up. I'll stay here.'

I took his advice, and drove away from the hospital towards Colleen's house. I resolved that when I returned to the hospital I would urge Glen to go home. He looked drawn and weary. I stayed with my girls for a short time, then restored and warmed by their company and hot coffee, I returned to the hospital. I glanced at my watch and saw that I had been away a little over half an hour. As I approached the hospital entrance, Glen stood waiting. I knew from his sombre face that during my short absence, on the afternoon of September 15, 1989, Sid had exercised his prerogative to go alone one last time. Tears of shock fell, shock that, after all those hours, he died as soon as I left. Tears fell as I contemplated his lonely, isolated life. His life had led him along a mostly painful pathway. Did he choose to wrap himself in a safe cocoon as a means of protecting himself? Did he withdraw into a shell to close his feelings off from the havoc of others and to avoid the discomfort of dealing with their emotions? I would never know whether he had the power to alter any of it. I felt certain, though, as I looked at his calm and strangely-youthful face, that whether it suited me or not, as much as he was able to care for another person, in his own compromised way, he did care for me. With the passage of time I was *almost* able to smile at the memory of that awful pale, silvery-blue, floor covering, and those neon blue bench tops. I was also able to wonder if it were possible that his intention had been not to diminish me, but rather to bolster himself.

One week later, although it was early spring, the wind blew capriciously, chilling and threatening to bring the rain down upon us on an overcast, dismal morning. I walked away from the cemetery with my four children, and we went home together.

Chapter 21

Good Shepherd Revisited

On a quiet, overcast Sunday afternoon, I reached for my jewellery box, selected an elegant diamond ring and slid it on to my finger. I have owned the ring for many years. I studied the sparkling jewel, and remembered the day when my son was leaving home. John had handed me a small jewellers' box, and told me the gift was for me for looking after him for twenty five years. I was going to miss my calm, thoughtful son more than he could ever imagine. Then I clasped a gold chain and nugget around my neck, a gift from my other son, Glen, on my fiftieth birthday. I wore my treasures on that particular day because I had a need to feel the love and protective aura that wearing them afforded me.

I valiantly made a decision to walk around the outside of The Home of the Good Shepherd, walk along the path, and up to the front door, just to see if I was able, now that I knew so much more about myself and that place. Over the years I had painstakingly avoided the building and, if I found myself unexpectedly in the vicinity, I drove by with my gaze averted and my breath held in. All was still and silent as I edged my car slowly through the gateway and past the rose bushes. I wondered if they were the same bushes that I had struggled by with my suitcase on that long-ago day. Not a soul was in sight when I parked my car. I sat for a while and I asked myself why I was there.

Alert and edgy, I walked away from the safe confines of the vehicle. The dull, grey limestone walls loomed ahead. On each side of the wooden door with the stained glass and leadlight panels, I noted six curved archways. Those arches were replicated on the upper level, making twenty four overwhelming grey openings that shed no light. I walked forward and stood close to the door – my extra height and added years had not made it any less intimidating. Few nuns resided there now. The insidious institution, with its laundries and ironing rooms, had long gone, but it still looked ominous and sinister to me. I remembered how my mother had been unable to meet my eyes as she stood beside me that day. I stared at that door for a few moments and then I moved hurriedly away, fearful that I might be drawn inside and trapped, unable to leave. I passed through a tall, unlocked gate and walked along a portion of the colonnade that I had once walked along so wistfully from the inside as I tried to see the flowers at the front of the building. In retrospect, what seemed an endlessly long passage to me as a child, I saw was really quite a short distance. I followed a narrow path around the colonnade and realised that I was at the door of the chapel, the door that parishioners on the *outside* were permitted to use.

I tiptoed in through the unlocked door and found myself in the silent, dim interior, which exuded the unmistakably-sharp scent of incense and the heady perfume of roses. I half expected to see myself, a dowdy, sad little figure, sitting on the opposite side, with my head down and my back aching, praying earnestly for release and freedom. From a habit learned long ago I made a move to genuflect before the altar, but a swift, sharp pain in my left knee prevented me from bending, perhaps reminding me not to be hypocritical. Nothing stirred. I left the chapel and continued around the side of the building. With old familiarity, apprehension walked with me through the gate and I had an uneasy notion that someone might come and lock me in. So strong was the feeling that I cast my eyes around to see if I had a means of escape if I did find the gate locked against me. A wire fence bordered the grounds. I decided that it was probably climbable, even though it was rather high. Perhaps an ungainly exit, but I would not be the first person to exit untidily from that place.

Rooftops and the distant blue of Lake Monger were visible and I felt better. Unexpectedly, as I walked gingerly around a corner, I found myself confronted with the area where the outside steps used to be that led up to the dormitories. The outside steps that I recalled from that first evening seemed to be missing, although the area above was definitely the dormitory area and the place where we sat for recreation. There were many changes and red brick additions and other alterations were obvious. I moved away and I imagined the laundry buildings clearly, even though they had been removed long ago. Just lawns, fences and an intangible air of sadness remained. I walked towards the former refectory and I imagined ugly, large Dolus, who taunted me at meal times. I smelt and tasted Epsom salts. When I looked through the window into the room, I saw no rows of tables with starched white cloths. I peered through another window into a different room and saw a beautifully polished table, which took up most of the room. Perhaps the room was now used for meetings.

There was the locked door through which I came with my mother, and through which I left with my mother again, two years later.

While I continued wandering, questions about my mother arose in my mind. Why was she sent to the nuns at The Home of the Good Shepherd? Why could she never find peace? That question would forever remain unanswered. Amy's path through life was choked and hidden with the weeds of ... don't tell anyone.

Feeling unnerved, I wished that I were not there alone. Clouds formed and a brisk wind sprang up. The wind rustled sharply, and it seemed to me, threateningly, through the trees. My senses sharpened and I heard voices, angry voices, and the wailing voices of sad souls lingering in that place. I heard my young voice crying and praying to God to send my mother to get me.

Recently I had become more overwhelmingly and irrationally afraid than usual of being locked in or out of places. I was afraid of being trapped behind a locked door with no one knowing where I was, even in my own home, and I sometimes bordered on hysteria if my front door did not open at the first turn of the key. The fear was with me again and I raced back to the gate fully expecting to find it locked fast against me. My ears roared and I stumbled awkwardly to the car as I fumbled in my bag for my keys. And along with my keys, my hands touched the smooth surface of my mobile phone. *I would not have been trapped after all.*

I felt no dramatic change after my return to the institution of my childhood. I experienced no particular relief because I had bravely confronted my demons. I certainly felt no better understanding of the body and soul destroying time I spent there. And perhaps sadly, my heart held no forgiveness.

Buoyed by my previous boldness, though, when I found myself driving along Newcastle Street one day, I decided to face the demons that I associated with *that* area. Over the years, I had driven through that particular area many times. But, with the passage of time and numerous changes later, Newcastle Street and its surrounds had become, to me, just streets on the way to a destination, and I usually passed by the house that I once knew without much thought. That day, however, my attention was drawn, and my eyes fixed upon a sign stating that the semi-detached, tiny cottages were heritage listed by the local authority. I drove past slowly, but traffic behind impatiently tooted me to hurry along out of the way. I manoeuvred abruptly around the corner to escape, and parked my car in Aberdeen Street, near St Brigid's Church. With no conscious thought, my feet took me across road, and I walked up to the church door. I was baptised, made my first communion and attended midnight mass in that church. I remembered my first days at the little school, which now no longer existed. Curiously nostalgic and drawn further towards the past, I attempted to push the church door inwards. It did not move and I pushed harder. It remained firmly shut.

A bearded young man called to me. 'You can't get in unless there is a service going on. Too many vandals.'

He joined me as I walked away and I told him that I used to attend the church, and the school, when I was a child and, at that time, the church door was never locked. We continued around the corner and I remarked that I was surprised to see that the presbytery was still standing, attached to the church. However, the land where the school and playground once stood was now lost to accommodate changes brought about by the busy Mitchell Freeway, which echoed with the noise of cars, trucks and police sirens, rather than with the sound of children's laughter and the ringing of playtime, lunch time and prayer bells. My temporary companion was familiar with the locality and seemed interested in my observations. I pointed to the opposite corner where there had once been a wine bar, and he laughed delightedly when I told him that I used to run like hell past the place in case some inebriate, or the devil, chased me with evil intentions. We parted company and went our separate ways.

I found that I did not mind that the church was locked to me.

Massive reclamation and demolition to make way for the freeway had rendered the area unrecognisable from the place of my childhood. I approached Bertram Street hesitantly and thought that I might weaken when I came to the corner. I looked around in puzzlement for a few moments, until I realised that Bertram Street no longer existed. The houses and the *very street* had all gone. What an air pumping surge of triumph I experienced, because it was not often that an entire street disappeared. Stella and the people from that time were dead and buried. The wood-yard and the Airedale dog had gone. *Hallelujah!!!*

I walked along Fitzgerald Street and continued around the corner. The grocery store was no longer there, it went years ago, nor was the fish and chip shop that once had devoted Catholics queued along the pavement on Friday evenings. The laneway that once led from Newcastle Street to Bertram Street was now a short connecting street, and its only function was as an entrance to an office and apartment building block, currently under construction.

Epilogue 2012

The laundry girl did not do too badly.

No more secrets, no more *don't tell anyone*.

What was next ... I would wait and see.

A small country town, about a one hundred and thirty kilometres from Perth, was where I came to call home. In the distance, the mournful whistle of a train beckoned enticingly, seeming to suggest a different life in another place.

My daughter, Colleen, once worked at a women's health care centre, situated in Aberdeen Street. I was surprised to learn that the location from which the centre operated was the same house I lived in all those eons ago. When I told Colleen of my childhood connection to the old house, she offered to take me through. Together, we stepped over the threshold and I waited for memories to surround me. I had not allowed for the passing of quite so many years. The once familiar rooms were now waiting rooms and offices, not bedrooms and kitchens. No spirit of Amy nor Alfredo lingered, nor of Laurie and Maxie, my childhood playmates. I had only the vaguest feeling of ever having lived there.

Several years ago my eldest son, Glen, and I drove to Somerville, near Kalgoorlie, and amazingly, we found the old house still standing – just. The screen door that I once peered through was, by that time, dilapidated, the mesh was missing and the door hung precariously from its one, remaining, worn hinge. The iron roof had rusted away, the paint had disappeared completely from the weatherboards and the earth around was barren. Although we saw no-one, from various broken bikes, rusted tools and empty paint tins scattered about, and a cockatoo in a cage, it did appear that someone dwelt there. I had a lone photo of myself from that time of my childhood. It showed a white-blonde little girl, quite chubby, with bare feet, sitting in a pedal car under a vine-covered archway. Standing there with my son, my spirit again raced across the yard to the wash pump. I felt again the freezing water on my face and in my mouth as I brushed my teeth. Glen took several photos of me under the grapevine, which was still growing, in spite of the general disrepair of the place. I think the old folks would love to know that something they had planted and nurtured so long ago still thrived. As I stood with my son under the vine, I recollected my pleasant existence at that place that sadly, all too soon, ended.

My cousin, Paul, moved to a distant Asian country many years ago. We continue to exchange emails and occasionally a phone call. I have a small dream that one day we will meet again.

I welcome the reminiscing and special times that I still spent with Elizabeth and John Brett's three daughters.

Recently, after a lapse of more than twenty five years, I met my girlhood friend, Nan, and her husband, Geoff. The years rolled away and we recalled our memories of dances and young love. I told them both briefly about this book and, during the conversion, I expressed surprise at myself for never having told Ron about having been in a home. Geoff stirred his cappuccino slowly and said thoughtfully, 'You would have told him one day, Faye. You just ran out of time.'

Information that I acquired only recently from the records of Thomas Street School told me that, when I was enrolled there, it was their understanding from my mother that I had been at St Brigid's in Lesmurdie, during the whole of 1949 and 1950, and that I had passed the necessary exams to advance to the sixth standard. *Oh Amy!*

When I was expecting our son, John, Ron suggested that we were about to create a dynasty. With four granddaughters, three grandsons and a *great grandson*, I am reminded that, for a moment in time, a man who will always be a part of me, loved me. He was my first love and the father of my children. In our own small way, we did create a dynasty.

To make my journey complete, and with a feeling reminiscent of making a confession, I mention that I did marry again in 1999. Living alone, the black demons of my childhood still bared their fangs and pursued me worrying away at my peace of mind, at dawn and dusk and on long dreary Sunday afternoons, bringing unsettling recollections of other Sundays waiting for my turn to move away from the wall. However, many mistakes have been made by many people in the erroneous belief that another person might be the answer to the search for tranquillity. Ultimately, we separated.

In Perth, one day, I found myself drawn to look again at the Newcastle Street house. I stood on the same spot outside the little semi-detached houses where I had stood as a child watching the women having their photo taken. Memories revisited. The faithfully-restored houses remained there, looking precisely as I remembered them.

The afternoon sun shone vividly, reflecting flashes of bright colours from tin roofs and nearby windows. I blinked and, for a fleeting second, I thought I saw a tiny, fair-haired girl dressed in red ....

I endeavour to be a worthy mother for my children.

They are my forgiveness for the times I got it wrong.

They are also my reward for the times I got it right.

With my great grandson Reece 2011.

Acknowledgements

When I approached my friend, former journalist and English teacher, Annie Girard (née Pougnault), about telling my story, my plan was to relate the details to her over a glass or two of some pleasant beverage and for her to ghost write the story for me. How wrong I was. Annie believed that the story was mine to tell in my own words and she showed me how to seek those words. However, it took an *incredibly* long time for my emotions and words to merge and for me to grasp the mysterious, unpredictable intricacies of the computer. I had never used one. Thank you, Annie, for giving me the benefit of your years of teaching, and for your editing experience. Above all, thank you for your friendship.

Thank you and love to my sons, daughters and grandchildren. Without your ongoing encouragement I may not have survived the writing of my protracted saga. Thank you, Lynette, for diligently reading my drafts several times and for your emotional support when the going got tough.

Thank you, too, to Dr Geraldine Wooller, PhD, novelist, essayist and teacher, whom I met towards the latter part of my writing and who kindly shared her professional experience so readily with me.

As well, I am indebted to Ron Gregor, husband of my girlhood friend, Lynne, whose encouragement and meticulous proof reading of the document helped me improve upon and tell my story.

In a life full of coincidences, one of the most remarkable happened when I learned that Sarah Brett – the same Sarah I'd known since she was a baby – operated a publishing company: *Spirit of the Boabs*. Thank you Sarah, for the co-operation, hard work, and valuable time spent on my behalf away from your Kimberley Vet Centre. I am overwhelmed by the love and respect you have shown me, the laundry girl.

I value the comments of Dr John Weiland, PhD, after his reading of my completed manuscript and thank him for his encouraging words about my story and the way I have written it. Those comments from an historian and writer of many years' experience and expertise mean a great deal to me.

www.ingramcontent.com/pod-product-compliance
Lightning Source LLC
Chambersburg PA
CBHW071859290426
44110CB00013B/1206